D0182694

The Development of a Discipline

The History of the
Political Studies Association

The Development of a Discipline

*The History of the
Political Studies Association*

Wyn Grant

WILEY-BLACKWELL

A John Wiley & Sons, Ltd., Publication

This edition first published 2010
© 2010 Political Studies Association

Blackwell Publishing was acquired by John Wiley & Sons in February 2007. Blackwell's publishing program has been merged with Wiley's global Scientific, Technical, and Medical business to form Wiley-Blackwell.

Registered Office
John Wiley & Sons Ltd, The Atrium, Southern Gate, Chichester, West Sussex, PO19 8SQ, United Kingdom

Editorial Offices
350 Main Street, Malden, MA 02148-5020, USA
9600 Garsington Road, Oxford, OX4 2DQ, UK
The Atrium, Southern Gate, Chichester, West Sussex, PO19 8SQ, UK

For details of our global editorial offices, for customer services, and for information about how to apply for permission to reuse the copyright material in this book please see our website at www.wiley.com/wiley-blackwell.

The right of Wyn Grant to be identified as the author of this work has been asserted in accordance with the Copyright, Designs and Patents Act 1988.

All rights reserved. No part of this publication may be reproduced, stored in a retrieval system, or transmitted, in any form or by any means, electronic, mechanical, photocopying, recording or otherwise, except as permitted by the UK Copyright, Designs and Patents Act 1988, without the prior permission of the publisher.

Wiley also publishes its books in a variety of electronic formats. Some content that appears in print may not be available in electronic books.

Designations used by companies to distinguish their products are often claimed as trademarks. All brand names and product names used in this book are trade names, service marks, trademarks or registered trademarks of their respective owners. The publisher is not associated with any product or vendor mentioned in this book. This publication is designed to provide accurate and authoritative information in regard to the subject matter covered. It is sold on the understanding that the publisher is not engaged in rendering professional services. If professional advice or other expert assistance is required, the services of a competent professional should be sought.

Library of Congress Cataloging-in-Publication Data
Grant, Wyn.
    The development of a discipline : the history of the Political Studies Association / Wyn Grant.
      p. cm. – (Political studies special issues ; 2)
    Summary: "By tracing the history of the PSA, The Development of a Discipline: The History of the Political Studies Association reveals the changing nature of the study of politics in Britain and the development of British higher education. Shows how the PSA developed from a small elitist club to a highly professional discipline. Offers parallels to the development of the study of politics as a discipline in the UK. Appeal extends to those who study higher education and political scientists." – Provided by publisher.
      ISBN 978-1-4443-3210-0 (pbk.)
    1. Political Studies Association of the United Kingdom.   2. Political science–Study and teaching (Higher)–Great Britain.   I. Title.
    JA88.G7G73   2010
    320.071´141–dc22

2010026571

A catalogue record for this book is available from the British Library.

Set in 10.5/13pt Minion by Toppan Best-set Premedia Limited
Printed and bound in Singapore
By Fabulous Printers Pte Ltd

1   2010

Contents

Tables, Boxes and Illustrations

Tables

Boxes

Figure 1:   Professor William Robson, a key figure in the formation of the PSA. *Source: National Portrait Gallery, London.*

Figure 2:   Professor Sammy Finer, giving a typically ebullient lecture at Keele where he built up the politics department. *Source: Special Collections and Archives, Keele University.*

Figure 3:   Sir Norman Chester, Warden of Nuffield College, Oxford and a key figure in the formation of the PSA. *Source: International Political Science Association.*

Figure 4:   Professor W. J. M. Mackenzie at the PSA conference in 1996. He was a leading figure in the foundation of British political science and PSA chair from 1960 to 1962.

Figure 5:   Professor Sir Bernard Crick at a PSA awards ceremony.

Figure 6:   Professor Sammy Finer (left) and Professor Jean Laponce at the IPSA conference in Edinburgh, 1976. *Source: International Political Science Association.*

Figure 7:   Delegates to the IPSA conference in 1976 wait in the courtyard of Edinburgh Castle for the reception. *Source: International Political Science Association.*

Figure 8:   Elizabeth Meehan presents the Sir Isaiah Berlin prize for lifetime achievement in political science to Professor Lord Parekh in 2003.

Figure 9:   The PSA has used its annual awards ceremony to develop links with practitioners. Here Elizabeth Meehan, the first woman to be chair of the PSA, makes a presentation to Shirley Williams.

Figure 10:   From left to right, Jack Hayward, William Paterson and Patrick Dunleavy. Jack Hayward became chair of the PSA at the time of the Oxford insurgency. William Paterson is a leading figure in German and EU studies and Patrick Dunleavy has made many contributions to the PSA for over 30 years.

Figure 11:   From left to right, John Benyon, Jon Tonge and David Denver. John Benyon has been treasurer of the PSA since 1992, Jon Tonge was chair from 2005 to 2008 and David Denver has been a prominent member of EPOP and served on the PSA EC.

Figure 12:   Rod Rhodes, secretary of the PSA after the Oxford-led insurgency and chair from 1999 to 2002.

Figure 13:   Paul Whiteley has been a prominent member of the PSA and is a member of the EC in 2010. He is one of the current generation of political scientists who started his career in a polytechnic.

Preface

This history of the Political Studies Association (PSA) seeks to place its story within the context of the development of the discipline as a whole and of British higher education. It is essentially a story of the modernisation and professionalisation of the PSA in response to the demands of a discipline that has become much larger, more diverse and increasingly centred around sub-disciplines.

The treatment is essentially a chronological one, tracing the way in which the discipline and its association have evolved, although there is a thematic chapter on women and diversity. However, each chapter returns to certain central themes such as the state of the discipline itself, the professionalisation of the PSA, its conference and journals and its relationships with higher education bodies and with practitioners.

The study is substantially based on the PSA archive, which runs from the formation of the association in 1950 until 1982 and is maintained at the London School of Economics and Political Science (LSE), supplemented by papers from the National Archives at Kew. From 1992 there is an electronic archive of executive committee minutes. In the references these are quoted as LSE, NA and PSA, respectively. Considerable efforts were made to locate the missing material for the period from 1982 to 1992, but without success. I have sought to cover the missing ten years through interviews and recollections obtained electronically. Such interviews have also contributed to the rest of the account.

I am grateful to the PSA for asking me to write this history and in particular to the treasurer, John Benyon, who has been supportive throughout (any royalties will accrue to the PSA). They have given me a free hand in what I write and any errors, misinterpretations or omissions are my own responsibility. I generally use the term 'political science' to refer to the subject throughout. This does not imply any particular view of how the subject should be constituted, but it simply serves as convenient shorthand. Political science is an eclectic discipline which thrives because it tolerates a variety of contrasting approaches.

I am particularly grateful to Jack Hayward. Not only did he act as a mentor to me when I was a young entrant, but he has carefully read each chapter of this book and offered constructive and helpful comments. Tony Birch provided me with extensive and very useful handwritten notes of his memories of the PSA. Rod Rhodes and I had a breakfast meeting in Hobart, Tasmania in February 2009 when we reviewed the time we worked together as secretary and treasurer of the PSA. Michael Shattock advised me about the higher education policy context at an early stage of the study.

I would like to thank the archivists at the LSE for their assistance and also the National Archives. The following individuals have all contributed to the writing of this book in different ways: Geoffrey Alderman; Hugh Berrington; David Butler; Sarah Childs; Richard Chapman; Philip Cowley; David Denver; Keith Dowding; Ian Forbes; Michael Goldsmith; Robert Goodin; Justin Greaves; Dilys Hill; Christopher Hood; Reverend Sarah Kilbey MBE; Joni Lovenduski; David Marsh; Ken Newton; Pippa Norris; Geraint Parry; Colin Rallings; Richard Rose; Matthieu St-Laurent; Colin Seymour-Ure; Maurice Spiers; Vicky Randall; Lord Trevor Smith; Jeff Stanyer; and Jean Woodall.

The photograph of Professor Robson was provided by the National Portrait Gallery, London. The photograph of Professor Finer lecturing was provided by Special Collections and Archives, Keele University Library. The photographs from the Edinburgh congress of 1976 were provided by the International Political Science Association. I would like to thank these bodies for finding these photographs and for permission to reproduce them. Other photographs are taken from the PSA archive.

I hope that this book is more welcome to PSA members than earlier free gifts and that understanding the past of the discipline and its association will stimulate reflection and debate on its future course.

Wyn Grant

Chapter 1

The Emergence of a Discipline

The history of an academic association must also be about the history of the discipline that it seeks to serve. To a large extent an association reflects changes in a discipline rather than shaping them. Indeed, there is always a risk that an association may fall behind the curve of those changes and reflect the agenda of an earlier generation now in positions of disciplinary influence. Such a story is part of the history of the PSA. In the 1970s the leadership of the Association was reinvigorated, and, following a series of further developments in the succeeding decades, the Association became a highly professional organisation which made a real contribution to sustaining the study of politics.

The story of a discipline, however, cannot be considered in isolation from the development of higher education as a whole. During the 60 years that the PSA has been in existence, higher education in Britain has been transformed from an elitist system largely reserved for a privileged few to a mass system, albeit still with inbuilt social biases. The aftermath of the 1963 Robbins Report in terms of the expansion of existing universities and the creation of new ones gave a major boost to the study of politics in British universities. The financial cutbacks under the Thatcher government at the beginning of the 1980s presented a major challenge for the subject. The conversion of the polytechnics into universities in 1992 and the increasing numbers of overseas students triggered a process of renewal. The Research Selectivity Exercise initiated by the then University Grants Committee in 1986 was the precursor of the Research Assessment Exercises (RAE) which came to determine the allocation of funding council research money to the universities and became the subject of major controversy.

What Is a Discipline?

One of the characteristics of an academic discipline is the existence of an association that provides a focus for its intellectual activities, operates journals and represents it to the outside world. In the case of the study of politics, this raises interesting questions about the relationship with international relations or studies, which will be returned to at various points in the analysis. With its own association and journal, has international studies become a discipline in its own right, or a sub-discipline? This is not a trivial question as in many respects it represents the fastest growing aspect of the discipline, in terms of student numbers and research activity. Elections and political parties, represented by the Elections, Parties and Opinion Polls (EPOP) group of the PSA, is a vigorous area of the discipline which has secured a substantial share of available research funding. It has its own journal and its own well-attended annual conference, but it operates under the umbrella of the PSA. 'More than elsewhere, perhaps, the primary attachments of scholars of politics and IS in the UK are to sub-disciplines rather than to some larger, overarching discipline' (ESRC, 2007, p. 11).

What do we mean when we talk about a discipline? Michael Kenny (2004, p. 566) reminds us that there is a debate 'about whether the very idea of a "discipline" projects a spurious unity, and misleading singularity, on to what are in reality internally diverse and loosely bounded fields of study'. Apart from the imposition of an artificial coherence, there is a serious intellectual objection to the kind of study being undertaken here:

> The naturalizing perspective understands political science as constituted by a pregiven empirical domain – politics – and a shared intellectual agenda, to make this domain the object of a cumulative and instrumentally useful science. It thus encourages a retrospective vision that focuses, first, on the establishment of an autonomous discipline, free from the clutches of history, law, and philosophy, and, second, on charting progress made in the subsequent development of that discipline (Adcock *et al.*, 2007, p. 3).

What is more, 'Disciplinary histories risk privileging the category of the discipline as if its institutional presence' – in this case the PSA – 'demarcates boundaries to the flow of ideas or explains the way in which ideas have developed within such boundaries' (Adcock *et al.*, 2007, p. 4). One needs to be aware of this danger and to an extent this study uses the story of the PSA as a lens through which to view the intellectual development of the discipline. However, resources and their organisation into institutional settings also shape that story, making some paths of intellectual development easier to follow than others. Moreover, when the PSA fell out of step with developments in the discipline in the 1970s, leading figures thought it sufficiently important to intervene to restore its focus.

When we examine the study of politics, what is apparent in many respects resembles a subject or a field of inquiry rather than a discipline because of its internal fragmentation. 'In academic parlance, a discipline refers to a branch of knowledge, but it also reminds practitioners of the rules that govern their activity' (Macintyre and Clark, 2003, p. 29). Some of these are general rules that apply to all academic scholarship, such as the acknowledgement of sources or the avoidance of plagiarism. Michael Moran reminds us that 'discipline' in English has a notorious double meaning: 'it can refer to academic specialisation and it can refer to activities of compulsion or punishment' (Moran, 2006, p. 74). He argues that the very root of the word's academic meaning links it to power and hierarchy: from the Latin *disciplina*, referring to the instruction of acolytes by elders. Disciplines, therefore, are about power, hierarchy and control in the organisation of knowledge (Moran, 2006, p. 74). The PSA is not like a professional organisation that disciplines its members who fail to adhere to accepted standards. It may, however, reflect and embody informal systems of power, such as those that for a long time underpinned a significant gender imbalance in the profession (see Chapter 8). How far that power was exercised within the context of the PSA is an open question to be pursued further in this book. For example, informants who recalled the period differed in their views about how far the PSA annual conferences in the 1950s were a mechanism for assessing and recruiting new members of staff.

Alex Warleigh-Lack and Michelle Cini (2009, p. 6) offer an elaborated definition of a discipline in terms of 'discrete sets of knowledge that share understandings about the most salient questions to ask, variables to explore and the most appropriate methods to employ'. Reflecting on his experience of interdisciplinary research, Justin Greaves (2008, p. 3) notes that a discipline may be distinguished in terms of 'language, techniques, problems or levels of organisation . . . In terms of language, a particular way of thinking will have its own jargons, symbols and conventions and this may only be understood in the context of the discipline'.

Reviewing the literature, Greaves suggests (2008, p. 2) that a discipline may have a number of defining characteristics including:

- 'a distinctive subject matter;
- a distinctive methodology;
- an area of expertise that needs specialised training in order to become a practitioner;
- a professional association which manages the profession and to which most practitioners belong; and
- a mission'.

The first two of these criteria present particular challenges for the study of politics. The subject has been widely viewed as 'more eclectic than most disciplines in borrowing the approaches of others' (Peters, 1999, p. 20). One of the leading early proponents of British politics, W. J. M. Mackenzie, thought that political science should be 'above all things eclectic in method, drawing on many approaches and indeed making this almost the defining characteristic of the discipline' (Birch and Spann, 1974, p. 19). As Brian Barry notes (1999, p. 429), 'The most striking feature of the study of politics in Britain during the first half [twentieth] century is its very weak tendency to disciplinary boundary-management'. It has led to questions being raised about 'whether political studies – or even political science – is in fact a discrete discipline' (Warleigh-Lack and Cini, 2009, p. 7). This dilemma reflects the origins of the subject in a variety of other disciplines such as history, philosophy and constitutional law. W. J. M. Mackenzie (see Box 2.2) was a classics don by origin.

From one perspective, this eclecticism has been a weakness. It has laid the subject open to the predatory ambitions of other disciplines. As Wilfrid Harrison recalled (1975, p. 186), '[the] other social scientists, including sometimes economics, could appear to be ready to put forward takeover bids by suggesting that whatever it was that political scientists were trying to do it could be done better by the practitioners of some other discipline'. At one time the major challenge came from sociology, which argued that there was a subject called political sociology, but not a distinctive discipline of politics. Within the International Political Studies Association (IPSA) in the 1950s, 'sociology was perceived as a discipline with hegemonic pretensions that were hardly compatible with the attainment of autonomy by political science' (Boncourt, 2009, p. 37). In the twenty-first century, John Trent notes that 'political sociology is in decline in many countries, partly because it no longer addresses itself to the big questions of society (Lipset's famous "why no socialism in the United States?") and partly because it has become an aggregate of causes that lose sight of the larger, macro-social picture' (Trent, 2009, p. 16). More recently the challenge has come from economics, which argues that its methodology provides the means for constructing a rigorous 'economics of politics'. The strength of this eclecticism has been openness to the insights of other disciplines, giving students of politics a broader education than is available in more narrowly focused subjects. It also places politics in a good position to engage in the interdisciplinary work being encouraged by the UK research councils.

It is possible to identify key themes that have been at the heart of the study of politics: power and its exercise; conflict and its resolution; democracy and, more recently, democratisation; the state and its relationship with civil society. In terms of methodology, a range of approaches are used in the discipline from social con-structivism to more positivist forms of analysis. Research techniques, both quantita-tive and qualitative, are shared across the social sciences. If anything, political scientists have become more ambitious in the range of techniques they have used in recent years, embracing participant observation (Rhodes *et al.*, 2007) and explor-ing the possibilities of experimental work (Stoker and John, 2009). If there is one technique that is particularly used by political scientists it is semi-structured or elite interviewing, which reflects the extent to which the discipline is involved in the study of the political class where standardised survey techniques are often not appropriate.

In terms of an area of expertise that needs specialised training, the Economic and Social Research Council (ESRC) has made increasing efforts to standardise the training available to doctoral students in politics, making sure, for example, that they have an understanding of qualitative and quantitative techniques as well as comparative politics and explanation in social science. There is a professional asso-ciation that gives the discipline an identity and to which the majority of practitio-ners belong. Whether the discipline has a 'mission' is more questionable given the variety of topics that are pursued. However, that does raise the question of what relationship there should be between the academics in the discipline and the practitioners of politics and policy makers more generally. Jack Hayward and Philip Norton point to a tension in the Aristotelian conception of politics as a 'master science' between 'a theoretical preoccupation with political science as a vocation on the one hand and public service as a vocation on the other'. In the USA the scientific vocation has predominated while the public service one has been foremost in France.

> In Britain, an ineffectual zig-zag has taken place in the no man's land between rigidly separated theoretical and practical spheres, in which a polite or contemptuous rejection of political science by those in authority as an aid either to promote democratic citizenship or public service is coupled with a half-hearted academic attempt to acquire a scientific role (Hayward and Norton, 1986, p. 8).

The issue of the relationship with practitioners of politics has arisen a number of times during the Association's history. Some civil servants hold a rather dismissive attitude to those who engage in academic study. When the teaching of public administration was being discussed in the civil service in 1974, a note scribbled by a civil servant on a memorandum stated: 'I have no great sense of need for what is being inchoately hawked here: but perhaps I am missing the real significance . . . "those who can't teach"' (NA, 1973). As Trevor Smith observed (1986, p. 431), 'Northcote-Trevelyan man has invariably regarded the political scientist as being largely irrelevant in relation to the *national* policy-making process, precisely because those areas where the academic might make a contribution (e.g., constitutional issues, machinery of government problems, policy analysis, etc.) coincide exactly with his own special skills' (emphasis in original).

Some British politics academics started their careers as administrative class civil servants, but left after relatively short periods, for example Nevil Johnson and Colin Seymour-Ure.

In recent years, the research councils have placed increasing emphasis on the value of research to a variety of external audiences and the Research Excellence Framework (REF) that is to replace the RAE will include an emphasis on the measurement of 'impact'. These developments led eventually to a systematic attempt by the PSA to build better relationships with the political class through events such as the annual awards ceremony. Relationships with politicians and other practitioners are a theme that will receive attention throughout the volume.

The Establishment of the Subject in British Universities

The contrast with the United States

Politics had been studied as a subject long before it became a discipline with departments in universities and a professional association. The systematic study of politics in Britain was a latecomer both by international standards and compared with cognate disciplines. In the United States the School of Political Science at Columbia University in New York was established by John Burgess in 1880, an event that has been described as marking the birth of political science 'as a learned discipline' (Somit and Tanenhaus, 1967, p. 21), followed by the establishment of departments elsewhere such as John Hopkins University in Baltimore. The American Political Science Association (APSA) was founded in 1903, the *American Political Science Review* (APSR) began publication in 1906 and 'by the 1920s [political science] was on the syllabus in over a hundred American universities' (Birch, 2009, p. 2). A number of other associations were also formed earlier than in Britain: Canada (1913), China (1932), Finland (1935), India (1938) and Japan (1948) (Boncourt, 2009, p. 4), but it was the American discipline of political science that was the largest and most active. How can the earlier and more rapid development of the discipline in the USA be explained?

America's universities expanded at an earlier date than those in Britain with the undergraduate population growing from '54,300 in 1870 to 597,900 in 1920' (Ricci, 1984, p. 53). This created a demand for new courses, informed by the rise of Darwinist thinking leading to a rejection of the dominance of theology in the old colleges. 'The main objective was to distinguish very clearly the new science from the old theology' (Ricci, 1984, p. 38). From the early days of the American study of politics, there was a clear commitment to scientific progress, underpinned by an American belief in the benefits of technological progress, and reflected in the title of the Association. '[Political] scientists shared in the widespread faith – a sort of "scientism" – that universities must rely on science rather than revelation to inform their teachings on natural and social phenomena' (Ricci, 1984, p. 66). The tension between this belief in the possibility of a science of politics and the British perspective which tended to be more sceptical, cautious and to emphasise the value of normative theory was to be a recurrent one over the century ahead.

British reservations about the very possibility of a systematic study of political phenomena were reflected in the slower establishment of politics as a single honours 'major' in Britain, although this trend was helped in the USA by the fact that law could not be taken as a first degree subject. Hence, this created a market for majoring in political science as a prelude to law school. In Britain, the tendency was to teach politics as one of two or three major disciplines, exemplified by Philosophy, Politics, Economics (PPE) at Oxford. Cambridge had established the teaching of politics as part of the History tripos in 1873 and Manchester offered politics and economics with the addition of politics and modern history in 1948. Tony Birch thinks (2009, p. 3) that 'there were no single honours politics degrees in Britain until the 1960s'. Even when new universities were established, as at Warwick, the foundation of joint honours degrees preceded single honours politics by several years.

Another driving force in America was the perceived need to socialise the waves of immigrants who entered the country in the last quarter of the nineteenth century into democracy, given that many of them came from despotic countries. This led to the development of civics teaching in high schools, which needed an underpinning in universities. In Britain, citizenship education was not taken seriously until the first decade of the twenty-first century. The progressive movement, a reform movement of the urban middle class, also made an important contribution to the development of political science and especially the study of public administration. Many American cities were dominated by corrupt machines whereas British cities were often well run and made municipal innovations that offered valuable policy lessons. In the USA this led to a call for electoral, public service and municipal government reforms. 'They found an enthusiastic reception among many political scientists who became activists and were in the forefront for public service reforms and the establishment of legislative reference bureaux and institutes of governmental research' (Dreijmanis, 1983, p. 196).

John Gunnell (2005, p. 598) has traced a 'protobehavioural revolution' in American political science back to the 1920s. A key role was played by the influential department at Chicago that provided six of the twenty presidents of APSA between 1954 and 1974 (Almond, 2004, p. 91). It was Chicago in the 1930s and 1940s that 'drove the intellectual movement reacting against the formal-legal-historical approach to political analysis of the nineteenth and early twentieth centuries' (Monroe, 2004, p. 95). British political studies has been characterised by a greater intellectual scepticism in what Jack Hayward has called 'a self-deprecating discipline' (Hayward, 1999, p. 1).

Slow and late development in Britain

Only the British Sociological Association out of the major social science disciplinary associations in Britain was formed later than the PSA (see Table 1.1).

Before the professionalization of politics as a specialized discipline in the latter half of the twentieth century, writing about statecraft was confined merely to part of the activities of philosophers, historians and jurists such as Hobbes, Hume and Bentham, or to politicians and journalists with intellectual inclinations, such as Burke, Bagehot and Bryce (Hayward, 1999, pp. 2–3).

Table 1.1: Formation Dates of Selected Major Associations in Britain

Royal Geographical Society	1830
Royal Anthropological Institute	1843
Royal Economic Society	1890
British Psychological Society	1901
Royal Institute of Public Administration	1922
Political Studies Association	1950
British Sociological Association	1951

Source: Derived from Smith, 1986, p. 421.

The development of the study of politics in Britain was smothered by the prevalence of the Whig view of history and its essential complacency, but a different course of development might have been followed if the Benthamite notion of a science of legislation had gained ground.

In late nineteenth-century Cambridge, advocates of a deductive approach that would have led to such a perspective lost out to advocates of an inductive approach based on history (Collini *et al.*, 1983). 'In Cambridge, the struggle between Marshall and Sidgwick for the soul of political economy led to the triumph of a deductivist economics over an inductivist political science, which was virtually eliminated as a serious subject of study in its own right' (Hayward, 1991a, p. 305). The subsequent situation of political science at Cambridge, although it has undergone a recent revival under the leadership of Andrew Gamble, contrasts with the Cambridge economics programme, 'which created a theoretical powerhouse that was to dominate the English field of economics for the next half century' (Fourcade, 2009, pp. 133–4). Ernest Barker (see Box 1.1) was the first holder of the chair of political

---

Box 1.1: Sir Ernest Barker, 1874–1960

Ernest Barker was the first, if somewhat reluctant, occupant of the chair in political science at Cambridge, which he accepted in 1927. He had previously taught at Oxford for 21 years in the History faculty at Oxford and spent seven years as principal of King's College London. The fact that he was held in high regard in the emergent discipline was shown by the invitation made to him to contribute an article to the first issue of *Political Studies*. He 'had retired from the Cambridge Chair in 1939, but had since done some of his best writing' (Chester, 1975, p. 158). Barker came from an impoverished family of seven children, but won a scholarship to Manchester Grammar School and Balliol College, Oxford. He was primarily a historian of political thought, but also wrote on the emergence of totalitarianism in the inter-war period. He saw himself as engaged in a 'form of inquiry concerned with the moral phenomena of human behaviour in political studies' (quoted in Den Otter, 2007, p. 58). 'The synthesis of the ideas of idealism, whiggism and pluralism characterized and informed Barker's thought . . . It was never an entirely stable and coherent synthesis' (Stapleton, 2009, p. 2). 'Barker's work plunged into a period of relative obscurity soon after his death' (Stapleton, 2009, p. 8). However, Harrison (1975, p. 186), while admitting that some of the content of his article in the inaugural edition of *Political Studies* 'may seem odd to younger members of today's profession', noted a revival of interest in his ideas. 'This interest was fuelled by the revival of pluralism and ideas of civil association as the statism and class polarization of the post-war decades began to recede' (Stapleton, 2009, p. 8). His 'abiding liberalism and his scholarship' have endured (Stapleton, 2009, p. 13).

science at Cambridge, but was unhappy at the title and attacked the scientific model in his inaugural lecture (Kavanagh, 2003, p. 598). Much of Barker's work 'was essentially a rearguard defence of the political order that prevailed before the First World War' (Kavanagh, 2003, p. 603; see Stapleton, 1994).

Developments at London and Oxford

The formation of the London School of Economics and Political Science (LSE) in 1895 with Graham Wallas as its first professor of political science reflected a more technocratic approach to the study of the subject and one designed to engage systematically with practitioners, particularly administrators. Sidney Webb, the co-founder with Beatrice Webb, 'was attracted, as a civil servant, by the idea of an administrative elite training institution and when a specialist department was established to teach the subject it was called not Political Science but Government' (Hayward, 1991a, p. 305). 'The Webbs were critical figures in articulating an empirical and neopositivist approach to the study of politics'. The syllabus was empirical rather than normative in its emphasis: 'lectures on comparative politics, political economy, and administrative history were staples of the program, though administrative history remained a bulwark of the discipline'. A book series published under LSE auspices 'defined political science as an empirical, positivist inquiry with utility for current public policy' (Den Otter, 2007, pp. 62–3). In practice the LSE often functioned as an institution that produced colonial administrators (exemplified by the appointment of Lucy Mair as Lecturer in Colonial Administration in 1934; see Chapter 8 for a discussion of her career) and later trained the new political and administrative elites of colonies about to be freed from British rule. There were also important links with the Labour party, exemplified by Wallas' successor, Harold Laski. As far as Wallas was concerned, his *Human Nature in Politics* was received far more favourably 'in the USA than in Britain where his arguments for a quantitative behaviouralism were received with scepticism' (Hayward, 1991a, p. 306).

Wallas was rejected by Oxford for the newly established Gladstone chair of political theory and institutions in 1911 (first established as a readership in 1910). He was in any case 'by background and temperament ill at ease in the establishment milieu of "Greats" at Oxford with its philosophical certainties and Whig historical assumptions and looked for an alternative framework in Darwin and science' (Ross, 2007, p. 35). The first two appointees to the Gladstone chair were practical men of affairs, W. G. S. Adams having been a member of Lloyd George's secretariat in Number 10 Downing Street, while his successor, Arthur Salter, was an MP from 1937 and later served for four years in Churchill's war cabinet (Kavanagh, 2003, p. 597). It was possibly examples of this kind that encouraged a reaction in terms of too great a separation of the study of politics and its practice in the post-war period. However, an alternative model was offered by R. H. S. Crossman who was a politics don at Oxford in the 1930s and went to on to serve as a cabinet minister and to reflect on his experiences in that capacity.

In 1920 Oxford had admitted the first students to study 'Modern Greats' or PPE. 'In its early years the School was predominantly philosophical and historical' (Chester, 1975, p. 155). Part of the plan was to offer students who were inexpert in Latin and Greek some kind of equivalent to Greats, Oxford's degree in Classics (Redcliffe-Maud, 1981, p. 21). 'Intellectual legitimacy in nineteenth-century British elite culture was heavily vested in "classics"' (Fourcade, 2009, p. 149) and this carried over into the twentieth century where Greats was one route into the administrative civil service. Oxford and Cambridge 'promoted an aristocratic conception of education, permeated by references to classical antiquity' (Fourcade, 2009, p. 47).

The modern form of PPE was introduced in 1932, 'which opened the way to a great increase in the amount of teaching required in politics' (Chester, 1975, p. 155). John Redcliffe-Maud, who claims to be the first politics don to be appointed in 1929, recalls that politics 'was an undefined subject' that 'was taught, often with some reluctance, by dons whose primary interest was in modern history or constitutional law' (Redcliffe-Maud, 1981, p. 21). One compulsory paper remained: British Political History and Institutions since 1760, but a comparative Political Institutions paper was introduced. Mackenzie (1975a, p. xxvi) recalls: 'Our perspective for country politics was in effect limited to Britain, America, France with a few side-glances at Switzerland and at the Dominions of the "old" Commonwealth, and there might be not more than two or three books on each'. A sub-faculty of Politics, the functional department in a non-collegiate institution, was established in 1938. A number of individuals who were to become significant figures outside Oxford taught there during this period, including W. J. M. Mackenzie, originally a classics don, and Wilfrid Harrison. One informant who had been at Oxford commented: 'PPE politics arose from the need to teach these people with the minimum amount of extra resources, mixture of constitutional and political history and political theory rooted in political philosophy, some less black letter law as applied to public administration, no psychology (still a great gap), no sociology'.

The other important development at Oxford was the founding of Nuffield College in 1937 as a postgraduate social science college with an endowment by Lord Nuffield of Morris Motors. '[For] various reasons the College, as a College, did not really get going until the end of the War' (Chester, 1975, p. 158). Many of the individuals who played a key role in the history of the PSA, either as its founders or its reformers, had links with Nuffield. It represented a break with Oxford traditions in a number of respects: it would be Oxford's first co-educational college; it planned to bring non-academics and academics together to pursue solutions to social problems; and it would be the first college to specialise in a specific area. This did not go down well in the more traditional Oxford circles where jokes were made about its location near the railway station on a former canal basin.

The intention was that it would be 'the expression of Oxford's purpose in social studies and a powerhouse for the development of the University at large' (Beloff, 1975, p. 136). In the 25th anniversary volume of *Political Studies*, Max Beloff goes on to make an extraordinary attack on Nuffield for exclusivity and an unjustified dominance of the subject in Oxford. Perhaps he had his own personal reasons for this attack. Drawing on his own experience as a graduate student there, Alan Beith (2008, p. 42) gives a generally favourable verdict on 'a college with an appearance of Cotswold cuddliness but with a fierce and generally productive competitiveness in academic fields in which the university had been underperforming'. Nevertheless, despite Nuffield's reputation as an ante-room to Whitehall, and the fact that a number of political scientists served as civil servants during the war, it was not so easy to break down the barriers between political actors and political analysis as had been hoped, in particular because 'the British disease of official secrecy . . . prevented senior civil servants playing any part in this work' (Hayward, 1999, p. 19).

As well as Nuffield, St Antony's College was a key element in Oxford's development, although representing a different approach to the study of politics. It opened in 1950 with the intention of being 'a centre of advanced study and research in the fields of modern international history, philosophy, economics and politics and to provide an international centre within the University' (http://www.sant.ox.ac.uk/about/history.html, accessed 13 October 2009).

The other centre of activity in politics teaching in the inter-war period was Manchester University. A combined honours course in economics and political science had been established in the 1920s (Birch and Spann, 1974, p. 2). Some of the teaching was driven by the needs of local government: 'Manchester offered a Bachelor of Arts in Administration for which evening lectures were available. Manchester Corporation, particularly the City Treasurer's department, were generous in providing the fees and time off for their staff' (Chester, 1975, p. 156).

The study of international relations was developing in these universities, especially the LSE, where the Montagu Burton chair was established in 1924 alongside one in Oxford, but also Aberystwyth where the Woodrow Wilson chair was established in 1919, stimulated by the events of the First World War and the search for a lasting peace. Spence argued that these chairs were established as a 'reaction to old conservative assumptions about statecraft' (LSE, 1978a, PSA/17). Although these were small-scale developments, Lucian Ashworth (2009, p. 16) argues that in the inter-war period international relations developed independently of political science and 'It was only in the 1950s that IR became attached to political science'.

Despite these various developments, the profile of political science remained low. A University Grants Committee return of professors and readers defined the social sciences as economics, economic history, anthropology, industrial relations, social psychology, demography, economic statistics and commerce. What might be regarded as sub-disciplines were thus included but not the study of politics. The British Association had five sections on what it called 'human institutions': geography, economics, anthropology, psychology and educational science. Admittedly, sociology was also omitted from this list, but there was a view in some quarters, referred to by Professor Simey in his evidence to the Clapham Committee, that it was not a 'respectable' subject. In a British Association report on research on human institutions, political science was mentioned in the report, but in terms of teaching provision 'in so far as factual' (British Association, 1943, p. 348).

While political scientists of this period were not insular and pursued systematic comparisons with other European countries and the United States (Kavanagh, 2003, pp. 608–9), a contrast with the post-war period was the lack of influence from American political science. '[One] is impressed by the general lack of British interest in contemporary developments in American political science in the inter-war years' (Kavanagh, 2003, p. 599). When W. J. M. Mackenzie took out a subscription to the APSR in 1932 'and for decades read it carefully and critically, [he] was virtually the only person in England who did so' (Rose, 1999, p. 469). Indeed, the British Library had discontinued its subscription in 1939 (Rose, 1999, p. 469n).

Dennis Kavanagh (2003, p. 594) emphasises that 'The inter-war years are a key stage in the development of the academic study of politics in Britain . . . the ideas of the post-war makers of the profession were shaped by the writers of the inter-war period'. The key features of the subject in the inter-war period are well brought out by Kavanagh:

- 'Politics was a small subject operating in the small world of British higher education. Before 1914, and for some time later, as a subject, let alone a discipline, it lacked a distinct identity; it was studied alongside economics, philosophy, law and history, all of which were more securely established as separate subjects and departments in the universities' (Kavanagh, 2003, p. 595).
- The subject 'was seen as part of a humane tradition, deeply rooted in the classics, literature and history, one which provided a liberal elite education' (Kavanagh, 2003, p. 600). This tradition was perhaps reflected in the keynote address given at a PSA conference the author attended at the beginning of the 1970s in which a professor of politics argued that 'we should all read more novels'.
- Most teachers of teachers were public intellectuals who made extensive use of the media of the day, served on government committees and, in some cases, wrote party programmes. 'Many were . . . active social reformers and believed that the study of politics could provide the knowledge to reform society' (Kavanagh, 2003, p. 610).

The Clapham Committee

'Wartime experience had shown the importance of the social sciences in public affairs' (Chester, 1975, p. 157). In its 1943 report the British Association had called for the establishment of a social science research council based on the American model. This may have influenced the deputy prime minister, Clement Attlee, who wrote to the chancellor of the exchequer, Sir John Anderson, informing him that he had come 'to the conclusion that a useful purpose might be served by adding a fourth Research Council to those at present in existence'. Those were the Department of Industrial and Scientific Research, the Medical Research Council and the Agricultural Research Council, all of which were concerned with the natural sciences. In Attlee's view:

> I feel that the time has come to do something for the *social sciences*. They are of increasing importance in throwing light on the problems of public policy, and I am given to understand that we are dangerously dependent upon American Foundations for funding research in this wide field and that, in any case, the total amount of money available is very small (NA, 1944a, emphasis in original).

Attlee got rather short shrift from the chancellor who replied after a delay of three weeks and made it clear, no doubt reflecting attitudes at the time, that the value of the social sciences was in his view open to question, as well as their impartiality:

> I think that the analogy of the existing Research Councils is rather misleading. The so-called social sciences, with the possible exception of economics, have not reached the stage of exact knowledge at which the natural sciences have strived. Moreover political considerations affect the study of sociology much more than they do that of the natural sciences. I think it would be a good thing to avoid using the term 'social *sciences*', partly for the reason mentioned above, partly because it may be held to include such fringe subjects as ethnology, linguistics, ecology and even dietics (NA, 1944b, emphasis in original).

Nevertheless, it was agreed to set up a committee under the chairmanship of the distinguished economic historian and president of the British Academy, Sir John Clapham (who died before the report was completed) to investigate the state of economic and social research, which was one way of kicking an awkward issue into touch. Its terms of reference were 'To consider whether additional provision is necessary for research into economic and social questions'. This wording led to an understandable focus on economics and sociology (which was rather broadly defined) in its early discussions.

In preparation for an interview with Sir John, Attlee was briefed as follows: 'After discussion with a number of distinguished social scientists we all came to the conclusion that since the number of vested interests was very great, and the difficulties of providing money very real, it would be best to set up a small Committee of Investigation in the first instance' (NA, 1944c).

Although the committee did not lead to the research council that Attlee wanted, it did enhance awareness of the social sciences and in particular it argued that there was under-provision of political science in the universities. Professor G. D. H. Cole, one of the subsequent signatories of the letter that led to the formation of the PSA, declined an invitation to serve on the committee and another signatory, Sir Hector Hetherington, was added. He soon proved his worth, Clapham noting in a letter about arranging the date of the meeting: 'Make sure of Hetherington. He is valuable' (NA, 1945). After Clapham's death, Hetherington took over as chair of the committee and produced the final draft of its report.

The state of political studies in 1945

The committee set out to collect information about the provision for the study of the social sciences, including politics. The work was undertaken in England and Wales by Professor Sir Henry Clay, then the warden of Nuffield College, and by Sir Hector Hetherington in Scotland. It was probably these data that led the committee to conclude in the earlier drafts that politics provision was 'woefully inadequate', although this was toned down, probably by Hetherington who was noted for his 'judicious' use of language in civil service circles, to the more restrained 'not enough' in the final version (Cmd. 6868, 1946, p. 8).

What the survey showed in 1945 was that the main numerical concentrations of expertise were at the LSE and Oxford. The LSE had the chair of political science and the Montague Burton chair of international relations. It also had readerships in public administration and political science and teachers in political science and economic and public administration. Cambridge was confined to its chair of political science, but Oxford had the Gladstone chair of government and public administration, plus a large number of college fellows and lecturers in politics. In the immediate aftermath of the war, Manchester was confined to a lecturer and assistant lecturer in public administration. Aberystwyth had its chair of international relations and lecturers in political science. There were isolated individuals elsewhere. Nottingham had a lecturer in political and social theory and Exeter had a lecturer in international politics. In Scotland there was a junior lectureship in political science at St Andrews and Glasgow had a sub-department of political philosophy. Edinburgh told Sir Hector that it had no lecturer in either political science or political philosophy.

The papers of the committee also included a privately circulated survey of social science research undertaken in 1945 by the National Institute for Economic and Social Research. There were five topics listed at the Oxford Institute of Colonial Studies of a relatively predictable kind such as 'The Government of the Anglo-Egyptian Sudan'. Fourteen projects were under way at the Royal Institute of International Affairs and they were mostly concerned with what would be called comparative government rather than international relations. A project on federalism had been completed and there were five projects on democracy, including one on 'The Modern Democratic State' in which 'The author will consider democratic disillusionment, the new challenges set to democracy by technical progress and how the democratic State has partially met and may more successfully meet these challenges' (National Institute, 1945, p. 40). Miss Mary Macdonald was studying the failure of democratic government in Austria, while the government of Ethiopia under Haile Selassie was being researched. The LSE had two political theory projects, one involving Professor Hayek engaged in a study of the letters of J. S. Mill.

Five public administration projects were listed at Nuffield College, one at Birmingham and one at the Institute of Public Administration. Some of these projects had a substantial political dimension. For example, the Nuffield College project on 'The Elected Personnel of Local Authorities', involving Miss E. I. Hardy, sought 'to throw light on the actual working of the electoral machinery of local government, and of any hindrances which may exist to the participation in local affairs of particular groups or sections of the community capable of playing a useful part in public work' (National Institute, 1945, p. 43). In other words, it was concerned with social biases in the recruitment of local councillors.

The final report of the committee referred to Graham Wallas' *Human Nature in Politics* as a work that had been 'inadequately followed up'. It also found that 'Political science, the study of the institutions of government and public administration is a subject in which sufficient work has been done to demonstrate its utility and importance. Yet there are only three chairs specifically devoted to this subject' (Cmd. 6868, 1946, p. 8). However, it considered that the proposal for a research council was unnecessary as it was 'both premature and misconceived'. What was needed was more routine research, otherwise there could be a 'premature crystallization of spurious orthodoxies'. There was simply not enough output and the scope of the subjects was not well defined. The whole field was understaffed and what was needed was to strengthen the various branches of the social sciences in the universities (Cmd. 6868, 1946, p. 12). This was very much a 'safety first' recommendation and it is interesting to speculate what the effect would have been if a social science research council had been established in the late 1940s. Given the immature state of politics, it would have probably lost out to other social sciences.

What the report did recommend, apart from more funding for the social sciences in universities, was the establishment of a social sciences sub-committee to advise the University Grants Committee, which was put into effect, and the formation of an Interdepartmental Economic and Social Research committee involving both social scientists and civil servants. This functioned until 1950 under the chairman-ship of the registrar-general, Dr North, as an energetic body that undertook a considerable amount of work to survey what might be possible. Its task was assisted, as the chairman noted at the first meeting, in that 'the presence of several members of University staffs who were closely associated with or have actually served in Government Departments was in the right line of continuing the valuable coopera-tion between the universities and the Departments which had developed so much during the war' (NA, 1945, p. 1). Unfortunately, these contacts atrophied over time and, as will be noted later, it was not easy to recreate them.

In appointing the academic members of the committee it was thought that 'There would be no harm if one were [*sic*] a Scot and women were by no means barred' (NA, 1946a). Hetherington was at least resident in Scotland, but was not available. Sir Henry Clay, the warden of Nuffield College, noted that G. D. H. Cole 'had obvious claims', but he did not want to serve. 'D. N. Chester seems to me to be the liveliest intelligence in the field, with the advantage that he combines a very practical sense with very high standards of scholarship' (NA, 1946b). The civil service view of 'the four outsiders' was that there should be 'one man from the London School of Economics' who in the event was the director, Sir A. Carr-Saunders. Other potential candidates having been dismissed as 'too much of an individualist', despite Clay's recommendation that 'he comes from the Provinces', or in another case as a 'windbag', it was noted that Chester 'would provide a link with Nuffield' and 'I think, would be better'. This comment was underlined and a 'Yes' scrawled in the margin and Chester came to sit on the committee (NA, 1946c).

Chester was an active and assiduous member of the committee and his interests ranged widely and were certainly not confined to political science or public administration. However, he was not slow to recommend making available data that might be useful for the study of politics. At the fifth meeting he noted that 'there was no reference in the replies of the Home Office on the General Register Office to the number and proportion of votes polled at Local Government elections. This was an unfortunate gap in published statistics' (NA, 1947, pp. 3–4). He was also concerned about the position of younger researchers in smaller universities: 'While some Departments did have formal or informal contacts with universities, he thought that more means should be found of ensuring that the interests of new people, especially those in the smaller universities, should not be overlooked' (NA, 1949, p. 7). However, reflecting a rather elitist conception of research activity that was apparent later in his career, he wanted to make a clear distinction between research and journalism and between university and commercial research:

> Mr Chester said that the Committee must confine their recommendations to accredited research workers, e.g., to those who were sponsored by a University research department or a recognized non-commercial research institute. In this way 'lame ducks' would be eliminated, for such departments would act responsibly in their recommendations. Departments must themselves discriminate between pure research interests and business or journalistic research (NA, 1948, p. 4).

These arguments would not be acceptable in the twenty-first century when funded research is supposed to have demonstrable positive impacts on the economy or society more generally.

The Formation of the PSA

The stimulus for the formation of the PSA came principally from UNESCO and its plan to set up an International Political Science Association (IPSA), founded in 1949, which would need national associations to be its members. A number of other national associations were also founded in 1950 (Israel, the Netherlands, Sweden) with Germany, Belgium, Mexico and Greece following in 1951 (Boncourt, 2009, p. 5). At a conference in 1947 UNESCO had selected political science as the first of the social sciences to be chosen for a stocktaking review. 'This led to a small meeting in Paris in September 1948 attended by Professors G. D. H. Cole [Oxford, see Box 1.2] and W. A. Robson [LSE, see Box 1.4]' (Chester, 1975, p. 29). One of the motives for forming the PSA was so that it could 'play an active part' in the work of IPSA. However, according to the 'Memorandum on the Proposed Formation of a British Political Studies Association' there was also a domestic motivation:

Box 1.2: G. D. H. Cole, 1889–1959

G. D. H. Cole was the first Chichele Professor of Social and Political Theory at Oxford University, a position he held from 1944 until his retirement in 1957. He was one of the individuals selected to contribute an article to the first issue of *Political Studies*. 'Yet in other respects his life and work is a challenge to today's academic political science (a term he always resisted, which is one reason why the association "studies" politics). Instead of a narrow discipline talking to itself in an obscure language, Cole wanted relevance, engagement, accessibility and breadth' (Wright, 2001, p. 13). From a middle-class commercial background, he was educated at St Paul's School London and Balliol College Oxford. He was a leading intellectual of the left in Britain, advocating a political theory of guild socialism which gave a high priority to individual liberty. He was first appointed to a readership in economics at Oxford and subsequently made a major contribution to the emerging discipline of labour history. He could claim 'to be the only leading academic expert in all three branches of Oxford's final honour school of philosophy, politics and economics' (Stears, 2009, p. 6). Over time 'his contributions to political theory increasingly attracted praise and attention' (Stears, 2009, p. 9). A polymath, he displayed 'a commitment to politics as an enterprise of public philosophy – including the academic practitioners of the discipline' (Wright, 2001, p. 14).

A considerable development of studies specifically termed 'political' has been taking place in our Universities during recent years. In each University this expansion is proceeding in relative isolation; and the level reached varies greatly from one University to another. The exchange of information about what is being done, and the discussion of the problems arising, would plainly be mutually helpful (LSE, 1949, PSA/15, p. 1).

Informal meetings took place in London and Oxford to plan an association. As one interview respondent commented, 'PSA was superimposed on an existing network'. In November 1949 a letter was distributed outlining the proposed formation of a 'Universities Political Studies Association' (see Table 1.2 for signatories). The relative balance of influence is reflected in the fact that six of the signatories were from Oxford (albeit Lindsay had just become principal of the new university college of North Staffordshire, later Keele University); three were from Cambridge (but one of those was emeritus and another, Wade, a constitutional lawyer); three were from the LSE; and one from Manchester. The exception, Hector Hetherington, was principal of Glasgow University where he had earlier lectured before becoming vice-chancellor of Liverpool. Ninety-eight individuals responded to this letter. The original plan was to base membership 'upon Groups functioning in each University

Table 1.2:   Signatories of the Letter Proposing Formation of the PSA

Ernest Barker (Cambridge)
D. W. Brogan (Cambridge)
D. N. Chester (Oxford)
G. D. H. Cole (Oxford)
Hector Hetherington (Glasgow)
H. J. Laski (LSE)
Lindsay of Birker (Oxford and University College of North Staffordshire)
W. J. M. Mackenzie (Manchester)
M. Oakeshott (Oxford)
W. A. Robson (LSE)
K. B. Smellie (LSE)
E. C. S. Wade (Cambridge)
K. C. Wheare (Oxford)
C. H. Wilson (Oxford)

Source: LSE, 1950b.

or University College; although provision will have to be made for individual membership in cases where no Group is practicable' (LSE, 1949, PSA/15, p. 1). In the event this idea of group or departmental membership was dropped in favour of individual membership.

An interesting omission from the list of signatories was any specialist in international relations. Birch recalls (2009, p. 7) that the substantial international relations department at Aberystwyth 'sent no members to the PSA inaugural meeting. Had it been sent the November 1948 circular letter, I wonder? If not, why not?' Chester comments (1975, p. 158n): 'We must have not thought International Relations to be an essential ingredient in the list of names, for I cannot recall anyone being approached from that field'. It is therefore even more remarkable that, as Ashworth argues (2009, p. 23), 'it was IR's capture by political science in the 1950s that closed off this link to other disciplines, and led to a thirty year isolation'.

It was acknowledged that 'No agreement exists, or is likely to be reached in the near future, about the precise scope of a systematic study of politics' (LSE, 1949, PSA/15, p. 3). For practical purposes, it was proposed to use the classification of subject matter used at the Paris conference. This divided the subject into four main areas: political theory; government; parties, groups and public opinion (what later came to be known as 'political behaviour'); and international relations. These were in turn subdivided so that, for example, 'government' encompassed the constitution, national government, regional and local government, public administration, economic and social functions of government and comparative political institutions. The objectives of the Association were decidedly modest: 'In our view the proposed Association ought not to embark on any ambitious functions or projects in its early stages' (LSE, 1949, PSA/15, p. 4). One proposed activity that was never followed up was the creation of a primary documentation centre, while the pro-

Box 1.3:   Harold Laski, 1893–1950

When the PSA made their 50th anniversary awards, they affectionately named them after one of the founders of the association, Harold J. Laski. He has been described as 'interesting, influential and dangerous' (Hirst, 2001, p. 12). Coming from a wealthy and cultured Jewish family in Manchester, he was yet another political scientist to have attended Manchester Grammar School. He read history at Oxford and then went to junior posts at McGill University in Montreal and Harvard before accepting a post at the LSE where he was promoted to the chair of political science in 1926 at the age of 32. His early works on pluralist theory with their emphasis on intermediary bodies and the value of decentralisation have stood the test of time well. Laski came to adopt 'a personal form of Marxism, which continued to be infused with liberalism' (Newman, 2009, p. 5) and as his involvement in practical politics increased, he became a kind of political lightning conductor who attracted attacks from the right. He served on Labour's National Executive Committee from 1937 to 1949, but his usefulness as a punching bag to Conservatives and his attempt to prevent Attlee becoming prime minister after he won the 1945 general election led to the latter's famous put down: 'a period of silence on your part would be welcome'. He was committed to the formation of the PSA and wrote to the inaugural meeting two days before his death to say that 'I had greatly looked forward to the occasion, and it is very disappointing to be held a prisoner by my doctor'. Views about the enduring impact of his work differ, and his reputation declined sharply after his death, 'but since the 1980s and 1990s it has risen steadily' (Hirst, 2001, p. 12).

posed research and information bulletin quickly metamorphosed into a journal. Perhaps the founding members were influenced by the letter sent to the inaugural meeting by the ill Laski (see Box 1.3) two days before his death in which he wrote: 'I hope we shall not forget how remarkably Lord Keynes and his colleagues made the Royal Economic Society a success by associating the Economic Journal with its fortunes' (LSE, 1950a, PSA/15).

Tony Birch, who attended the inaugural meeting held at the LSE on 23 and 24 March 1950 as the sole representative of Manchester University, recalls: 'It was not an exciting occasion as the effective decisions had been taken a few months earlier by a group of senior scholars whose members had been co-opted by Chester and Charles Wilson at Oxford' (Birch, 2009, p. 5). Despite the effort to construct a minimalist conception of the PSA, a number of controversies arose when the inaugural meeting discussed its constitution. The most fundamental of these was about whether the Association should be one of political *studies* or political *science*. As Hayward notes (1999, p. 18), 'Scepticism about the possibility of political science was deeply rooted in the British intellectual tradition, represented notably by the University of Oxford'. The memorandum claimed that 'Both the Oxford and LSE groups strongly favour the term "studies" as against the term "science"' (LSE, 1949, PSA/15, p. 2). In fact, the LSE preferred the term science, as was evident in Laski's use of it in his letter to the inaugural meeting.

Professors Robson (see Box 1.4) and Smellie (see Box 1.5) from the LSE proposed that the association should be called 'Political Science Association of the United Kingdom'. Birch recalls (2009, p. 6) that 'Alfred Cobban of UCL proposed that the term "political science" in the draft constitution should be replaced by "political studies"'. (Cobban was a historian who worked and wrote on French history, but he also wrote two books on political theory.) 'Robson spoke against the resolution,

Box 1.4:   William A. Robson, 1895–1980

William Robson was very active in the formation of the PSA, urging that it should have 'science' in its title. He also served as the second president of IPSA from 1952 to 1955. He was the son of a Hatton Garden pearl dealer whose circumstances changed when his father died when he was fifteen. Wartime service in the Royal Flying Corps led to a chance meeting with George Bernard Shaw who gave him an introduction to the LSE where he completed his PhD in 1924, having been called to the bar in the meantime. His broad subject was public administration including administrative law, local government and city planning. One book was written jointly with the future Labour prime minister, Clement Attlee. He was actively involved in the foundation of the *Political Quarterly* in 1930 and continued as a joint editor until 1975. Like most political scientists of his generation, he worked in the civil service during the Second World War, but his personal style was not one that most civil servants found congenial. He burned his boats with the Labour party in the late 1950s by supporting the sensible but politically inconvenient plan for a Greater London Council. The Labour leadership formed the view that he 'was not politically reliable, too independent, too big for his boots, and certainly too big for theirs' (Crick, 2009, p. 2). 'An austere and forbidding man', he 'certainly did not suffer fools gladly' (Crick, 2009, pp. 2, 3). He customarily arrived at the LSE by bicycle and was a keen sportsman, particularly in hockey. He fell out at the LSE with successive heads of department, Harold Laski and Michael Oakeshott, and was also not on speaking terms with Kingsley Smellie (see Box 1.5). It is perhaps appropriate that Crick wrote his entry for the *Dictionary of National Biography* as they were both engaged in public debate, somewhat polemical and prickly yet inspiring respect. Crick's interests were, however, wider both intellectually and personally than those of Robson.

> **Box 1.5:** Kingsley Bryce Smellie, 1897–1987
>
> K. B. Smellie, a Cambridge history graduate, is not one of the political scientists like Laski and W. J. M. Mackenzie who have entries in the *Dictionary of National Biography*, but he was nevertheless an influential figure in the early years of the discipline and the formation of the PSA. He was a popular and respected teacher at the LSE where he was originally Lecturer in Public Administration but became Professor of Government in 1949. When Laski was too ill to address the inaugural meeting, Smellie was called on to give an address on 'The General State of Political Studies in Britain'. Smellie chaired the PSA from 1957 to 1960. He and his wife (Stephanie) were recruitment headhunters in an informal way, operating as a placement agency. They facilitated first posts for leading political scientists such as Andrew Dunsire, Maurice Vile, (Lord) Trevor Smith, Derek Crabtree and Ken Minogue. David Butler recalled in interview: 'Smellie said we had a very bright young man who should get away from London: that was Hugh Berrington', who became Butler's doctoral student. The Smellies lived in a large rented house in Wimbledon where they hired a butler for parties. Smellie had lost both legs, one below the knee and one above the knee, in the First World War but he was a good ballroom dancer and liked to drive at Brands Hatch. His principal books were historical, including *Great Britain since 1688: A Modern History*, *A Hundred Years of English Government*, *A History of Local Government* and also *The British Way of Life*.

but there was quite a large majority in favour of the change' (Birch, 2009, p. 6). The amendment substituting the word 'Studies' for the word 'Science' was carried without being put to a vote. 'The titles of both the PSA and its journal reflected a degree of dubiety in this country about the label "political science"' (Harrison, 1975, p. 61). From an Oxford perspective, 'There was also a feeling that "studies" was a wider umbrella than "science", a particularly important consideration when so much of the writing was political history' (Chester, 1975, p. 153). A 'science' title might have allowed the discipline to distinguish itself more clearly from political history and constitutional law and more clearly define its boundaries as an autonomous discipline. However, in what was then a small and eclectic discipline, it was important for the PSA to be as inclusive as possible.

The question of who should be a member also provoked some debate. The original memorandum had stated that a general aim of the Association should be 'to promote the *disinterested* study of political ideas and political practice' (emphasis added). What was at stake here was the relationship with practitioners, which was to be the subject of continued uncertainty and some friction. Chester recalls (1975, p. 154) that there was 'a good deal of discussion about whether membership should be confined to University teachers or be thrown open to non-University institutions or to practitioners, e.g., MPs and civil servants'. Clause 2 of the constitution as adopted stated that 'Any person holding an appointment in political studies and allied subjects in a University or University College in the United Kingdom or Colonies shall be eligible for membership'. Brogan had insisted on the phrase 'and allied subjects' as a saving clause, claiming: 'It's necessary for Cambridge!' (Chester, 1975, p. 154) At the meeting the wording 'or Colonies' was added by amendment. However, the inclusion of Eire was ruled out on the grounds that it would be inconsistent with the constitution of IPSA. Clause 3 left it to the committee to decide whether non-academics could be admitted: 'Any other person whose participation in the activities of the Association is likely, in the opinion of the Committee, to be advantageous to political studies may be admitted to membership'.

Birch, in his only contribution to the meeting, suggested that the Association should be called the 'British PSA',

> but this was rejected politely by Chester, who said it was unnecessary as we would always know who we were and if some person outside Britain should think that we were the Turkish association, then that person 'would be genuinely in error' (I remember the last words distinctly as they struck me as a very Oxford way of saying that somebody was an idiot) (Birch, 2009, p. 6).

This anecdote is quite revealing as it shows how dominant Chester (see Box 1.6) was in the proceedings and also the phrase 'we would always know who we were'

Box 1.6:   Sir Norman Chester, 1907–86

Sir Norman Chester played a key role in the formation of the PSA as its founding chair from 1950 to 1957 and subsequently served as President of the International Political Science Association from 1961 to 1964. Chester came from a relatively humble background and was obliged to start work in the treasurer's department of Manchester City Council at the age of fourteen. However, Rose (1999, p. 472) names him as the exemplar of the 'able and ambitious young lads from town halls in the North West' who was able to pursue an evening degree in Administration at Manchester University. He subsequently became a lecturer there, but on the outbreak of the Second World War he was drafted into the Economic Section of the War Cabinet secretariat where he remained until 1945. During this period he served as secretary to the Beveridge Social Insurance Committee. He was effectively one of the northerners drafted in to reinvigorate the southern establishment in its hour of need and he made subsequent good use of the wartime contacts he developed among politicians and administrators. In 1945 he went to

Nuffield College, Oxford as a fellow and became its warden (head of college) in 1954. He held this post until 1978, skilfully developing it as an intellectual powerhouse of the social sciences. His own authoritative work was principally on administration and public utilities. He served on a number of government committees, but his interest in sport (particularly Oxford City football club) and his wartime friendship with Harold Wilson led him to chair a government committee on football from 1966 to 1968. He remained a key figure in the game, holding a number of posts. He was a formidable individual who could seem abrasive. He thought that admitting the polytechnics to the PSA would devalue the currency and he was opposed to the ousting of the existing Executive Committee of the PSA in 1975. Although he remained very much a northerner in his manner, he was quite at ease in establishment circles and had absorbed an elitist view of higher education in the sense that he believed in the pursuit of research excellence by individuals drawn from diverse backgrounds.

suggests a clear identity as a network of individuals familiar with each other if not as a discipline with a well-defined and distinguishable intellectual core.

The committee of ten elected at the end of the meeting was less exclusive than the original group of signatories, although Chester as the first chair 'effectively co-opted the first members' (Birch, 2009, p. 9). However, no doubt he realised that the 'golden triangle' universities could not be allowed to become too dominant. Oxford and LSE universities had just two members each and Cambridge was confined to one. Apart from Kingsley Smellie, the LSE was represented by Professor Sir Charles Webster, 'who was in effect head of the International Relations department there, which covered economic and legal relationships as well as international relations' (Birch, 2009, p. 7). Manchester University had two members, one of whom was W. J. M. Mackenzie and the other Harry Street from the law department who had an interest in civil liberties. The other committee members were drawn from Bristol, Leeds and Glasgow. In addition, Richard Bassett from the LSE, described by Birch (2009, p. 5) as 'a very sensible man who died tragically early' was elected as honorary secretary and treasurer. The post was not divided into separate secretary and treasurer roles until 1961.

Conclusions

At the end of the 1940s, there were around 50 teachers of politics in Britain (Chester, 1975, p. 61). This was a very small number on which to base a discipline, even if it had shown greater confidence about its distinct identity and its boundaries. Kenny claims (2004, p. 572) that 'Political studies at the start of the 1950s functioned as an intellectual community, not as a professional discipline in the contemporary sense of the term'. It was therefore not surprising that the formation of a subject association required an external stimulus, although it was also facilitated by well-developed domestic networks.

> What is striking about this small group of scholars is the extent to which they sat at the same table . . . This was a consequence partly of the small London and Oxbridge axis but also of their shared educational background, employment in a handful of universities and interest in both political institutions and political theory (Kavanagh, 2003, p. 611).

It is also worth noting that three of the six pioneers featured in boxes in this chapter came from financially impoverished backgrounds and were markedly upwardly mobile, four of them went to Oxford (Smellie went to Cambridge) and none of them were women although this was a period of increased activism by women as they fought for and obtained the vote. Admittedly, women politicians were thin on the ground, but political scientists even more so.

A clear legacy of this period was the eclecticism of the study of politics in Britain and the resistance to 'scientific' approaches to the discipline. That this was the predominant view was evident in the discussions over the title of the PSA. This reflected 'The continuing importance of history and philosophy . . . Many of the founding members still regarded politics as a subject that properly borrowed from these allied subjects; a more practical consideration was that historians and philosophers formed a large number of those teaching politics' (Kavanagh, 2003, pp. 610–11). In its early years the discipline lacked a clear identity, well-defined boundaries and often collective self-belief in the validity of its contribution. This only encouraged the view that it did not require any special skills or training: 'Thus, in Britain, political science, insofar as it is regarded at all, is seen very much as a gentleman's hobby in which anyone so minded may participate' (Smith, 1986, p. 431). The intellectual openness and tolerance of eclecticism has its merits, but if it is allowed to become too uncontrolled it can lead to a lack of rigour in the deployment of methodologies and techniques, which undermines the systematic comparison that the subject has to offer if it is to be distinguished from polemic or idle speculation. Although it has developed in many ways that would not be recognised by its founders, the study of politics in Britain is still heavily influenced by its origins.

Chapter 2

An Elitist Discipline? 1950–63

This chapter reviews the period from the formation of the PSA in 1950, to 1963, which saw the publication of the Robbins Report on higher education which was to have a major impact on the study of politics in Britain. This division into periods is slightly different from that used by Hayward, whose first phase lasts from 1950 to 1960. The point being made here is that the PSA, and the discipline, expanded very slowly until 1963. Membership of the PSA expanded by 20 per cent (from 129 to 155, excluding 'other' members who were mostly outside the UK) in the six years from 1953 to 1959 and another 16 per cent in the four years to 1963.

Incremental Expansion

To put it another way, in the decade after the establishment of *Political Studies*, the membership of the PSA expanded by a little less than 4 per cent a year, a slow incremental growth. For example, if we examine the period from 1953 to 1959, the membership at smaller 'civics' like Exeter (where government was then a sub-department of economics) increased from five to seven and at Leicester from three to five. Perhaps the most striking increase was at the University College of North Staffordshire, later Keele University, from two members in 1953 to eight in 1959 and eleven in 1963. This was not just a numerically significant development, for as well as the inspired leadership of Sammy Finer (see Box 2.1), the department included such important future figures as Frank Bealey, Jean Blondel and Hugh Berrington in 1959. Finer 'used his exceptional lecturing gifts to proselytize for his subject. The result was that a large number of students chose politics as an option for their honours courses, which in turn enabled him to expand his department' (Pulzer, 2009, p. 2). John Easom, alumni officer at Keele University, commented: 'he invariably comes up in conversations with our pioneer alumni of the 1950s and 1960s. They hold him in great respect

Box 2.1: Sammy Finer, 1915–93

Sammy Finer was a founder member of the PSA, although in 1950 he was not the major influence he became later, and he was its chairman from 1965 to 1969. It is difficult to capture the essence of an exuberant phenomenon like Finer in print, although Peter Pulzer's entry in the *Oxford Dictionary of National Biography* is exemplary in this respect. Finer was a larger than life character who had a 'lifelong love affair with the sound of his voice' (Pulzer, 2009, p. 4). Bill Proctor considers that 'Sammy Finer was essentially an academic historian of the old broad-brush school, and the new discipline of political "science" was not something he was much good at or at any rate took to naturally, although he believed in it passionately' (Personal communication, 9 July 2009). Nevertheless, he made a considerable and original contribution to the study of politics, especially comparative government. Jack Hayward (2001, p. 13) described him as 'a protagonist of the best of old institutionalism' who 'stood out for his imaginative range of conception and panache in execution'. He came from a large family of Romanian origins and 'was one of the many children of pre-1914 Jewish immigrants from eastern Europe who were to play such prominent roles in British economic, cultural and political life' (Pulzer, 2009, p. 1). His older brother, Herman Finer, was also a distinguished political scientist, first at the LSE and later in the United States. Proctor thinks that in writing *Comparative Government*, 'Sammy was determined to demonstrate to himself (more than anyone else) that he was his brother Herman's equal: Sammy simply didn't appreciate the true value of his own unique abilities as a communicator, and as an inspiration to young people' (Personal communication, 9 July 2009). After taking PPE at Oxford, Sammy Finer was elected to a junior fellowship at Balliol in 1949 following war service, but quickly took up the post of Professor of Political Institutions at the newly founded University College of North Staffordshire (later Keele University). It was here that he was at his most creative, pioneering, for example, the study of pressure groups in Britain. In 1966 he went to Manchester which offered less scope for his energies. Bill Proctor recalls: 'Sammy never seemed entirely at ease amongst his peers in a larger department than Keele's, and frequently admitted to missing the stimulation of Keele students' (Personal communication, 9 July 2009). In 1974 he became Gladstone Professor at Oxford. His personal style, including his extravagant dress, did not always go down well in Oxford and 'his attempts to change the philosophy, politics and economics syllabus came to nothing' (Pulzer, 2009, p. 3). He had a new period of creativity in retirement, producing the three-volume posthumous *History of Government from the Earliest Times*. As Hugh Berrington remarked in his memorial address, 'Sammy was an experience' (quoted in Pulzer, 2009, p. 4). He belonged to a generation when professors could be ebullient, even mildly eccentric, figures.

and affection as perhaps the most brilliant teacher of that time' (Personal communication, 30 June 2009).

In the two years to 1965 the membership grew to 270, an increase in 27 per cent or 13.5 per cent a year over the unadjusted figure. It then increased again to 400 in 1967. Of course, the membership of the PSA is not the same as those engaged in the discipline, as the PSA included members who did not teach in politics departments, while not all those so employed were in the PSA. However, the proportion of politics academics who were members was probably higher in the earlier years when social pressures to join may have been stronger and the trends in membership do give a picture of the increasing size of the discipline.

The precise dating of the beginning of Hayward's second era of expansion and technocratic reforms is less significant than his characterisation of the first phase:

> The first decade (1950–60) was marked by a retrospective Whig inclination to complacent description of traditions inherited from the past reflected in the continued teaching of constitutional history and the history of ideas, coupled with a predominantly atheoretical empiricism in the study of political institutions not being seriously threatened by lively but inconclusive debates within political philosophy (Hayward, 1999, p. 20).

Kenny is also critical of the moralistic discourse that celebrated an essentially nineteenth-century liberal constitution embodied in the Westminster model (Kenny, 2004, p. 572). However, he cautions us against 'the tendency to construe this period as a kind of amateurish prequel to the establishment of a modern autonomous discipline' (Kenny, 2004, p. 567).

What was evident was the domination of the big three departments of London, Oxford and Manchester during this period. 'Outside Oxford, the London School of Economics and Manchester, political studies led a beggarly existence in the 1950s' (Pulzer, 2009, p. 2). In 1953, 1959 and 1963 the three leading departments accounted for over 50 per cent of UK academic members of the PSA. They also 'provided 55 per cent of the authors in [*Political Studies*] between 1953 and 1957' (Boncourt, 2007, p. 283). Oxford was always predominant in numbers of PSA members with between 21.8 per cent (1959) and 23.2 per cent (1953) of the total. This reflected the need for colleges to have politics tutors. With a very large post-war rise in the numbers reading PPE, 'Before long most Colleges had at least one Tutorial Fellow in both Economics and Politics, Nuffield College and, to a lesser extent, St Antony's College, also appointed a number of Fellows in Politics . . . out of their own resources' (Chester, 1986, p. 177). Membership of the politics sub-faculty grew from 47 in 1949 to 54 in 1959 and 72 in 1969 (Chester, 1986, p. 179). There was a widespread view that Oxford had something special to contribute, reflected in a request at the 1956 PSA annual general meeting for the Oxford PPE Bibliography in Politics to be brought up to date and used for a more general bibliography in politics. 'Although Oxford University is often cited in the profession as a major institutional obstacle to the maturation of an indigenous political science, it actually performed a more ambivalent role in these years' (Kenny, 2007, p. 169).

London (largely LSE) had between 17.4 per cent (1959) and 19.5 per cent (1963) of the total membership. It did rather less well in terms of *Political Studies* articles, 5 per cent between 1953 and 1957 and 13 per cent between 1958 and 1962 (Boncourt, 2007, p. 284).

The Manchester Department of Government

Manchester accounted for just over 10 per cent of the total of UK academic members of the PSA, but had a greater significance than the numbers would suggest because of the role of W. J. M. Mackenzie (see Box 2.2) and the fact that 'the Manchester Department of Government became the most productive nursery in Britain for professors of politics: the great majority of those who were lecturers at Manchester in the '50s got chairs before they were forty' (Birch and Spann, 1974, p. 7). Richard Rose (1999, p. 25n) lists 24 members of the Manchester department who subsequently obtained professorial appointments in Britain or across the world.

Box 2.2:   W. J. M. Mackenzie, 1909–96

Bill Mackenzie was a founding Executive Committee member of the PSA and a key figure in the development of political science in Britain. 'In achievement as well as appearance he was a big man, white haired from early days with a ruddy complexion and a wide, blue-eyed gaze both friendly and quizzical' (Rose, 1999, p. 465). His department at Manchester produced a considerable number of those who went on to hold chairs of politics in British universities at the time of the 1960s expansion and he was also prominent as an assessor at appointments and an examiner of PhDs. An intimidating experience for the author as an MSc student was to give a paper before Mackenzie at a weekend 'country house' event in Scotland on a subject on which I had no prior knowledge but of which he had personal experience. He was the first chairman of the Social Science Research Council politics committee when it was created in 1965. Mackenzie was a Balliol Scot who changed from being a classics fellow at Magdalen College, Oxford to teaching PPE. Like many of his contemporaries, he was a civil servant during wartime and made good use of the contacts he developed in government. He had an impressive record of service on a wide range of government bodies and inquiries, taking a special interest in Africa. He became Professor of Government at Manchester in 1948 and built up a department that had a wide influence. He moved to the University of Glasgow in 1966 and took a keen interest in constitutional issues surrounding Scottish independence, although it is uncertain whether he ever voted for the Scottish National party. His 'translation' of the Plowden

Committee Report out of civil service code, using his knowledge of classic tongues, remains a highly original piece of work that has continuing relevance. His book on *Politics and Social Science* draws on the impressive range of his erudition. Yet it had no overarching theme, other than perhaps eclecticism, and there was no Mackenzie 'school' of politics. He would not have wanted one, however, beyond a sceptical, questioning, searching approach to the study of the subject which sought to deepen and broaden understanding. He is recalled with deep affection by those who worked with him and his influence on the study of politics in Britain was subtle yet profound.

Although it only had ten members by the end of the decade, the influence of the Manchester Department of Government was considerable and this was because Mackenzie took both political science and the need for research seriously. As one informant commented, there was a different sort of work ethic at Manchester to Oxford and Mackenzie made it clear to his staff that they had 'got to produce a book every so often'.

It would be misleading to say that for Mackenzie in the 1950s political science was a subject that had yet to be created, but he certainly saw it as a struggling infant which he had a special duty to nurture . . . He even liked the term 'political science' itself, at a time when most of his British colleagues . . . fought shy of it (Birch and Spann, 1974, p. 5).

'Mackenzie saw particular benefits in the project of bringing the American and British disciplines into closer proximity' (Kenny, 2004, p. 575).

But what did Mackenzie understand by political science? He 'regarded politics as a very peculiar discipline' (Birch, 2009, p. 4). In many ways he saw it as an exploration in which the destination was uncertain, something reflected in the title of his retrospective volume, *Explorations in Government*. In the introduction to this volume, he explained: 'I see "the discipline" as a group of people rather than a set of principles, as a continuing debate rather than an enquiry in the style of natural science' (Mackenzie, 1975a, p. ix). Indeed, 'in the 1950s Mackenzie doubted, as did his contemporary Michael Oakeshott [see Box 2.3] whether political science could properly be regarded as an academic discipline at all'. In particular, 'He shared Oakeshott's scepticism about social scientism and about political theology of the Laski or Lindsay kind' (Birch and Spann, 1974, p. 4). At its worst, this could degenerate into a kind of polemical pious moralising which was far removed from academic analysis. Nevertheless, Mackenzie 'could find no satisfaction in Oakeshott's answer, which was to use political writings as a way of inducting his students into an understanding of historical explanation' (Birch and Spann, 1974, p. 4).

Box 2.3:   Michael Oakeshott, 1901–90

Michael Oakeshott was a distinguished and influential political philosopher who was unsympathetic to the notion of a discipline of political science. He 'preached scepticism about the idea that methods and approaches other than those of the historian or philosopher were applicable to the study of politics' (Kenny, 2004, p. 573). He argued 'forcefully against the idea that a proper understanding of the political necessitated an independent disciplinary field and distinctive methodologies and theories' (Kenny, 2004, p. 574). Oakeshott was the son of a Fabian civil servant who had played a part in the founding of the LSE. After studying history at Cambridge, he became a fellow of Gonville and Caius College in 1925. In 1949 he became a fellow of Nuffield College, Oxford and in 1951 he succeeded Laski to the political science chair at the LSE. 'The contrast between the public profile and enthusiastic socialism of Harold Laski . . . and Oakeshott's sceptical conservatism made the LSE appointment a dramatic one, and his famous inaugural lecture, *Political Education*, made an appropriate splash' (Minogue, 2009, p. 3). He had no time for ideologies of any kind, not least socialism or Marxism, and R. H .S. Crossman led the critical charge, in which Bernard Crick (see Box 2.4) joined, by describing Oakeshott as a 'cavalier iconoclast' who was determined to destroy the 'School dedicated by the Webbs to the scientific study of the improvement of human society' (Crossman, 1951). William Robson, an established professor at the LSE (see Box 1.4), called Oakeshott 'irresponsible and obscurantist' (Crick, 2009, p. 4). 'His love of freedom was so radical that his conservatism had anarchic tendencies' (Minogue, 2009, p. 1). Perhaps this helps to explain his arrest for indecent exposure after he was seen bathing naked in Dorset in 1955. The LSE archives contain his own account of the incident along with an enthusiastic letter of support from a committed Canadian nudist who sent him ten shillings towards his legal expenses, stating: 'I have for years been an advocate of nude bathing and it is people like yourself who will bring this about' (LSE, 1955a). Oakeshott also co-authored a book on *A Guide to the Classics* which did not refer to early political philosophers but gave advice on how to pick the Derby winner. Along with W. J. M. Mackenzie, he was described by an informant as a 'king maker' in chair appointments in the 1950s and early 1960s. Oakeshott's idea of civil association 'represents a highly original contribution to political philosophy' and he 'offered a persuasive political theory base[d] on the ideas of individuality, civility and conversational politics' (Parekh, 2001, p. 14). His opposition to state action 'led to Oakeshott becoming a guru in the 1980s, appealing to all shades of Conservatism' (Bevir and Rhodes, 2007, p. 246). He was no friend of political science, narrowly conceived, but he made an important contribution to the wider conversation about politics.

Mackenzie's task was not made easier by the fact that the department had historically been concerned with teaching public administration and it was evident that he had serious reservations about the way in which the subject had been taught (Mackenzie, 1975b; 1975c). Thus, 'one had to start a Politics department with the politics left out, and it required a good deal of time and patience to inject it' (Mackenzie, 1975a, p. xxix). He was, however, helped by the strength of the economic and social studies faculty at Manchester. There was a 'high degree of mutual respect between the senior professors, such as Ely Devons, W. Arthur Lewis, Michael Polanyi, and Max Gluckman' (Lee, 2009, p. 2). After this intellectually formidable group 'had imperceptibly disintegrated', Mackenzie wrote *Politics and Social Science* as 'a rather desperate effort to state the outcome of that experience in an impersonal way' (Mackenzie, 1975a, p. xxxii). What Mackenzie managed to achieve was to 'legitimate a conception of political study that was more social-scientific in its orientation, and more interdisciplinary in its ethos' (Kenny, 2004, p. 576).

Even though it was far smaller than most politics departments in American universities, Rose claims (1999, p. 466) that 'Dover Street' as it was known after its location in a former girls' school 'was the closest that England has ever come to the excitement of the University of Chicago in the 1930s'. Under Mackenzie's inspiration 'it became the first research-oriented centre for the study of politics in Britain' (Rose, 1999, p. 471). As a head of department he managed to combine the tasks of support, guidance and direction in a way that was both authoritative and informal. When Tony Birch was confined to a dreary Cheshire hospital, he was given a psychological boost when an untidy Mackenzie arrived there wearing muddy boots to disturb the solemn atmosphere with his booming voice (Birch and Spann, 1974, p. 14). 'He hired promising young persons as assistants, encouraging them to think for themselves and then cautioning them when they started going off the deep end' (Rose, 1999, p. 466).

The Friday afternoon seminars for staff and graduate students were a key part of the atmosphere of intellectual discovery and were followed by informal gatherings at the Mackenzie house in Stockport. Maurice Spiers recalls:

> Mackenzie did quite radical things for those days, though there was occasionally a slightly surrealistic feel to some of his Friday afternoon staff student seminars, e.g., when he got hold of a French member of the national Assembly who spoke very typical but limited French/English. Mackenzie was, as you will perhaps know, not exactly a shy man, but one who was easily embarrassed, and did his best to translate both ways with some slightly comic results (Personal communication, 26 June 2009).

As Birch and Spann note (1974, p. 11), 'there can be no doubt that his greatest impact on British political science has been made through his personal influence on colleagues and students'. Although Manchester remains one of the key politics departments in Britain, the special and distinctive atmosphere did not survive the post-Robbins expansion and the departure of Mackenzie to Glasgow in 1966.

The Nature of the Discipline

What kind of discipline constituted political studies in the 1950s in terms of its intellectual orientation? Smith (1986) emphasises the twin effects of logical positivism and linguistic analysis on political studies in the formative years of the PSA in the mid-twentieth century. He argues (1986, p. 423):

> political philosophy all but disappeared from the curriculum with the result that the teaching of political ideas was mainly confined to courses in the history of political thought; while the study of political institutions became detached from the examination of ideas. Thus, the syllabus effectively compartmentalized thought and action in a quite unprecedented and unfortunate manner.

In 1956, Peter Laslett, expressing a more widely shared view, had proclaimed that political philosophy was dead in the 'sense that the questions animating political philosophy had now been revealed as essentially meaningless' (Buckler, 2002, p. 172). 'While positivism made its assault on traditional political philosophy, the study of politics was developing in a way that aligned itself with natural-science enquiry' (Buckler, 2002, p. 176), although this process was more apparent in the US than in Britain.

At Oxford, beyond the first year in which candidates were required to take British Constitutional History from 1660 to 1914 (ultimately replaced by Political Institutions), the politics subject offered in List I was 'Political History, 1871–1914'. List II offered candidates a choice of: 'Political Theory from Hobbes'; 'Local Government in England since 1830'; 'Modern British Government'; 'Labour Movements 1815–1914'; 'Political Structure of the British Empire'; and 'International Relations' (Chester, 1986, p. 170). Three of the six subjects thus had some historical emphasis and there was no general as distinct from historically based political philosophy course (but by 1971 there was a compulsory course in the 'Theory of Politics'). In 1961 'International Relations' was promoted to List I in place of 'Political History' (Chester, 1986, p. 171). The offering at Oxford had a broader relevance as its courses were often reproduced by its graduates who went to teach elsewhere.

Although it was undergraduate teaching that enabled emergent politics departments to make a claim on additional staff, postgraduate studies were beginning to develop. 'What has happened is that during the last ten years graduates have been creeping into Oxford by stealth in ever-increasing numbers. Suddenly the University woke up to the fact that there were almost two thousand of them' (Committee on Graduates Council of Junior Members, 1962, p. 4). It remained the case that 'many more scientists and technologists, proportionately, go on to graduate work than do students of the Arts and Social Studies' (Seymour-Ure, 1963, p. 32). By 1960–61 there were 1,290 men and 402 women engaged in postgraduate work in social studies (Seymour-Ure, 1963, p. 35). Fifty-seven per cent of postgraduate students in England were at Oxford, Cambridge and London and the proportion for politics students may have been even higher given the availability of studentships at Nuffield (35 students working on social studies at the beginning of the 1960s) and St Antony's (figures derived from Seymour-Ure, 1963, p. 33).

In 1946 Oxford had introduced a BPhil. which Chester regarded as a more 'significant development than the introduction of the DPhil. after the First World War'. It 'opened the way for the clever PPE man to spend a fourth year concentrating on the subject in which he wished to specialise' (Chester, 1986, p. 164). It thus provided a form of postgraduate training that could be a prelude to undertaking a thesis, although some institutional obstacles on the way to a DPhil. had to be overcome (Chester, 1986, pp. 166–7). It is also possible that in a period in which a PhD was not required for the university post, it was a sufficient qualification to teach politics in a provincial university, particularly when rapid expansion occurred. For example, at Leicester, which by this time had a small group of politics staff, 'At present the University offers no postgraduate courses of formal lectures . . . or seminars leading to a higher degree, both the Master's degree, as well as the Doctor's degree, being virtually a research degree'. Funding was not readily available for Arts (which included Social Studies) students:

> If more awards are to be made available to Arts students, they will probably have to come through the Ministry of Education, or through the altruistic endowment of scholarships for this purpose by private bodies. The difficulty is, of course, that whereas it is generally accepted that a scientist is likely to be of more use to the community if trained in research methods, the value of a higher degree in an Arts subject is less obvious outside the academic field (Bamford, 1963).

Some funding for graduate students was nevertheless available. Maurice Spiers completed his postgraduate education at Manchester with a grant from the Leverhulme Trust.

The relationship with the United States

British political studies was certainly aware of American political science, if only to repudiate its assumption, language and techniques as Bernard Crick with his 'caustic pen' (Jeffery, 2009, p. 464) did to such great effect in *The American Science of Politics*. Crick's volume may be regarded as offering an inoculation against the excesses of the American approach, but the British approach was perhaps astutely captured by Hayward's phrase of 'homeopathic doses of American political science' (Hayward, 1991b, p. 104). As in most matters, Wilfrid Harrison, the editor of *Political Studies*, was a bellwether of orthodoxy, reflecting mainstream opinion: as he once told the author, 'I would not regard myself as in any way outré'. His view was that when the PSA was founded, American political science was 'transitional' and that it was in about 1953 that 'political science approaches in the United States began to be drawn together' (Harrison, 1975, p. 184) in a way that could offer a coherent narrative which could be subjected to a critical but friendly reading.

Bernard Crick's (see Box 2.4) doctoral thesis was on 'The American Political Science' and three years later it was published as what became a very influential book (Crick, 1959). What Crick was complaining about with some justification was the depoliticisation inherent in American political science which sat uneasily with the British tradition, classical in its origins, which emphasised the normative and ultimately moral dimensions of the study of politics. The nature of the American science of politics proceeded from some features of American society which included 'a concept of science widely held by American social theorists, a concern with citi-

---

Box 2.4:　Sir Bernard Crick, 1929–2008

Sir Bernard Crick was one of just six political scientists given lifetime achievement awards at the 50th anniversary celebration of the PSA. He was born in London and educated at University College, London and the LSE where he took his doctorate. He went on to teach at Harvard, McGill in Montreal and Berkeley before returning to the LSE in 1957. In 1965 he became Professor of Political Theory and Institutions at Sheffield, maintaining his base in London where he returned as Foundation Professor of Politics at Birkbeck in 1971. He took early retirement in 1984 and moved to Edinburgh. His *American Science of Politics* and *The Reform of Parliament* are discussed in the text of this book. He regarded his 1980 study of George Orwell as in many ways his magnum opus. *In Defence of Politics* 'remains a brilliant republican polemic that has had a profound impact on how we view politics as theory and practice' (Arthur, 2009, p. 8). 'It laid a foundation for his thinking about how the study of politics might interact with the practice of politics' (Jeffery, 2009, p. 465). This was expressed in his interest in the work of the Politics Association, of which he served as inaugural president, and his long-standing editorship of *Political Quarterly*. When his former student, David Blunkett, became Secretary of State for Education in 1997, Crick had the opportunity to introduce citizenship and political literacy into the school curriculum. When Blunkett moved to the Home Office he was appointed to chair the committee to devise a test of minimum competence in English language and British culture for immigrants. Crick was not 'your ordinary common or garden political scientist' (Arthur, 2009, p. 8). Indeed, Crick himself once wrote: 'I have got so bored with political science' (LSE, 1974c, PSA/15). He could be polemical and argumentative and it was entirely in character that his funeral notice advised 'Dress flamboyant'. He hoped for an Oxbridge chair, but did not fit in, and wanted a peerage, but had to settle for a knighthood. He was often critical of the PSA, not without reason, but frequently attended the annual awards ceremony in the years leading up to his death which stimulated a great outpouring of affection for this unique individual.

zenship that was entrenched in American political life, the generalisation of the habits of American democracy, and a faith in progress or manifest destiny for American society' (Adcock and Bevir, 2007, p. 225). In practice, of course, despite the attempt by some of the more extreme behaviouralists to claim that it was possible and desirable to create a value-free political science, Crick argued 'that behaviouralism was culture bound and, rather than being value free, was actually shot through with liberal American values' (Kavanagh, 2007, p. 115). Given that American political science had little practical influence at this time on what British political scientists researched or taught, this might seem to be tilting at windmills. However, for Crick, the construction of a democratic order and the defence of politics against totalitarianism required a historical study of politics rather than the scientism of the behaviouralists.

Even W. J. M. Mackenzie, who was at least sympathetic to the notion of political science, displayed 'a quirky anti-Americanism' including 'a rather curt comment about the behavioural movement in *Politics and Social Science*' (Birch and Spann, 1974, p. 19). Oxford probably had more contacts with American scholars than anywhere else because of its function as a gateway to British academia for foreign scholars. However, for many British academics working in the field of politics, American political science was 'the other' that helped to give a meaning to their own rather inchoate subject.

The Contribution of the PSA

Although the day-to-day life of the discipline in this period took place within a small number of politics departments, the PSA had its role to play in institutionalising and developing the new discipline. The two most important activities were the organisation of the annual conference, which gave members a chance to meet together and exchange ideas, and the establishment of the journal *Political Studies* in which they could publish their work.

Annual conferences

An informant who held a post in the period thought that the conference was probably less important to the departments that had critical mass than to the relatively isolated individuals in institutions where there were just one or two politics specialists. One of the first tasks of the new committee was to organise the PSA's first conference, held at St Hilda's College, Oxford from Friday 16 March to Sunday 18 March 1951. The wish had been expressed at the inaugural meeting 'that papers should be read on the development and present position of political studies at Oxford, Cambridge, London and other Universities' (LSE, 1950b, PSA/15). David Butler from Nuffield College was appointed as what today would be called the local conference organiser. Some 70 individuals attended. David Butler recalled in interview: 'Robson, Smellie, Norman Chester and Wilfrid Harrison most remain in my memory but Ken Wheare must have been around. The conference didn't divide into distinct sessions'. Mackenzie recalls this conference 'in the days when the PSA was comparable to the Fourth Party of the 1880s when all could go to Parliament in the same cab. The total membership was said to be about fifty' (Mackenzie, 1975b, p. 2). (In fact, there were 100 members.) 'I remember giving the paper to a plenary meeting of perhaps fifteen or twenty in a rather dark dining room in Magdalen' (Mackenzie, 1975b, p. 2). Mackenzie may be confusing the location with his old college, and the audience does seem to be rather small given the overall attendance. However, his comment does convey the sense of a very small discipline, as one (Oxford) informant put it: '[A] relatively small elite of Oxford and LSE people who could talk to each other on the phone'.

It was suggested that the conference performed an informal recruitment function, allowing professors to identify promising talent. However, relatively few posts were available and those that did occur were often filled by internal candidates or through pre-existing personal networks. One respondent from the period who was asked about the conferences said that he did not think that they served as a job market like the APSA. This function was performed informally by individuals like Professor Smellie (see Box 1.5). Nevertheless, another respondent recalled that the conferences were quite intimidating for new entrants, particularly given that people in those days did not wear name badges so it was not possible to identify them.

The 1953 annual general meeting had agreed that conferences should be organised on a circuit involving Oxford, Cambridge, London and the 'provincial universities'. In the event, in the decade between 1951 and 1960 only one conference was held in Cambridge. Four were held in Oxford, three of them at St Hilda's, but one informant commented: 'Oxford were prepared to host our conferences, but disdained having much to do with us'. Two conferences were held in London, but at Queen Elizabeth College and Bedford College rather than at the LSE. The other conferences were held at Birmingham (1953), Sheffield (1957) and Durham (1958).

The annual conference was the location of the annual general meeting and provided the opportunity for a ballot to elect the Executive Committee (EC) should one be needed. In effect, the committee was self-selecting. However, at the 1955 annual general meeting, the usual processes seem to have broken down. Initially, there were fewer nominations than vacancies, but then further nominations meant that a ballot had to be held for the first time (LSE, 1955b, PSA/15). A ballot was not held again until 1963 when two candidates were unsuccessful (both from provincial universities).

There was certainly not a book display of the type that is a central feature of contemporary PSA conferences. In 1963 the Executive Committee considered a request from the publishers Random House 'to mount at the Conference a display of their publications in the field of political studies'. This proposal received a cold reception from the committee and 'was negatived' [sic]. Instead, it was decided to ask the conference secretary to contact Blackwell's the booksellers in Oxford 'to ask if they planned to arrange a window display for the Conference, as in previous years' (LSE, 1963, PSA/15).

The establishment of a journal

Along with an annual conference, a journal would give a focus and meaning to the activities of the PSA. In the twenty-first century its expanding family of journals constitutes one of its most important activities, both in terms of advancing scholarship and also providing a key income stream for the work of the PSA. However, the challenge that the founders of the PSA faced was selling enough copies to what was still a very small discipline to make a journal viable. The decision-making pattern of the time was followed in the discussions about the founding of a journal which 'took place between a few people at the LSE and Oxford' (Chester, 1975, p. 159), although Cambridge was also consulted.

The Oxford publisher Blackwell was approached initially to produce the journal. The original plan of Blackwell's had been to install Charles Wilson as the editor of a new politics journal. He had been assistant editor of *Politica* which had been established by the LSE in 1934 but had been suspended on the outbreak of war. The LSE was prepared not to revive *Politica* if a new journal was established (Chester, 1975, p. 159). This scheme collapsed when Wilson was appointed principal of University College, Leicester from April 1952. The original discussions 'had largely turned on the close and friendly relations he had with Henry Schollick of Blackwells' (Chester, 1975, p. 159).

In the absence of its favoured editor Blackwell required guaranteed sales of 500 copies. Even sales at that level would lead to a loss and the future of the journal would have to be reviewed after two years. Given that the membership of the PSA had not reached 150 and that extensive library sales could not be anticipated, this did not seem to be a promising way forward (Chester, 1975, p. 159). Blackwell soon lost any interest and Kegan Paul quickly decided not to become involved. Fortunately, the delegates of the Oxford University Press (OUP) came to the PSA's rescue and offered to publish three numbers of a journal each year. 'They did not ask for any financial guarantee, but stipulated that the arrangement should be reviewed after 5 years' (Chester, 1975, p. 160). This was clearly a loss-making venture for OUP and it may be that Oxford members of the PSA exerted influence behind the scenes. The Nuffield Foundation also provided a grant of three years to provide secretarial assistance to the editor, Wilfrid Harrison, then at Queen's College Oxford. The first number appeared in 1953. By 1960 it was reported that there had been a 'considerable increase in the circulation of *Political Studies* and the consequent profit' (LSE, 1960a, PSA/15).

Wilfrid Harrison (see Box 2.5) seems to have 'emerged' as editor. As he recalled (1975, p. 188),

Box 2.5:   Wilfrid Harrison, 1909–80

Wilfrid Harrison was the founding editor of *Political Studies* from 1952 to 1963. He was born and educated in Glasgow, but as was typical for able Scots at the time, went south to take PPE at Oxford. He was one of the pioneers of the subject there, becoming a lecturer and then a fellow at Queen's College. Like many of his generation, he worked as a civil servant during the Second World War. After the war he published a widely used textbook on *The Government of Britain* which ran to many editions, but also undertook well-regarded work on Bentham. In 1957 he became Professor of Political Theory and Institutions at Liverpool and then went to the University of Warwick where he founded what was to become a large department of politics, recruiting what he regarded as promising young individuals (all men) who were allowed to develop their particular research interests in accordance with his view that no one orthodoxy should prevail in the study of politics. He was also the first Pro-Vice-Chancellor of Warwick University, playing an important role in the establishment of a successful new university. A contemporary described him as not 'interested in the real world of politics, very much a dour Scots political theorist who didn't believe you should have contact with real politicians'. His generation believed that one should conceal one's political preferences and it was only after his retirement that his colleagues discovered that he was a lifelong Labour voter. An accomplished cook, he had a liking for large and boisterous German Shepherd dogs, one of whom is alleged to have attacked an external examiner. Despite an attachment to domestic pleasures, Harrison could be a hard and meticulous worker when the occasion required. For example, he 'worked 16 hours with [Hans Daalder] over a weekend to get an article into shape' (Hayward, 1999, p. 28).

> The simple position was that the PSA wanted to have a journal, but there appeared to be no great enthusiasm for taking on the editorship of it, and I seem to have become editor, therefore, in a fit of absence of mind as far as I was concerned, and by some sort of process of elimination as far as others were concerned.

The editor would probably have had to be from Oxford given that the Clarendon Press was to publish the journal. In the days before electronic communication this had practical advantages and it also would have reassured OUP. As Harrison rather self-deprecatingly put it (1975, p. 188), 'I was of about middling seniority in a small profession in which it was possible to know practically all of one's colleagues'.

Harrison had interests in both political theory and government, two of the major areas of the discipline. He saw it in terms of 'the general study of government and of political ideas' (Harrison, 1953, p. 2). In a discipline that celebrated eclecticism,

Harrison's approach was based on a willingness to consider a variety of approaches and perspectives. 'To use language that has since become more popular, there was no paradigm' (Harrison, 1975, p. 185). He wanted 'to try and keep as many doors as possible open, not to try to move quickly to the establishment of any paradigm, but to proceed cautiously and see whether one could discern what might be emerging' (Harrison, 1975, p. 186). In his view, a paradigm never did emerge and he was probably relieved that it did not. He was very conscious of the fragility of the emergent discipline, particular in terms of challenges from historians and philosophers.

> There were, particularly at Oxford, the historians, who often appeared to resist any approaches other than those with which they were familiar, and even, in some extreme cases, appeared to hold that no approaches could be accepted that were not based 'entirely on documentary evidence' (which seemed to me to suggest that no approaches at all could be accepted). The new political scientists and the historians looked askance at one another (Harrison, 1975, p. 185).

Harrison's concerns about history were well founded. 'History as a cultural genre and academic study commanded greater authority in England than in the United States and hence had greater power to keep political science in its orbit' (Ross, 2007, p.19). The *English Historical Review* had been founded in 1886, nearly 70 years before *Political Studies*. 'Moreover in the principal universities, history was conceived of as primarily political: constitutional history remained paramount' (Den Otter, 2007, p. 47). As a discipline at this time, political studies lacked numbers and identity in terms of separate departments at most universities. This contributed to a lack of intellectual self-confidence which could be reinforcing and led to a somewhat diffident approach to the subject.

Harrison was given a very free hand in how he edited the journal. There was an Editorial Board, but it did not meet 'and never did anything collectively, let alone seek to issue policy directives'. Moreover, 'There were scarcely any adverse comments on the journal at meetings of the PSA Executive or at Annual General Meetings' (Harrison, 1975, pp. 187–8). Harrison had no lack of material coming forward and the page budget was increased in 1956. This is not surprising given that it was the only non-specialised politics journal in existence at the time and what he published reflected the interests of the discipline during his editorship (see Table 2.1). The existence of *Political Quarterly* meant there was already an 'intermediary' journal bridging the gap between academics and practitioners, leaving the more academic ground to the PSA's journal (Boncourt, 2007, p. 281): 'Almost all the authors who published in the journal between 1953 and 1957 were affiliated to a university. In addition, while they did not reach the level of scientific rigour achieved by political scientists, they were nonetheless careful to back their assertions with the results of previous work' (Boncourt, 2007, pp. 280–1). The first number of *Political Studies* appeared in February 1953 and cost 10*s*. 6*d*. (52.5p) a copy, but the 130 members of the PSA received the three annual numbers for 25 shillings (£1.25) out of the 30 shillings (£1.50) they paid as an annual subscription.

Table 2.1: Foundation Dates of Early Politics Journals

International Affairs	1922
Public Administration	1923
Political Quarterly	1930
Parliamentary Affairs	1947
Political Studies	1953

Table 2.2 shows the principal topic of articles during Harrison's editorship between 1953 and 1963 (including one issue in 1963 when he was no longer formally editor). A number of caveats have to be made about these data. In constructing the table all articles were assigned to one category on the basis of their principal theme, but clearly some articles covered more than one category. The categories are necessarily arbitrary. For example, it would have been possible to construct a category for federalism which was a popular subject during the period and formed the theme of the 1963 PSA conference. The fact that articles on topics such as communism or the UK parliament were rare does not reflect a lack of interest on the part of political scientists or any editorial bias, but more likely the existence of other journal outlets in these fields.

Nevertheless, some interesting patterns do emerge in what after all was the official journal of the PSA. Over 25 per cent of articles were about political theory or the history of political thought, reflecting received perceptions of the discipline at this time. It is important to bear in mind that 'doubts about a science of politics could become a shared trope among many British students of politics, rather than a fissure line between theorists and others' (Adcock and Bevir, 2007, p. 214). There were also quite a large number of articles about constitutional or public law, although it should be noted that Harrison had announced his intention to embrace articles on the law in the first issue as part of his strategy to make the journal appeal to those who would not regard themselves as engaged in political studies. Moreover, 'The new administrative political science had its roots in the empiricist methodologies of the legal historians' (Den Otter, 2007, p. 51). Seventeen per cent of the articles were about the UK, a number that could be boosted to around 20 per cent by counting most of the constitutional and public law articles. UK elections and parties were the most popular British topic and some of these articles deployed statistical techniques. Outside the UK, France and the US were the most popular countries covered in the developed world, while there was a relative lack of articles on Germany. There was a sprinkling of articles on the 'Old' Commonwealth and relatively few on developing countries. Those that did appear tended to focus on India and East Africa. None discussed South Africa and there was not a single article on Latin America. While international relations were represented, Harrison's wording in the original issue that the study of government did not involve 'the exclusion of international relations' (Harrison, 1953, p. 3) is perhaps significant.

Table 2.2: Analysis of Articles in *Political Studies* between 1953 and 1963

Political theory, conceptual/analytical	31
History of political thought	29
UK elections and political parties	26
International relations	16
France	14
United States	13
Comparative government and politics	10
Constitutional and public law	10
Asia (mostly India)	7
Discipline of politics	7
Other countries, Europe	7
Pressure groups	7
Africa	6
Communism	6
European unification	5
Republic of Ireland	5
Canada	4
Germany	4
Local government UK	4
Commonwealth	3
Devolution UK	3
Public administration UK	3
Australia	2
Cabinet and ministers UK	2
Foreign policy UK	2
New Zealand	2
Parliament UK	2
Research methods	2
Comparative Third World	1
Developing countries comparative	1
Education policy UK	1
Middle East	1
Political behaviour	1
N	237

Notes on calculation: research notes, replies to articles and review articles were included, but not book notes or correspondence. Articles published in two instalments, a not uncommon practice, were counted as two articles.

Many of the articles that did appear were commissioned review articles, perhaps reflecting a view that this aspect of the discipline needed to be included in the journal, but it was evident that the leading international relations scholars were largely publishing elsewhere.

Entitlement to membership

This occupied a considerable amount of the Executive Committee's time. The underlying motivation was clearly to maintain the PSA as an exclusive and high-status disciplinary association. However, sometimes financial considerations intruded. In 1958, the secretary reported to the Executive Committee:

> that university teachers in Canada and New Zealand had applied for membership of the Association. In view of the undesirability of increasing the Association's costs and of overseas subscriptions from the OUP it was agreed to maintain the policy of confining membership to applicants working in universities in the British Isles and the colonies (LSE, 1958, PSA/15).

However, it is not clear that this ruling was actually applied in practice.

Particular admission decisions could be long drawn out, as is illustrated by the cases of Dr Koeppler and Mr Thole. Dr Koeppler was the warden of Wilton Park, a highly regarded conference centre for opinion formers. Dr Koeppler was not qualified for membership, but the committee was asked to consider admitting him under Clause 3 in July 1959. 'The Committee decided to defer any decision until the next meeting and asked the Secretary to ask Professor Beloff (who had prompted Dr Koeppler's application) whether there were any exceptional circumstances which would justify Dr Koeppler's admission' (LSE, 1959a, PSA/15). A decision was deferred at the next two Executive Committee meetings and it was not until September 1960, fifteen months after his initial application, that a doubtless grateful Dr Koeppler was admitted to this somewhat exclusive club.

Lecturers at colleges of advanced technology and similar institutions were less fortunate. In 1960 it was reported that John Thole, lecturer in political philosophy at the Northampton College of Advanced Technology, had applied for membership. 'The difficulty was that this College was not part of London University although it included teachers recognised by the University. Mr Thole was not so recognised' (LSE, 1960a, PSA/15). A decision was deferred and at the committee meeting at the annual conference 'The Secretary was instructed to write to him and find out certain relevant facts, e.g., academic record and publications, number of students taught' (LSE, 1960b, PSA/15). At the September meeting it was reported that 'Mr Thole had not completed an application form [whether he had been asked to is unclear] and it was agreed that this application should be presumed to have lapsed' (LSE, 1960c, PSA/15).

In the meantime, at the behest of Professor Finer, who had raised 'the question of extending the membership of the Association to new categories especially teachers in technical colleges', the committee decided to ask Professors Finer and W. J. M. Mackenzie 'to prepare a scheme for the extension of membership and to frame a motion which could then be put to the Annual General Meeting' (LSE, 1959a, PSA/15). At the 1960 annual general meeting, Professor Mackenzie and Professor Finer proposed a motion that would create two new categories of members:

(a) 'Members of the staff of technical and commercial colleges and other similar institutions who teach a substantial number of students up to final honours or ordinary degree standard in politics or public administration.

(b) Members of the teaching or research staff of other bodies carrying out work of a high standard in the field of politics or public administration' (LSE, 1960d, PSA/15).

It was part of the motion that 'Applications under these two headings shall be considered individually by the Executive Committee on the basis of the academic qualifications and, where relevant, the teaching responsibilities of the applicant, and the status of the institution which he serves'. Despite these provisos, it was clear that a number of members were concerned about the dilution of membership standards.

> During the discussion several members indicated that they would not be willing to support the motion as an amendment to the Constitution but that they would be willing to support it if it was phrased as an instruction to the Committee to make a more liberal use of its power to accept as members persons who were not University teachers.

Professor Mackenzie was obliged to amend his motion substantively so that it became an instruction to the committee 'to use its discretion more liberally than hitherto' (LSE, 1960d, PSA/15).

As it so happened, something of a test case involving Professor Mackenzie quickly arose within the next few months. Mr R. S. Burgess, who had been a student at Manchester, and was now a lecturer at Wigan Mining College, applied for membership. Professor Mackenzie 'hoped to let the Committee know more about Mr Burgess's record at the next meeting' (LSE, 1960c, PSA/15). Whatever he provided cannot have been sufficiently convincing for it was decided that Mr Burgess would not be admitted, which suggests that the committee's discretion was not being used more liberally.

It transpired that the needs of lecturers teaching in government in technical colleges in Lancashire were addressed, perhaps as a consequence of these events, by the formation of an organisation for them called the Government Lecturers' Society in 1960. It seems to have petered out after a few years, but its Yorkshire branch became the regional branch of the Politics Association when that organisation was formed under the auspices of the Hansard Society in 1969. For over 30 years it provided a solution to the need for an organisation for those teaching politics in schools and colleges.

A somewhat different course of action was followed in the case of Mr C. Martin who was the Director of Studies at the Hansard Society. 'There was some doubt as to whether Mr Martin was a graduate' (LSE, 1960c, PSA/15). At a subsequent meeting, 'It was agreed that Mr Martin should be invited to attend the Conference and the question of his admission be deferred until after the Conference' (LSE, 1961c, PSA/15). Presumably he could be informally vetted at the conference to inform a decision about his suitability to be a member.

In 1963 the Executive Committee took something of a landmark decision by agreeing to admit Maurice Spiers, lecturer in politics at the Bradford Institute of Technology. However, the committee warned, 'The decision was taken on the basis of Mr Spiers' personal qualifications and was not to constitute a precedent regarding the eligibility of Lecturers in colleges of technology for PSA membership' (LSE, 1963, PSA/15). However, the following year Michael Goldsmith, a future PSA chair, was admitted into membership from The Royal College of Advanced Technology, Salford, so the defences were beginning to crumble.

As it was, some existing members were causing difficulty by falling in arrears with their subscriptions. At the beginning of 1959 £250 of subscriptions was in arrears (LSE, 1959b, PSA/15). This figure had been reduced by the summer, but £40 of subscriptions for 1958 and earlier years was still unpaid (LSE, 1959a, PSA/15). The problem persisted and two years later 'It was agreed to write off some arrears, but Professor Robson would speak to Mr Miliband' (LSE, 1961c, PSA/15).

Relationships with practitioners

These were somewhat *ad hoc* during this period, but not non-existent. Dame Evelyn Sharp was invited to address the 1953 conference on 'The Civil Service in the Modern State'. The Executive Committee responded gratefully in 1961 to an invitation from the Iron and Steel Board for an expenses-paid trip to its headquarters. There were also contacts with the emergent European institutions, particularly the Coal and Steel Community.

Relationships with the media, now an important part of the PSA's activities, were viewed with some suspicion. The irrepressible Professor Finer 'suggested that . . . the BBC, ITV, certain MPs and administrators and representatives of certain newspapers be invited to our Annual Conference and that the Conference should be announced in The Times'. This suggestion evidently did not go down too well with the committee and 'After discussion, Professor Finer agreed not to press his proposal in the Committee, but gave notice his intention to raise it at the AGM' (LSE, 1959a, PSA/15).

An explanation of what was concerning members is given in a letter from Tony Birch to Peter Woodward, then the secretary, in 1973 explaining his response to a telephone call from a reporter from the *Times Higher Education Supplement* asking if she could attend the conference:

> My first reaction was to tell her that she could come to the academic sessions but not to the AGM. However, I discovered a couple of days later that on more than one occasion in the past members resolved not to permit representatives of the Press to attend the Conference because of the fear that the Association might be drawn into a political controversy or to be thought by the Press to be taking a stand on some issue or other (LSE, 1973d, PSA/20).

International links during this period were largely conducted through IPSA, but in 1961 it was reported that Mr Hanson of Leeds and Mr Abdel-Rahman of Manchester would be attending the annual conference of the Lebanese association. The Japanese Political Science Association more than once tried to persuade the PSA to sign up to statements on nuclear weapons, but the Association insisted that it could not pronounce on such divisive political questions.

The PSA received communications on a variety of matters on which it was expected to act but had no capacity to do so. In 1961 the secretary reported that he had received a letter forwarded by Mr W. Pickles, a French specialist at the LSE, 'from a French lady living in Avignon drawing attention to the deterioration of John Stuart Mill's house. Mr Pickles had suggested that the Association were the appropriate body to deal with the matter'. Not surprisingly, the committee 'agreed the letter should lie on the table' (LSE, 1961d, PSA/15).

Conclusions

Kenny downplays the significance of the PSA during this period. 'Both the PSA and *Political Studies* had at best a small influence in the development of politics as a university subject in the [1950s]'. Neither the Association nor the journal 'attempted to institute a particular intellectual approach or to lay down prescriptive norms for the discipline, though both reflected the prevailing Whiggish understanding of British political development and the values associated with it' (Kenny, 2007, p. 161). Thus, 'The formation of the PSA was an important moment in terms of the constitution of a fledgling community of researchers within the field of political studies, but was not necessarily a staging post towards the conscious formation of a new discipline' (Kenny, 2007, p. 162).

The PSA in the 1950s was a rather exclusive, club-like organisation of people who knew each other, but in that sense it reflected the society of which it was a wider part. As Moran comments (2003, p. 7), 'The crisis of the club system amounts to the exhaustion of a historically ancient project – preserving oligarchic government in the face of democratic institutions and a democratic culture'. Although many political scientists came from relatively economically and socially deprived origins, or if not, from the middle rather than the upper class, the British higher education system was run by an elite with the intention of providing the members of an elite. That relatively static, slowly evolving system was about to change in the early 1960s. British higher education was about to undergo a major expansion which would greatly increase the number of politics posts and place new demands on the PSA as the subject faced pressures for intellectual change. The PSA did not always deal with these changes well as the comfort blanket of the 1950s was removed.

Chapter 3

The Stirrings of Discontent: 1964–75

The period from the mid-1960s saw a major expansion of higher education which benefited the social sciences including the study of politics. As a consequence, the number of academics teaching politics and hence the membership of the PSA doubled from 270 in 1965 to 540 in 1971. The last year in which a detailed list of PSA members was published in *Political Studies* was 1967, and the data actually related to 1966, but there was already a marked contrast with the figures for just three years earlier in 1963. Then only four departments had more than ten members of staff in PSA membership. By 1966 the number of such departments had increased more than three-fold to thirteen. Two of them were new universities, Essex and Sussex.

For Hayward (1999, p. 20) this was 'an enthusiastic and optimistic phase of technocratic reformism (1961–74), coinciding with the University expansion of political science and the belief that institutional nostrums could be suggested for national decline'. The creation of a binary system of higher education made up of universities and polytechnics with the designation of 28 polytechnics by the then education secretary, Antony Crosland, led to tensions with the PSA about the eligibility of polytechnic staff for membership. The Social Science Research Council (SSRC) was established in 1965, giving a considerable stimulus to research in politics, especially that which involved quantitative analysis and large and costly data sets. The foundation of the *British Journal of Political Science* challenged the hegemony of *Political Studies* as the leading domestic journal. The formation of the European Consortium for Political Research (ECPR) gave politics academics a new focus for their research activities. Some members considered that the PSA was not responding with sufficient speed or determination to these developments in the discipline. David Butler recalled in interview:

In the early 1960s I got on the committee. Tony King was very active, [I was] asked to stand down next year to prevent a contest, but there was one anyway. The committee was not very activist. It made very little impact on me. My impression is that it got through its business with less strain than most other institutions, certainly APSA. I don't remember much in the way of feuds.

Stirrings of discontent became apparent and some of their manifestations during this period are discussed below. These eventually led to a major challenge to the existing leadership of the PSA in 1975 which is discussed in the next chapter.

The Expansion of Higher Education

The 1963 Robbins Report on the development of higher education was significant because it ushered in a considerable expansion of British universities. 'The thesis of the Report which the Government has accepted is that we have a moral and social duty to make available higher ["university" deleted] education to all those who have the will, and the qualifications of the benefit by it. This is part of the philosophy of a free society' (NA, 1963a, p. 1). The envisaged expansion 'would achieve remarkable social change in one decade. At present 13 per cent (men) and 6 per cent (women) of each age-group successfully complete a course of higher education. By the mid-1970s, it would be about 22 per cent (men) and 12 per cent (women)' (NA, 1963a, p. 2).

It is important to emphasise that some expansion of higher education had already been under way before the publication of the Robbins Report. Indeed, in many ways the Anderson inquiry of 1960–61 on student funding was as significant in paving the way for a new era (Alderman, 2009; NA, 1961). In 1952/3 there were 81,500 students and 9,000 staff in higher education and by 1963 (including colleges of advanced technology) 128,700 students and over 14,000 staff. 'The Government committed itself to all this and to massive forward targets in the later 60s and in the early 70s long before the Robbins Report. They also appointed the Robbins Committee in order to know on the basis of expert advice and fully adequate statistical information whether the course they were steering was correct' (NA, 1963b). In particular the 'plate-glass' universities had already been approved by the time of the Robbins Report. Each of these universities (East Anglia, Essex, Kent, Lancaster, Sussex, Warwick and York) established departments or schools of politics and some of them, notably Essex, were to make a major impact on the discipline.

Nevertheless, there were those within government, notably the Treasury, who resisted the move away from a small universities system providing high-quality graduates to a mass system of higher education. As recently as the mid-1950s:

[The] official view was that student numbers if anything were slowing down and there was a serious danger of having to lower standards to maintain the level of intake. Two demographic factors were to shake this complacency. The first was the effect of the post-war bulge in births which was forecast to produce a peak in the 18-year old age group between 1964 and 1967, and the second was evidence of an increased staying-on rate in schools (Shattock, 1991, p. 12).

The Treasury's 1958 forecast included a provisional allocation for a new University of Sussex at Brighton. 'In March 1959 the UGC had set up a New Universities Sub-Committee whose task was to establish criteria for the founding of new universities and put the claimants into a "batting order" if new foundations were to be permitted' (Shattock, 1991, p. 16).

There was a particularly rapid expansion of posts in politics in the late 1960s. Beith (2008, p. 44) recalls how he was invited to apply for a post after one year of graduate study:

> [They] were great days to look for a university job in politics, because universities were expanding and the teaching of my subject was expanding. Early in my second year I received a visit in college from a head of department of a Scottish university, inviting me to apply for a prematurely vacant post. I declined it.

The Formation of the SSRC

The PSA had been alert to the importance of the formation of the SSRC and had established a sub-committee in March 1963 made up of Professors Campbell, Finer and Morris-Jones to submit a statement on the research council. The sub-committee circulated a questionnaire to all politics departments. In January 1964 the PSA made a submission to the Heyworth Committee which was preparing the way for the SSRC's formation and it was invited to give oral evidence in April 1964.

The evidence given by the PSA stated that 'Great difficulties had been experienced in filling vacancies adequately in University teaching staffs' (PSA, 1964, pp. 265–6). It was considered that the study of politics was disadvantaged as it was not closely related to any external profession. Although this might also appear to be a disadvantage shared by sociology and even economics, as distinct from law and social work, the PSA was insistent that 'this disadvantage would be liable to reduce the number of first-class students seeking to specialise in politics' (PSA, 1964, p. 266). The generally held perception of the discipline among members was reflected in the statement that 'political studies tended to straddle Arts and Social Science: there might be some danger of political studies being held to be purely an arts subject' (PSA, 1964, p. 266), thereby cutting it off from SSRC funds. The submission also emphasised the importance of the provision of MA degrees in politics given that the subject was so often studied at undergraduate level in joint honours schools.

The formation of the SSRC in 1965 gave a considerable boost to research in politics and postgraduate study. A document prepared for the Social Studies committee of the University Grants Commission (UGC) in 1972 pointed out that 'Political Science is, with Sociology and Economics, one of the largest of the Council's constituent fields. This is not the result of accident or favourable treatment, but reflects the scale of Political Science at the universities and elsewhere'. As evidence of the rapid growth of the subject, reference was made to a 'six-fold' increase in the membership of the PSA. 'Yet the increase in SSRC awards to Political

Science has been noticeably smaller than that enjoyed by several other subjects' (NA, 1972a).

The document pointed to 'the generally accepted fact that Political Science embraces an unusually wide range of sub-disciplines, some of which might under other administrative arrangements have separate committees of their own'. Reference was made specifically to International Relations, Comparative Politics, 'domestic' Politics and Public Administration and Local Government. It was also argued that postgraduate students in political science were more dependent on SSRC financial support than those in more vocational subjects. If British political science was not to fall behind other countries, more funds would have to be made available.

> The importance and the theoretical and practical progress made by Political Science in recent years has been reflected in rapid and impressive extension of work in other countries, notably France, Germany and Canada. Britain can no longer rest upon the advantages of its long established and distinctive national tradition in political studies (NA, 1972a).

Nevertheless, the allocation of quota awards was not ungenerous. In 1968, political science received 132 awards, a number that increased to 228 in 1970–71, although it slipped back to 188 in 1971–72, no doubt influenced by public expenditure cuts (NA, 1972a). In these early years, the SSRC seems to have followed a policy of distributing awards as widely as possible combined with an element of selectivity. Only six higher education institutions that applied for awards received nothing. Thirty universities received at least one award, but more typically between two and four. However, 50 per cent of the quota allocations went to five institutions. The LSE received 23 with International Relations being allocated 11 and Government 12. Essex was second with 14, followed by Manchester with 12, Oxford with 9 and International Politics at Aberystwyth with 8. As Ian Budge recalled (2006, p. 318):

> [Only] Essex had the necessary flexibility and (it must be said) ruthlessness to recruit 12 MA students in the short time available and enter them for the 1965–1966 session. Most failed the year but the great principle of budgetary inertia meant that departments, which had once held studentships continued to get them as long as they had applicants. At one stroke, therefore, Essex acquired the largest and soon the best graduate school in political science in Britain.

W. J. M. Mackenzie was appointed the first chair of the political science committee at the SSRC. He sent a letter to the 1966 PSA annual general meeting 'which stated he wished to have advice for [sic] all university politics staff and not just from Heads of Departments about the research situation in the Social Sciences and the strategy and policy which the SSRC should follow'. Somewhat predictably, 'It was pointed out that this meeting was not the place to present a considered consensus'. A suggestion that a questionnaire should be circulated to members about research policy was 'left in the hands of the Executive Committee', where it remained. Members of the PSA were encouraged to write to Professor Mackenzie, but preferably via the PSA secretary (LSE, 1966b, PSA/15).

The SSRC was keen to encourage closer cooperation between the PSA and other disciplinary associations, especially the British Sociological Association. In 1970 they organised a meeting of representatives of learned societies and professional associations at their headquarters. One theme that emerged from this meeting was the fact that universities had been paying hidden subsidies to such associations by underwriting secretarial and other costs and it was questioned how long this arrangement could continue. It was perhaps with this in mind that at a meeting with the secretary of the SSRC and of the political science committee that the PSA was told that 'the SSRC expected to move premises in the fairly near future and they might then have surplus space which would enable them to place at the disposal of the PSA an office or a share of an office at a reasonable rent' (LSE, 1970a, PSA/15). If anything had come of this proposal, it might have accelerated the organisational development of the PSA.

Some subjects that received research grants could be controversial with government departments. Objections were made to the award of a grant to Professor Robson (see Box 3.1). As the Department of Education and Science (DES) pointed out, 'It is of course appreciated that Research Councils take their own decisions on such matters and a major part of the philosophy attaching to the Research Council system is that they should be able to do so' (NA, 1969a). As it happened, the 'force of our own [Ministry of Transport] objections to the project had been considerably reduced by the support which the CSD and Treasury had given it'. In the Ministry of Transport's view, 'we feel that in a case like this, where Transport's interest is strong and specific, we should have been consulted before comments were made to the SSRC by CSD and Treasury' (NA, 1969b). The DES outlined the underlying dilemmas that arose in the relationship between government and funded researchers and also cast light on relations between the departments and the SSRC:

> In this particular instance it emerged that the Department had not given SSRC the real reason for their dislike of the project and SSRC in their turn had not fully explained why they decided it should go ahead. I have had a word with the Chairman of the SSRC on the latter aspect and I told him that I would remind Departments likely to be concerned in these cases of the need for a full explanation of their views to SSRC. This may not always be easy in formal correspondence or on paper at all but other means are available. An informal exchange of views can always be channelled through the Academic Liaison Officers appointed by Departments to collaborate with SSRC – but apart from this there is no reason why any other officer responsible for a line of work should not make direct contact with the SSRC, and speak quite frankly. I hope they will do so, as I hope SSRC will do in return. These projects are sometimes a bit tricky and mutual confidence between the Research Council and the executive Departments is essential (NA, 1969a).

This dispute led to prolonged discussions in Whitehall and with the SSRC about how departmental views might be coordinated and communicated to the SSRC.

Box 3.1: Professor Robson's Controversial Research Project

The following extract from a letter from Sir David Serpell to the Civil Service Department outlines the Ministry's concerns about the project by Professor Robson funded by the SSRC:

'Earlier this year we were invited by the [SSRC] to comment on a project by Professor Robson of the Greater London Group and LSE for the examination of existing institutional arrangements for the co-ordination of transport in Greater London with the aim of suggesting possible improvements. Mr J. Thomson (a former employee of this Ministry) was named as the investigator under whose general guidance the research staff would work.

We criticised the proposal on the following grounds:

(a) Part of the proposal was to carry out case studies on a small selection of important decisions such as those concerning the Victoria Line, the Motorway Box and the Inner London Parking Area. We pointed out that the importance, size and political nature of such decisions was likely to make their passage through the decision-making procedure untypical of most decisions which are made and to reduce the validity with which comparisons can be drawn.

(b) The information in the papers submitted on methodology to be employed was sparse.

(c) The timing of the proposal seemed to us unfortunate, since some of the institutions with which it would be concerned were in process of being reorganised.

(d) Sufficient information was unlikely to be available to the researchers to enable them to form rational judgments on present arrangements for taking decisions and to reach sound conclusions as to how they might be improved.

(We were also influenced by the fact that Mr Thomson was considered by the Department to be not altogether suitable for an academic project of this type; but this was not said to the Council)' (NA, 1969b).

The Development of the Discipline

There is no doubt that the discipline was developing in new directions in the 1960s and early 1970s. 'The model of the political scientist that gained credence in the 1960s involved an emphasis on specialisation, particularly in terms of methodological and theoretical knowledge, the adoption of a technical language, and greater value upon the ideal of disinterested, impartial analysis' (Kenny, 2007, p. 178). There was a new openness to perspectives from the United States, reflected in the willingness of election studies experts to make visits to the summer school at the Survey Research Center at Ann Arbor, Michigan. The author, having completed a relatively conventional politics degree in 1968, sought training in statistics and survey methods and went to take the MSc in Politics established by Richard Rose at the University of Strathclyde.

The influential Nuffield election studies established in 1945 had provided an authoritative and increasingly analytical account of successive general elections, as they continue to do today. 'The introductions to the studies, penned by Butler in the 1950s and 1960s, reveal his adoption of an "insider's" approach to Westminster and informed judgements about the tactics and personalities of leading political figures' (Kenny, 2007, p. 169). The risk was that the statistical appendices to the Nuffield studies threatened to dominate the whole book. In 1960, Butler went to an international round table at the University of Illinois after an APSA meeting and 'This was the origin of Butler and Stokes' (1969). One informant commented that one of Butler's strengths was that he had good self-knowledge and that he realised that collaboration with Donald Stokes would bring him techniques and knowledge he could not readily develop himself. This book represented an important milestone in the development of more systematic election studies in Britain. Up to that point, much of the work that had been done had taken the form of studies of particular constituencies which, although not without value, were not a good basis for generalisation.

Local community studies were very much in vogue, influenced by the community power debate between pluralists and elitists in the USA, but also by the debate about the reform of British local government. The SSRC funded a number of such studies which produced results of variable quality or in one or two cases no discernible results at all. However, the better studies made significant contributions to the literature, for example George Jones (1969) and Ken Newton (1976). There were also important developments in political theory. Brian Barry's *Political Argument* (1965) 'introduced the new political theory that was about to break open the academy, most dramatically with Rawls' *Theory* six years later' (Dowding, 2009, p. 459). The discipline was in a state of intellectual ferment with new paradigms being developed and new approaches being applied. Yet even the staunchest supporters of the PSA considered that it was not engaging as well as it might. At the annual general meeting Norman Chester 'reminded the meeting that one of the reasons for the founding of the PSA was to provide opportunities for the younger members to give papers. This had tended not to happen' (LSE, 1965a, PSA/15).

Many departments also followed the Finer strategy of successful undergraduate teaching to build up their departments. According to Beith (2008, p. 46) this was the strategy followed by Hugh Berrington at Newcastle, who had been with Finer at Keele and built up a department more or less from scratch in a university that had only recently broken away from Durham:

> His technique for building up the department was to make the courses so popular and so well taught that student demand generated increasingly unacceptable staff/student ratios, leading in turn to faculty approval for additional posts in the department. The drawback of this strategy was, inevitably, very heavy teaching demands on

the staff which did not allow for effective research programmes, and it was an emphasis that was eventually corrected.

The Work of the Association

Stirrings of discontent: the Blondel Memorandum

With the influx of new members, not everyone was content with the quietist way in which the PSA had been run in the past. In 1966 the Executive Committee was told about what were termed 'The Essex Proposals': 'The Chairman reported correspondence between himself and Professor Blondel and Potter who had suggested that the PSA should expand its activities, to act as a clearing house of information, and to foster joint-ventures between departments' (LSE, 1966b, PSA/15).

Having been elected to the committee, Professor Blondel produced a memorandum in November 1968 entitled 'Extension of Activities of the PSA', which is referred to here as the 'Blondel Memorandum'. It is an important document both in terms of its analysis of the challenges facing the PSA and of possible solutions. In a conversation with Ian Budge in 1975, Blondel pointed out that it set out many of the proposals that were only acted on then. Blondel's starting point was that:

> the very welcome growth of the political science profession in the UK called for a re-examination of the scope of activities of the PSA. We started fifteen years ago as a well-integrated group of people who knew each other and could, by informal channels, come to hear about the interests and research activities of colleagues; we have now become, by virtue of our own success, a much less closely-knit body of people (LSE, 1968a, PSA/15).

It was impossible for new members to become acquainted with more than a small number of colleagues, but the need for collaborative research was greater. 'Informal channels have . . . become much more haphazard and the communication network has become unsatisfactory'. No other body was really in a position to improve links between colleagues. Blondel thought that advertising was no longer a satisfactory way of filling vacant posts and wanted the PSA to function as a 'clearing house' between applicants and departments. In terms of academic activities, 'the PSA should both help to prepare its conferences by organising meetings of panels, as IPSA does, and support specialists in particular fields by enabling them to run seminars under its sponsorship' (LSE, 1968a, PSA/15).

Professor Blondel expanded on his theme at the first meeting of the Executive Committee in 1969:

> He felt that membership spanned a larger profession and the Association did not do enough. He would like to see the Association become more active and with a stronger bureaucracy. In particular he would like to see the Association keeping regular files

of information of interest to members (vacancies, etc.) and a more active role taken in sponsoring conferences (LSE, 1969a, PSA/15).

On this occasion 'No decisions were taken'. At the meeting in July, 'A considerable amount of scepticism was expressed about some aspects of the "Clearing House" scheme' (LSE, 1969b, PSA/15). In October, it was agreed that 'it should be dropped for the time being' after the SSRC said that it could not provide assistance (LSE, 1969c, PSA/15). Professor Blondel had never really produced any evidence that demonstrated that the Clearing House was needed or that the proposal was feasible. The argument for more specialist groups was a stronger one and was reflected in the success of the new Comparative Politics group in which Professor Blondel was a leading member. However, Professor Blondel would have understandably been disappointed by the unenthusiastic response of the PSA and this may have encouraged him to divert his efforts to form the ECPR rather than trying to reform the PSA.

Professor Crick also became something of a thorn in the side of the PSA. In 1973 he wrote to Tony Birch as chairman stating that 'I have heard nothing further about my request that the Association should try to compile – which can be found in no reference book – a list of titles of what courses are actually given, which would be immensely useful to school teachers advising pupils where to apply' (LSE, 1973a, PSA/15). Tony Birch replied 'that it strikes me as odd that you should wait eleven months without doing anything to follow up on your request and then . . . write me a somewhat aggressive letter about the subject!' (LSE, 1973b, PSA/15) A decision had been taken that this request could not be met, but Professor Crick had not been informed because of the illness of the PSA secretary. Crick replied to Birch:

> You will pardon my saying, but this seems to me to be so typical of the lack of initiative and responsibility for the concerns of the profession of the committee of the [PSA]. This is why I got off when I discovered the body was so inactive. . . . With the PSA I never imagined that there was lack of resources so much as lack of will; and your letter confirms this (LSE, 1973c, PSA/15).

These exchanges have a broader significance because they show a dissatisfaction among some leading members of the discipline with the activities and energy displayed by the PSA as the study of politics in Britain underwent a rapid expansion. It forms a backcloth to the removal of the existing Executive Committee in 1975 and possibly to the formation of a separate British International Studies Association (BISA) in the same year.

Political Studies: 'dull and poor'

In 1969 *Political Studies* became a quarterly journal. Nevertheless, this was a period of considerable discontent within the PSA about the journal, while considerable turbulence surrounded the foundation of the *British Journal of Political Science* which first appeared in 1971.

By 1964 *Political Studies* was selling about one thousand copies per issue, of which about a quarter went to PSA members. When the subscription price increased to £2.50 in 1964, 'Professor Moodie asked [at the annual general meeting] whether the Executive Committee had considered asking for quotations from other publishers; he thought this was an unusually expensive journal'. Professor Campbell replied that for most of its life *Political Studies* had been published at a loss which had been borne by Oxford University Press. 'In view of past subsidies, he did not think it would be proper to leave the OUP'. In any case, as Professor Harrison pointed out, the journal was owned by the Clarendon Press and not the PSA. Mr Brown 'asked to what extent losses might have been due to inefficiency. Professor Campbell could not say . . . Mr Chester said that the main cause of loss was the paucity of sales; very few journals were in a different position' (LSE, 1964, PSA/15). This discussion represented the first time the PSA had reflected on where the journal might be published, but there was no realisation that it might be their most valuable asset.

For some time, as David Butler recalled, there had been a sense that *Political Studies* 'wasn't that good'. This came to a head in December 1966 when a series of complaints were made from the Executive Committee to the editor, Peter Campbell, who was not present at the meeting but had sent a letter to it. The minutes stated that the points made in the ensuing discussion implied 'no criticism of the Editor', but it is difficult to see what an alternative reading might be. The most damaging charge was that 'With the increase in the number of specialised journals, there was a tendency for articles to become residual, general, dull and poor'. It was also suggested that the look of the journal 'was dull' and that it might be a good idea to follow the practice of the *American Political Science Review* and organise reviews under headings. It was pointed out that 'The Executive Committee was the appropriate place for periodically discussing *Political Studies*'. Such interest had not been very evident before then, but Campbell subsequently argued that one reason for abolishing the Editorial Board had been so that the committee could function as an informal editorial board. Somewhat pointedly it was recorded that 'The Chairman and Secretary were asked to convey these points to the Editor . . . the Committee would appreciate hearing his comments at a future meeting of the Committee' (LSE, 1966c, PSA/15).

Professor Campbell arrived at the April 1967 meeting with a one-page memorandum giving his response to the criticisms. He stated that he was 'rather puzzled by the criticism that articles are "general" . . . after all, the Association is a general one and members in different fields can legitimately hope to find articles of interest to them'. There is certainly a difference between editing a general and a specialised journal and one of the challenges in editing *Political Studies* has been to serve an eclectic discipline with fuzzy boundaries. Professor Finer having surrendered the chair for this item and left the meeting, Professor Campbell said that he would try to commission more articles and also increase the amount of controversy, as well as discussing the typography and layout of the journal with Clarendon Press. He also agreed to consider the idea of reviving the Editorial Board (LSE, 1967a, PSA/15).

At the next meeting the editor reported that he would take on an editorial board of ten to eleven members. Professor Campbell also 'gave notice that he was to retire in 1969, having completed his five year term. This announcement was greeted with dismay' (LSE, 1967b, PSA/15). He was subsequently asked to stay on for two years (LSE, 1968b, PSA/15). At the 1968 annual general meeting, he apologised for the delay in sending out the current issue of *Political Studies*, explaining that Clarendon Press had recently changed its printers (LSE, 1968c, PSA/15). At its October 1968 meeting the Executive Committee agreed that successors to Professor Campbell would be approached in the following order: P. Williams (Nuffield College), F. F. Ridley, G. C. Moodie (LSE, 1968d, PSA/15).

Professor Ridley was appointed as the next editor, but the transfer does not seem to have been seamless:

> Professor Ridley reported that very little had yet been transferred to him from Professor Campbell, but he understood that Mr Cordy at the OUP had visited Reading on the previous day to collect the material in Professor Campbell's possession. He therefore had no idea what was 'in the pipeline' for future issues (LSE, 1970b, PSA/15).

At the annual meeting in 1970, Professor Campbell 'apologised for the lateness of recent issues and wished to make it clear that he took full responsibility for this' (LSE, 1970c, PSA/15).

Reflecting on this episode, Tony Birch (2009) recalled:

> We had some complaints about slow replies to authors who had submitted articles for publication. I believe that Peter Campbell and his assistants had perhaps been a bit dilatory in sending out manuscripts for assessment and dealing with the responses. But I do not think this was Campbell's fault, as some referees were appallingly slow in making their assessments.

Controversy over the British Journal of Political Science

The perceived failings of *Political Studies* created an opportunity for the creation of a new general journal that could respond to new developments in the discipline. The first issue of the *British Journal of Political Science* (BJPS), edited by Brian Barry from Essex University, appeared in 1971. Formal theory, tables, graphs and even equations were much in evidence. The consultative committee included six members from the USA.

These developments did not go down well with the PSA. Professor Finer wrote to the Executive Committee in January 1970:

> I would like to let the Committee know that I strongly disapprove, as does Bernard Crick, of the new journal (Essex) styling itself The *British* Journal of Comparative

Politics [*sic*]; and I hope that the Committee will be unanimous on this matter and that it will be able to write a polite but very firm letter to this effect to the Cambridge University Press (LSE, 1970d, PSA/15).

When the Executive Committee met, Professor Crick proposed that a motion be tabled at the annual general meeting condemning PSA members on the editorial board of the new journal. This was subsequently withdrawn, but shows how high feelings were running. To some extent, however, the PSA was faced with a fait accompli:

> Professor Ridley informed the Committee that he had spoken to Mrs Skinner of the CUP and understood from her that the CUP itself had originally been opposed to the incorporation of the word 'British' but that the editorial board had been determined that it should be included. Since printing had already begun and CUP would therefore incur considerable costs if any alteration was now made, it seemed to him unlikely that the title would be changed.

Nevertheless, after some discussion it was agreed that:

> [Professor] Moodie should write to the CUP on behalf of the Committee strongly regretting that the journal had incorporated the word 'British' in its title since this suggests that it is the official journal of British political scientists, which is certainly not the case since there is already such an official journal, and informing them that if the title is retained the Committee will be compelled to circulate foreign universities and libraries to correct this misleading impression. (The letter should point out however that the Committee did not object to and indeed positively welcomed a new journal on politics.) (LSE, 1970b, PSA/15)

The matter was raised at the 1970 annual general meeting. Following an article in the *Times*, the chairman felt obliged to deny 'that the Executive Committee had been involved in any "squabble" over the *British Journal of Political Science*':

> The Committee had discussed the inclusion of the term 'British' in the title but the only official action taken by the Committee had been to write to the Cambridge University Press suggesting that it might give rise to some misunderstanding by giving the impression that the Journal was the *official* publication of British political scientists. The CUP had replied declining to alter the title. The Executive as a whole felt there was plenty of room for another journal and had been in no way motivated by a desire to suppress this new one.

Professor Barry responded, saying:

> that the editorial board of the *British Journal of Political Science* had been at pains to make it clear that it was not in any sense an official journal. He regretted the controversy that had arisen and stressed that the journal was not an instrument of a clique. Articles were to be selected on the best academic basis (LSE, 1970c, PSA/15).

Professor Moodie subsequently met the chairman of the Cambridge University Press (CUP) syndics, Sir Frank Lee, at a conference in Cambridge. Sir Frank was used to taking a firm line in his previous post at the Treasury and he 'confirmed the fact that CUP did not feel it necessary to change their previous decision' (LSE, 1970a, PSA/15). There is a sense that the PSA was making rather heavy weather of this issue. After all, the journal was edited from Britain and published by a British university press and although two of the six members of the initial editorial board were from the USA, it could hardly have been called *The Mid-Atlantic Journal of Political Science.*

Tensions continued, although this time the BJPS made the first move. Brian Barry wrote to Graeme Moodie as PSA chair in January 1971 expressing surprise that 'A junior colleague who has agreed to do a paper for the next PSA conference has just been shown a note to the effect that *Political Studies* had first refusal on all papers given at the conference'. Professor Barry asked for this decision to be rescinded, arguing that 'it simply seems to be wrong to prevent someone who has given a paper to the annual conference submitting it to whichever journal has the readership he most wants to reach'. He expressed the hope that the Executive Committee would withdraw the note that had been circulated, but failing that a proposal should be put to the annual general meeting relating to the next year's conference. Professor Barry finished the letter by stating: 'The alternative, a motion from the floor condemning the executive committee's actions introducing the rule without consulting members, could only lead to an acrimonious discussion' (LSE, 1971a, PSA/15).

For some reason the letter only reached Professor Moodie in March. However, he stated:

> when *Political Studies* became a quarterly it was made very clear to everyone that the extra issue would be earmarked, at least in part, for the publication of papers delivered at the Annual Conference . . . The Committee also felt that it was not unreasonable for the Association to assert a claim on papers delivered at its own Annual Conference.

Moodie then called Barry's bluff by saying that if the committee did not change its decision, which he implied it would not, 'you will have no alternative but to attempt to censure the Committee at the AGM' (LSE, 1971b, PSA/15). This exchange cannot have pleased Brian Barry and may have been a contributory factor in his decision to move against the Executive Committee in 1975.

Relationships with practitioners

One might expect those engaged in the study of public administration and public policy to have a particularly close relationship with government, but it was evident that this was not the case. By the 1970s the old contacts forged in wartime had atrophied. 'When Professor W. J. M. Mackenzie retires from his Chair at Glasgow at the end of the present academic session, there will not be a single teacher of public administration in a UK university who has held a rank higher than Principal in the Civil Service' (NA, 1974b, p. 2). In the civil service's view, 'There is no doubt that there is a gap between British academics and practitioners in the field of public administration' (NA, 1974b, p. 2). The view was that there was 'a vicious circle: academics do not understand government well enough, because there is very little empirical research evidence; government does not look to academics because they do not understand the governmental process, and because it is not always easy to provide greater access' (NA, 1974b, p. 3).

In 1970 Professor Peter Self, who was then Chairman of the Public Administration Committee (PAC), tried to secure Civil Service Department (CSD) support for the setting up of a Committee of Enquiry into teaching of public administration, with terms of reference similar to those of the Hayter Committee on East European and Oriental Studies and the Parry Committee on Latin American Studies. This argument found little favour within the CSD:

> The analogy with the Parry and Hayter enquiries is a little misleading. When these Committees were set up, it was easy to concede in advance that the country would benefit from an increased number of people with knowledge of areas such as the Middle East and Latin America, and that it would be worth while to devote a modest proportion of national resources to the promotion of such studies. There is no *prima facie* reason to believe that an increase in the number of people with an academic knowledge of public administration would produce similar benefits for society (NA, 1973).

The Public Administration Committee subsequently produced its own report, authored by Dr Richard Chapman, entitled *Teaching Public Administration*. This report ruffled feathers in government with its criticisms of the Civil Service College which it considered was teaching a very traditional syllabus. It is within this context that one should place the judgement of Eugene Grebenik, then the principal of the Civil Service College, that 'We find this a disappointing document. Nowhere does Dr Chapman give a definition of public administration' (NA, 1973, p. 1). The contribution of administrative theory was relatively rapidly dismissed: 'a good deal of this is of American origin and seems somewhat culture-bound; so far relatively few studies in administrative theory have been made in a British context' (NA, 1973, p. 2).

Grebenik considered that it was essential 'to distinguish between the teaching of public administration in universities and polytechnics for undergraduate and graduate students as part of a general education, and teaching for public administration, i.e. to meet the needs of students preparing for administrative careers in the public service'. He was not optimistic about the prospects for conventional public administration topics: 'it might be noted that studies in the machinery of government are less glamorous, and less likely to appeal to the present day undergraduate than are the grand theories of sociology and political science. Undergraduate demand for courses in machinery of government is unlikely to be buoyant' (NA, 1973, p. 3).

He did agree with Dr Chapman's prediction that the subject might develop more quickly in the polytechnics, particularly in relation to local government, a forecast that was largely verified. However, 'since the Fulton recommendation of "preference for relevance" was rejected, it would require a change in the recruitment policy before any positive encouragement for courses in public administration could be given' (NA, 1973, p. 4).

Another suggestion that had been put forward was the establishment of a school of public affairs on the lines of such bodies in American universities or some kind of public policy 'think tank'. The notion of a 'British Brookings' surfaces again from time to time and private think tanks have become more prominent in the policy process. However, it overlooks an important difference between the organisation of the higher levels of the administration in Britain and the US with the phenomenon of 'in and outers' who join or leave government with each change of administration. Some of these are academics, although it is possible to exaggerate their numbers. Many of them find refuge in think tanks while waiting for another change of administration.

The view within the CSD was that there were already a number of institutions dealing with particular areas of policy such as Chatham House in foreign policy, the Institute of Strategic Studies in defence policy, the Centre of Advanced Urban Studies in the field of planning land use and the Institute of Local Government Studies at Birmingham University:

> It is difficult to see what would be gained by bringing these subjects together under one roof, even if this were politically possible, nor is it clear what special expertise someone concerned with problems of public policy as such would add to the consideration of these problems. It seems to me that any discussion of public affairs has to be soundly based on the basic underlying academic disciplines if it is to avoid being just another manifestation of the higher journalism (NA, 1973).

It was concluded that 'it is difficult to see what the Unit could do, and what it could contribute over and above the work of comparable centres in specific fields of activity'. Moreover, it might be difficult 'to make out a case for such a Unit to be staffed by specialists in public administration, rather than by economists, statisticians, sociologists and other specialists' (NA, 1974b, p. 3). An underlying issue here is that when one has a generalist civil service, they see themselves as the specialists in the machinery of government. This helps to explain why, while it was acknowledged that there might be a gap in studies of machinery of government and administration, the appropriate place to pursue them was the Civil Service College.

Andrew Dunsire, as chair of the PAC, proposed a meeting with Ian Bancroft, the second permanent secretary at the CSD. Bancroft was not initially enthusiastic about the meeting, noting that 'There is a lot of fairly inchoate thought churning about here. It would be practical and sensible to try and channel it into one or two practical areas rather than having people's time wasted in pursuit over too wide a range'. A handwritten note on Bancroft's memorandum added: 'I have no great sense of need for what is being inchoately hawked here' (NA, 1974a). Despite this rather inauspicious beginning, including a negative briefing he had received from Eugene Grebenik, Ian Bancroft wrote a minute about the meeting reporting that he had 'an interesting chat' and 'was interested in Mr Dunsire's practical approach and was glad that at any rate he had dropped the notion of a grand new initiative' (NA, 1974c). Andrew Dunsire's approach seems to have been to admit shortcomings on the academic side of the relationship with government: 'to the extent that public administration academics felt like poor relations, this was largely their own fault. If they had something useful to say to Government, then he was sure that Government would listen to them'. A practical approach was needed: '[The] academics must stop repining and wishing things were different. They must start from where they actually were now, i.e. with not very strong public administration faculties in the Universities, with the Civil Service College in being and with a relatively poor standing in the eyes of central Government' (NA, 1974c).

'At the end of this amicable discussion, I [Ian Bancroft] suggested that Mr Dunsire should get in touch with the Minister of State in order to have a chat with him' (NA, 1974c). This lunch was held later in May 1974 with thirteen academic guests (see Box 3.2). Some of the academics were in self-deprecating mood. Andrew Dunsire 'recognised that academics had not in the past done enough, and Mr [Nevil] Johnson (Nuffield College, Oxford) added that an element of realism was necessary: the views of all those engaged in public administration were not of equal value' (NA, 1974d). These discussions seem to have had relatively few practical consequences, although a seminar series for academics and civil servants was set up which the author attended.

Box 3.2: Ministerial Lunch 1974, Academic Participants

Dr R. G. Brown, Senior Lecturer, University of Hull
Sir Norman Chester, Warden, Nuffield College, Oxford
A. Dunsire, Senior Lecturer, University of York
Professor L. Gunn, University of Strathclyde
N. Johnson, Fellow, Nuffield College, Oxford
Dr G. Jones, Senior Lecturer, LSE
Professor M. Kogan, Brunel University
Dr D. Regan, Lecturer, LSE
Professor F. Ridley, University of Liverpool
Professor P. Self, LSE
L. J. Sharpe, Lecturer, Nuffield College, Oxford
Professor F. Stacey, University of Swansea
Dr M. Wright, Lecturer, University of Manchester

Source: NA, 1974d.

At the same time the civil service was considering the future of the Royal Institute of Public Administration (RIPA) which also published the well-regarded journal *Public Administration*. Indeed, one of our informants thought that it was a better journal in this period than *Political Studies* because it had a clearer focus. As far as the civil service was concerned, RIPA was something of a 'chosen instrument' of government, yet they were unclear what sort of body it was or in which direction it was or should be going. Certainly it had received substantial government encouragement and support:

> The Institute of Public Relations [*sic*] (IPA) owed its establishment to the initiative of individual public servants in central and local government: the notes remaining on the file show that this encouragement has persisted over the years, particularly in the period after the Second World War, by highly placed officials in the Treasury, including Sir Henry Wilson Smith, Sir Thomas Padmore and later by Sir Edward Bridges (NA, 1974e, p. 1).

In 1974 the CSD was paying RIPA a corporate membership fee of £16,850 on behalf of all government departments.

From a civil service perspective, 'the RIPA is a mixture of service agency and learned society. It is not a professional or occupational association. Nor is it a "Centre of Excellence" like the Centre for Environmental Studies on the one hand or Chatham House on the other' (NA, 1974f, p. 3). The view expressed within the civil service was that RIPA had been most successful 'as an agency of Government' (NA, 1974e, p. 3). However, despite this expressed preference, 'A close reading of the papers on relations with the RIPA reflect "a clear ambiguity" about the Institute's nature and purpose'. In 1970 Ian Bancroft had served as a member of a committee that reviewed RIPA's role:

> The Committee – like the Government – had difficulty in defining its nature between that of a professional institution and academic body, and as a service institution often on a consultant/contractor basis. It concluded that it had become a learned society acting as a service organisation for public authorities and that the aim of its founders to establish and develop the public services as a recognised profession was an 'unrealisable ambition'. Public administration tended to be regarded as a field in which there are many professions rather than a profession in its own right and the RIPA does not in any case attempt to set any professional standards (NA, 1974f, p. 2).

RIPA was placed in receivership in July 1992. As Chapman reflected (1992, p. 520), 'Any analysis will ... have to consider the relevance of an administrative culture, especially in the British civil service, that has never really believed public administration is a respectable subject for study or that it can make valuable contributions to good practice'.

The PAC was making the running on relationships with practitioners during this period, while the PSA's stance was more tentative. At the 1966 annual general meeting, Geoffrey Marshall had proposed that an informal group of members should get together to produce proposals to be put to the Fulton Committee on the civil service (LSE, 1966a, PSA/15). The Committee subsequently wrote to the PSA asking to give evidence.

> It was decided that the Secretary should inform the Fulton Committee that the PSA as an organisation did not exist to present such evidence, but that individual members would give evidence. It was felt that if groups of members presented evidence, it would be better for them to do so under the umbrella of the PAC rather than the PSA (LSE, 1967c, PSA/15).

In the event, 'The PAC did not submit evidence to the Committee, although a significant number of its members contributed in various capacities' (Chapman, 2007, p. 18). This represents something of a missed opportunity for both organisations and contrasts with the PSA's response to the 2007 Green Paper on constitutional reform when a critical analysis was published by the PSA with contributions from various members while making it clear that it did not represent an official PSA statement.

Another important development that took place away from the PSA during this period was the formation of the 1964 Study of Parliament group. This took place against the background of demands for the modernisation of parliament, a recurring theme. In 1964 Bernard Crick published his book *The Reform of Parliament* which was reprinted twice even though he was subsequently criticised by Henry Fairlie for advocating 'crick crack reforms' (Fairlie, 1968). In his preface to the second edition, Crick noted that in 1964 there was 'the crest of a wave compounded of the flood tide of an opposition drawing near to power and of the ebbtide of a government facing defeat and preparing itself for the salutary novelty of forming the Opposition. Nearly everyone had a good word to say for Parliamentary reform' (Crick, 1968, p. ix).

The initial memorandum that led to the formation of the group was drawn up by Bernard Crick and Michael Ryle, a senior clerk in the House of Commons. The immediate stimulus was the promised establishment of a Select Committee on Procedure whoever won the election. More generally, the memorandum stated:

> the suggestion has been made that it would be mutually useful, both for practical and academic reasons, for people in the universities and in the Palace of Westminster interested in the study of the modern Parliament to have the chance to meet each other on some known and regular basis, however informal, to study and stimulate studies of Parliament (quoted in Englefield, 2009, p. 2).

Among those to whom the memorandum was sent were individuals active in the formation of the PSA, including Norman Chester, W. J. M. Mackenzie and William Robson, although none of them attended the inaugural meeting. Three academics who were particularly active in the group were Harry Hanson (Leeds), Peter Richards (Southampton) and Victor Wiseman (Exeter). Both Hanson and Wiseman were later to die in the precincts of the House of Commons. The group has continued to flourish, but not anyone can join as candidates have to be proposed by an existing member and approved by the Executive Committee.

Conferences, specialist groups and the graduate conference

In many respects the annual conference during this period continued to be organised on relatively conventional lines. For example, 'It was agreed to stick to the same pattern of papers for the 1969 conference' (LSE, 1968g, PSA/15). This meant organising the conference around the conventional categories of British Politics, Comparative Politics, Political Theory and International Relations. Compared with 1963, the principal innovation was the splitting of Political Institutions into separate Comparative Politics and British Politics sections. However, the increasing size of annual PSA conferences and the influx of new members were recognised with a decision in 1974 that badges would have to be worn in the future.

Probably the most important development during this period was the emergence of the first specialist groups. In 1967 a Committee on Comparative Politics was formed which was to concern itself with research projects requiring inter-university cooperation, convene and organise research groups and endorse projects put forward to the SSRC. The underlying model was very much one of moving from the lone scholar to team working. Its membership included some key members of the discipline such as Professor Blondel, Norman Chester, Sammy Finer, W. J. M. Mackenzie and Richard Rose.

A Political Sociology group was formed jointly with the British Sociological Association in 1968. This was followed by the formation of the American Politics group in 1973 and the Franco–British Political Science group in 1974. These specialist groups were to play an increasingly important part in the work of the PSA.

Perhaps the most important development during this period in terms of conferences was the establishment of a graduate conference in response to the needs of the growing number of politics postgraduates. The first of these conferences was held in London in December 1968 and one question raised was why membership of the PSA was not open to postgraduates. In a theme that was to remain an issue 40 years later, there was 'A demand for nationally organised courses on statistics and methods' (LSE, 1968e, PSA/15). Out of the 45 students present 24 had received no instruction at all in this area.

The author attended one of these conferences in the Christmas vacation 1970–71 and his main recollection was of being told that the best hope of employment for those present was to be found in the polytechnics. The report on the 1972 conference stated: 'I had taken note of complaints at earlier conferences that the elders of the profession had been at times disposed to engage in cloudy wisdom, instead of getting down to the real practicalities of research' (LSE, 1972, PSA/15). There were also limits to how far the PSA was prepared to engage with postgraduates. At the first meeting of the Executive Committee in 1969 there was 'some discussion of the position of graduates vis-à-vis the Association and although there was general agreement that more should be done to involve them with the PSA, there should be no specific item relating to this on the agenda' (LSE, 1969d, PSA/15).

Entitlement to membership: the polytechnics are admitted

With the establishment of a binary system of higher education the PSA had to consider whether those teaching in polytechnics could be admitted to membership. First, however, the Association had to tackle the question of overseas members. In 1965 the Executive Committee agreed to create a new category of Associate Member for persons wishing to join the PSA from foreign or Commonwealth countries. They would not have voting rights or be eligible for office in the Association. 'The purposes of the amendment were to clear up anomalies, to associate University teachers all over the world with the PSA and to increase the income of the Association' (LSE, 1965b, PSA/15). When the motion was put to the annual general meeting in 1966, an amendment was proposed to amend clause 2 of the constitution so as to enable any university teacher of politics from anywhere in the world to be a full member of the PSA. This was lost by 37 votes to 17, but a motion to amend clause 2 which would have the effect of offering full membership to any in a university or university college in the Colonies or the Irish Republic was adopted (LSE, 1966a, PSA/15).

In 1968 the annual general meeting had a lengthy but inconclusive debate on the criteria for membership of the PSA: 'Some speakers wished membership to be open to all who wished to apply and others felt it should be restricted to the academic staff of universities. A compromise view, whereby those engaged at various further education institutions in teaching politics full-time, should be accepted for membership automatically, was urged' (LSE, 1968c, PSA/15).

Following this discussion, an amendment was proposed to the PSA constitution by Leslie Macfarlane of Ruskin College, seconded by David Griffiths of Sheffield, which would open membership to all those employed in Institutes of Education (presumably a deliberately vague and all-encompassing description). It was agreed to write to the Association of Teachers in Technical Institutions and the DES to find out what information they could provide about the teaching of politics in non-university institutions (LSE, 1968g, PSA/15). Not surprisingly, they were not able to provide much information and the PSA did not feel able to carry out its own survey of those engaged in the teaching of politics. There was a range of views expressed in the Executive Committee:

> Professor Blondel felt that membership should be open to all who wished to join. Mr Minogue felt membership should be open to all who contributed to research. Professor Moodie suggested that all full-time teachers of politics should be open to membership. Professor Crick argued that the rules should be applied more liberally (LSE, 1969a, PSA/15).

At the 1969 annual general meeting, Leslie Marcfarlane and David Griffiths proposed a new constitutional amendment, 'That membership of the Association be open to all persons in Institutions of Further Education in the United Kingdom who spend not less than two-thirds of their teaching-time, teaching politics or government at University degree or equivalent level'. From the Executive Committee, Graham Moodie and Peter Campbell moved an amendment, 'That membership of the Association be open to all full-time teachers of politics in new polytechnics'. Professor Moodie raised two problems about the motion: 'it would require a national survey to discover all teachers of politics in the country and it would further require a lengthy and complex process of policing the two-thirds criterion'. However, 'he recognised that a new situation whereas in the past there had only been university institutions, new "university-type" institutions were being created and the Association must cater for the needs of these new teachers of politics'. Undaunted, Mr Macfarlane 'continued to urge that there was a real need to bring outsiders into the Association, for whom university-type criteria need not apply'. Professor Crick pursued his own distinctive argument, calling on the meeting to reject both motions and asking the PSA to publicise clause 4 of the constitution and apply it more liberally. The Executive Committee amendment was carried by a substantial majority and lecturers in polytechnics became eligible for membership of the PSA (LSE, 1969e, PSA/15).

Not all members were happy about this decision. One informant recalled that Norman Chester thought that 'Letting people in from polys would devalue currency because they weren't supposed to be doing research'. Beith (2008, p. 47) recalls that Newcastle Polytechnic, later Northumbria University, was just across the road from the university but 'So rigid was the binary divide that there seemed to be almost no contact or cooperation between the University and its higher education neighbour. In the Politics department we began to change that . . . working with each other in areas of common research interest'. In fact, most lecturers in polytechnics were doing so and their number included figures later to play a prominent role in the discipline, such as Michael Moran, now the W. J. M. Mackenzie Professor at Manchester University, who started his career at Manchester Polytechnic, Paul Whiteley, who had his first job at Kingston, and David Judge, who began at Paisley.

The polytechnic lecturers did not exactly rush to become members. At the 1970 conference existing members did have the opportunity to inspect this new type of member as it was reported that 'A feature of the Conference was the attendance of 4 members from polytechnics' (LSE, 1970e, PSA/15). By that time only nine full-time teachers of politics in polytechnics had joined the PSA. Michael Moran recalls that he eventually joined in 1976 for the contingent reason that he was giving a paper at the annual conference. More generally:

> The binary divide meant that people in Polys were not very well integrated into professional political science. Politics departments were fairly uncommon – I was fairly typical in being in a wider department of social sciences, with a fairly small politics group. I also think that there was a perception – I certainly had it, and I recall hearing it occasionally from others – that the PSA was the association of the old universities (Personal communication, 7 July 2009).

There was certainly something of that attitude. David Marsh recalled a meeting with the Executive Committee in January 1976:

> The then PSA Executive had decided they needed to make links with the Polys. My recollection is that Bob Dowse was on the Exec and he suggested my name. Anyway a group (3 or 4) of us went to meet the PSA Exec at LSE. The only other person I remember from that delegation was Mick Ryan – who was an expert on penal policy at one of the other London Polys [Thames]. Anyway the meeting was OK, but some of the older members of the Exec were definitely sniffy and one said he wasn't too impressed with the Daves, Micks and Petes (there must have been a Pete on the delegation, I suppose!) from the Polys influencing the direction of Political Science (Personal communication, 11 June 2009).

There were eight participants from polytechnics in this meeting.

The Executive Committee still had to take decisions on individual applications made under clause 4. In the context of the discussion of the admission of members from other than university institutions, this had been used as something of a defence for the status quo. Mrs P. Skinner of Cambridge University Press was rejected 'on the grounds that to admit a representative of a publishing company might create a precedent for admitting many more' (LSE, 1967b, PSA/15). Professor Finer wrote to the then PSA secretary, Geoffrey Alderman to the effect that 'Mr Bodfish, with whom I have some limited acquaintance of the Harris College, Department of Language and Social Studies (God help us all) has written asking for my support in an application for membership to PSA. He says that he has written to you and you replied that you felt that he was not eligible'. Professor Crick reflected on what had been in the Executive Committee's mind on the 'additional membership' clause: '[The] trend of the discussion was certainly that we would favourably consider people in Further Education who had written some *worth-while* books, even if textbooks, or had published the results of some research. We let in a grammar school master who is a notorious writer of text books, Colonel Frank Benemy, a few months ago' (LSE, 1969f, PSA/15). As for Mr Bodfish, it was suggested that he should submit a CV for consideration.

Structure and election procedures

Sammy Finer had resigned as chair at the 1968 conference. At the October meeting of the Executive Committee, Graham Moodie had to take the chair and became chair in 1969 (the 50th anniversary booklet records Professor Finer continuing as chair until 1969). Professors Finer and Crick had advanced the idea of a president who would be 'a senior, elder of the profession and a Vice-President who would nominally chair the EC' (LSE, 1968f, PSA/15). These developments prompted a consideration of the Association's structure and it was agreed to consider a constitutional amendment to create a new post of president 'who would have mainly a nominal and honorific position and who would carry out the major social functions of the Association at such meetings as the IPSA Congress'. There would also be 'A Vice-Chairman who would chair Committee Meetings in the President's absence and upon whom would devolve generally, executive work' (LSE, 1968d, PSA/15). In 1969 W. J. M. Mackenzie became the first president of the PSA. The current position is that the chair, elected by the Executive Committee, serves for three years and then serves three years as president. This sometimes causes confusion in the US where it is thought that the president is the real head of the association rather than an honorific position.

Attendance at committee meetings fell away towards the end of the 1960s and at the beginning of 1969 'Some concern was expressed at the sporadic attendance at the last meetings of the Committee. It was suggested this could perhaps be remedied by organising meaningful elections at the AGM' (LSE, 1969a, PSA/15). Quite how one organises a meaningful election is a moot point, but at the 1969 annual general meeting there was a contested election with four unsuccessful candidates including Brian Barry and Richard Rose. There was a contested election again in 1971, but this time there was only one more candidate than the number of vacancies and the spread of votes was much smaller than in 1969 with the unsuccessful candidate receiving 49 votes and the candidate topping the poll receiving 66. There was a contested election again in 1972.

The increased frequency of elections led to a series of complaints at the 1974 election about the way in which the PSA's elections were conducted. It was suggested that some form of proportional voting might be introduced and the Executive Committee subsequently received a four-page letter from Miss Enid Lakeman, the campaigner for proportional representation, explaining the merits of the Single Transferable Vote (STV). A paper prepared for the Executive Committee (the identity of the author is unknown) stated:

> In theory there would appear to be no real objection to introducing some form of PR. However, there are very considerable practical difficulties imposed by the association's lack of resources (we would hardly want to purchase an electronic calculator merely for this purpose) and the burden of work such methods would inevitably involve for the returning officer.

The paper then went on to make an argument that would be criticised if it was submitted in a first-year undergraduate essay: 'In any case, as was pointed out by several members at the AGM, there is already an implicit weighting of preferences in the method we already use. No voter is obliged to use all his nine votes, any decision to use less means that those selected receive an extra weighting'. Finally, this aspect of the paper showed an unusual understanding of the role of theory when it commented: 'All in all, it seems to me that any decision to change the existing system of voting, however valid in theory, involves more practical difficulties than it is worth'. PSA elections today use the STV system.

The second issue was that all that voters were told about the candidates was whether they were sitting members of the executive. 'This was variously criticised as being too much (on the ground that it induced a vote for the status quo) or too little (particularly, on the ground that many of the younger members and those from Polytechnics might well be unacquainted with a majority of the candidates).' It was admitted that this criticism had some validity:

> Those who have been in the association a long time may know about most of those who offer themselves as candidates, but even they may know relatively little about the occasional 'Young Turk' who puts his head on the electoral chopping block. Furthermore, the current system may effectively disenfranchise those younger or more isolated colleagues who have attended few meetings or are new to the profession.

However, it was feared that providing more information to voters might encourage factionalism: '[It] may be argued that, since the PSA is not a sectionally divided organisation, it would be wrong to provide implicit factional programmes by a long listing of qualifications and views held. Moreover, on practical grounds, an [sic] huge quantity of information would again impose intolerable burdens on the Secretary'. Nevertheless, it was conceded that for a trial period some limited types of information might be provided such as institution, status, previous membership of the PSA executive and major teaching interest. Presumably it was felt that entrusting voters with any more information would provoke factionalism.

Finally, it was observed that very little use was made of the opportunity to make nominations before the conference. Beyond some redrafting of the secretary's letter, it was considered that 'there is very little that can be done about this problem' (LSE, 1974a, PSA/15). When the Executive Committee considered the issue, it opted for the status quo. 'It was decided that there should be no change in the method of voting currently employed. It was agreed that no information about any of the candidates should appear on the ballot papers' (LSE, 1974b, PSA/15). It was conceded that brief personal information on the candidates similar to that circulated by the ECPR could be posted on the conference notice board.

Admittedly the Association then had no paid staff, which now organise the whole election process, and the changes proposed would have placed additional burdens on the volunteers who ran the PSA. Nevertheless, the picture that emerges is of an organisation very resistant to change or to expressions of discontent from its members and this forms part of the backcloth to the challenge to the Executive Committee in 1975.

Charitable status

At the 1969 annual general meeting members unanimously approved a motion to convert the PSA into a recognised charity. 'The conversion would make it easier for foundations to offer financial assistance to the Association and likewise the Association would escape tax liabilities' (LSE, 1969e, PSA/15). Professor J. A. G. Griffith was subsequently asked for advice on how this might be achieved and he obtained a legal opinion for the PSA. This proposal met with some resistance with the DES writing on its behalf and that of the Inland Revenue to state that the PSA appears to be a members' organisation without a sufficient degree of public benefit to be considered charitable (LSE, 1971c, PSA/15). In response a lengthy lecture was drafted by Geoffrey Marshall to be sent to the DES. This led to a request for further information, noting that membership was confined to university and polytechnic teachers. Charitable registration was achieved in 1973.

This decision was of considerable importance for the PSA. First, it reduced tax liability and meant that Value Added Tax (VAT) did not have to be levied on the annual membership fee and the PSA has been able to recover the VAT it incurs on various items of expenditure. In 2008 this amounted to a financial benefit of £30,000 in that year, although from 2008 5 per cent of membership subscriptions have been treated as relating to taxable supplies. Second, it effectively brought to an end disputes about membership as no one could be excluded. Third, as the 'public benefit' test for charities came to be more stringently applied, the PSA had to ensure that its activities were of benefit to the wider public as well as its own members.

The Formation of the ECPR

Although important contributions were made by Rudolph Wildenmann and Stein Rokkan, Jean Blondel was the driving force behind the creation of the ECPR. It was 'Blondel's enthusiasm and energy, which drove the organisation forward and created a unified European political science around it'. Blondel believed 'passionately in an information-led, comparative political science' (Budge, 2006, p. 315). Blondel had evidently become irritated with the lack of response by the PSA to his suggestions for expansion of his activities. 'Meanwhile, confronted with the British political scientists' lack of faith in the relevance of their research, he had taken a stance in favour of a behaviouralist orientation for political science and maintained relations with American colleagues' (Boncourt, 2008, p. 369). With a Ford Foundation grant for the development of European political science, Blondel used the American model of the Inter-University Consortium for Political Research (ICPR) to set up the ECPR. He was also able to make use of the networks developed by the Essex Summer School.

The foundation meeting was held in 1970 with Essex, Nuffield College and Strathclyde being the British institutions present. The ECPR was set up as an organisation of departments and research institutes paying a subscription with the advantage that those attending research workshops received partial reimbursement of expenses from collective funds. The first Joint Sessions of Workshops, based on a week's work around a theme during which everyone had to give a paper, was held in 1973. 'Special attention was paid to attracting young members of the profession whose status in the workshop was the same as that of all other participants' (Budge, 2006, p. 322). For some younger political scientists, the ECPR Joint Sessions became a priority over the PSA conference.

Conclusions

On some issues the PSA was relatively proactive during this period. It recognised the importance for the discipline of the formation of the SSRC, it had the foresight to recognise the value of charitable status and it moved *Political Studies* to a quarterly publication and replaced the editor when there was dissatisfaction with the journal. The formation of specialist groups was not hindered, even if the initiative for their formation came from the membership rather than the Executive Committee. As the numbers of postgraduates expanded, a regular graduate conference was established. The committee was meeting more frequently and its agendas were longer.

However, on other issues, the PSA seemed resistant to change. The *British Journal of Political Science* was seen as a threat rather than as evidence of the vibrant state of British political science. While one can understand the position of those who wanted the PSA to focus on research, there was some delay in sorting out the membership issue and the polytechnic lecturers were not welcomed all that warmly. The systematic development of relations with practitioners was largely left to the Joint University Committee (JUC). The debate over election procedures showed a great reluctance to change, largely on grounds of convenience.

Yet the discipline was undergoing a process of transition, reflected in a rapid growth in PSA membership, although this levelled out in the early 1970s with a net increase of just thirteen members from 1972 to 1974 (550 to 563). The PSA often seemed to react rather belatedly, if at all, to these developments. Advocates of reform like Jean Blondel and Bernard Crick were evidently viewed with a lack of enthusiasm if not suspicion and they diverted their energies elsewhere, Blondel to the ECPR and Crick to the Politics Association. The PSA was ripe for change and it came in quite a dramatic fashion in 1975.

Chapter 4

The Oxford-Led Insurgency: 1975

This chapter discusses the 'Oxford-led insurgency' of 1975 which led to the replacement of the PSA's Executive Committee by a slate which had been organised by Brian Barry. Most of the members of the slate went on to be prominent members of the discipline they had shaken up. This was a very important development in the history of the PSA which laid the foundations for the highly professional association in the twenty-first century. The new committee was relatively young and full of energy and new ideas which they pursued in a systematic fashion. Not all of these ideas worked, but many of them did, and the PSA was transformed as a result, although not for the better in the opinion of everyone and there were costs in the terms of the loss of the involvement of some senior professors. This chapter examines the insurgency of 1975, its immediate aftermath in terms of the editorship of *Political Studies*, the efforts the Association made to expand its membership and the resource constraints it faced. Chapter 5 examines the major policy initiatives undertaken by the new EC and the way in which they were followed up in the period to 1979 when the effects of cutbacks in public expenditure on the social sciences began to be experienced.

The instigators of this change were seeking to rectify what they saw as some deficiencies in the organisation and operation of the PSA, but it may be that political science was facing an intellectual crisis that was deeper than its organisational one. One manifestation of this crisis was the formation of a separate British International Studies Association (BISA) in 1975, a division that became particularly important with the development of the RAE. Hayward (1999, p. 20) labels this period after 1975 as one that could be described as 'sceptical professionalism, nourished by the failures of the 1960s' ambitions and the reversal of University expansion of the social sciences'. Political science as a discipline was becoming more professional, but possibly more distant from its original engagement with the political process and from the ferment of ideas in society. One professional success came in 1976 when, after two earlier failed attempts, the PSA staged a Congress of IPSA in Edinburgh, which is discussed in Chapter 5.

The Insurgency

Robert Goodin attended his first PSA conference at St Catherine's College, Oxford in 1975, which was the 25th anniversary conference. He recalls: 'That was the year the Old Guard was decisively routed by a slate of Young Turks, organized by Brian Barry and consisting more or less wholly of the professionalized subprofessoriate who formed the Editorial Board of the *British Journal of Political Science* at the time. The revolution succeeded' (Goodin, 2009, p. 43). There is some disagreement about how these events should be described. Some have talked of a 'coup', but all that happened was a legitimate use of the electoral process. Tony Birch, who was one of those ousted but was immediately co-opted back on to the Executive Committee, uses the term 'quiet revolution' (Birch, 2009). Barry (see Box 4.1) talks of 'the insurgent camp' (Barry, 1975).

Box 4.1: Brian Barry, 1936–2009

'Brian Barry was a phenomenon, a character almost larger than life: a big bear of a man who could delight and intimidate at almost the same moment. A man full of ferocity because he believed everything he wrote and said: about justice, about equality, about our duties to others now and the future' (Dowding, 2009, p. 459). Barry read PPE at Oxford and stayed on to complete a doctorate there. He held positions at a number of universities and in a number of countries including Essex, Oxford, the European University Institute and Columbia University in New York, but found his eventual academic home at the LSE. Together with Anthony King he founded the *British Journal of Political Science* in 1971 which became a leading journal in the discipline. Later he rescued *Ethics* which was in danger of closing, 'turning it into the liveliest publication in normative political theory in its day' (Weale, 2009, p. 22). Barry was the instigator of the slate that toppled the 'old guard' of the PSA in 1975. Although he had collaborators, he was the prime mover. What he did particularly well in his academic work was to combine philosophical argument with the lessons of the social sciences in a way that informed current debates and reflected his personal concern for liberalism and social justice. In the 1990s he made his flat the venue for the Rational Choice group of the PSA. The PSA three times awarded him the W. J. M. Mackenzie prize for the best book published in the previous year, as well as giving him a lifetime achievement award as part of the 50th anniversary celebrations. He was the only British scholar to be awarded the nearest thing political science has to a Nobel Prize, the Johan Skytte Prize in Political Science. Barry suffered from bipolar disorder all his life. The tributes paid to him after his death left no doubt about the esteem and affection he commanded.

What is evident is that this was a carefully planned operation by Barry with close attention to strategy and tactics. Since he was unable to stand himself because of his prospective departure to the United States, he designated himself as campaign manager. He was assisted by Jim Sharpe, also at Nuffield College, much to the irritation of the warden, Norman Chester, who did not approve of what happened. On 12 February 1975 it was Barry who sent the list of nominees to the then secretary, Peter Woodward. They were: Rod Rhodes as secretary; Ian Budge; Bob Dowse; Jack Hayward; Dilys Hill; Dennis Kavanagh; Geraint Parry; Jim Sharpe; and Jeff Stanyer. Only one nominee was from Oxford (Sharpe) and there was no one from the LSE, but two nominees from Exeter (Dowse and Stanyer).

The choice of candidates was not accidental:

> I think Bob Dowse, Jim Sharpe and I all decided independently that after years of grousing about the PSA it was time to do something about it. Everybody we asked to stand accepted and the only two possible people I can think of that might have been added are Blondel and Rose, but Blondel is busy with the ECPR, and Rose is standing anyway (we believe) . . . I certainly think we've got just about everybody who has ever given any sign of having two ideas to rub together (Barry, 1975).

Barry undertook to 'act without inhibitions' as campaign manager and he was noted for not using the restrained, coded language that was prevalent in British academia, for example: 'with respect' (I think you are misguided); 'with great respect' (I think you are foolish); and 'with very great respect' (I think you are an idiot). Sharpe described Barry in the humorous lexicon he produced as 'a rather astringent fruit' (Sharpe, 1990, p. 16). Barry did not pull his punches about the existing committee about whom he thought there was 'a great fund of ill-will . . . waiting to be tapped':

> The electoral base of the incumbents is Reading, LSE, Oxford and York, both for personal reasons and because these are conservative departments the bulk of whose members find the slothful complacency of the present Committee quite to their taste. It will hardly escape your notice that three of these departments are in or within easy commuting distance of Oxford [Barry gave a Didcot home telephone number] (Barry, 1975).

Barry was convinced that it would 'be a tactical mistake to adopt a "low key" approach and hope to slip the new candidates on to the committee without anyone noticing, as a number of good chaps who just happen to be standing for the first time' (Barry, 1975). He was one of the two conference convenors, which helps to account for the presence of many of the slate on the programme. Jack Hayward recalls: 'the fact that I gave the opening paper on "Institutional Inertia and Political Impetus in France and Britain" had an intentional ironic implication for the challenge to the outgoing EC' (Personal communication, 14 August 2009). Barry emphasised that high turnout was important and recommended targeting large departments without a representative on the EC such as Lancaster, Strathclyde and

Warwick. (Arguably Warwick was no less conservative at the time than Barry claimed Reading or Oxford were). He argued that non-members of the PSA were a 'promising target' and they should be persuaded to join and attend the conference. They should be told: '(a) that this year's programme is quite attractive so the meeting should not be too painful and (b) that they need only join for the year, so that if the insurgent challenge fails at the elections they can drop out again next year'. Departmental chairs were told that they should be advised to bust departmental budgets to make sure that everyone who wanted to go to the PSA conference could do so. He thought that 'sortez les sortants is quite a good slogan, or if you prefer it in English You have stayed in this place too long for any good that you have done. In the name of God, go!' (Barry, 1975)

Jack Hayward, who enjoyed a reputation for sagacity and sound judgement, reined in some of Barry's unrestrained enthusiasm and gave more direction to the effort. He thought that there had to be more than just a negative call to get rid of the old guard, but also a positive programme of action. Addressing Barry, no doubt tongue in cheek, as 'Dear Campaign Manager', he wrote:

> As I see it, the main problem is that quite apart from the individual merits of the candidates (and here, I must say, I think we are lacking in 'weight') we do not seem to have a programme of reform. While I know this might be very difficult to agree in advance and there are doubtless advantages in not having a programme at all, fighting simply in a Poujadist style with the slogan 'Sortez les Sortants', the result will be that we shall only replace two or three of the old guard.

Hayward suggested that what was needed was a programme if 'we are simply to avoid a worthwhile initiative going off on half-cock. We shall undoubtedly be pressed, when lobbying, to say what we stand for, so perhaps we should be clear on this ourselves' (Hayward, 1975).

Barry himself was doubtful 'whether [the candidates] can get elected'. He had already sketched out a rough set of objectives:

(1) 'Revitalization (or vitalization) of PS, making more use of it as the PSA mag., probably new editor.
(2) Higher level of activity all round, including a big effort to get sections, regional meetings, etc., to flourish.
(3) Prevent the IPSA meeting at Edinburgh in 1976 from being a fiasco.
(4) Housekeeping matters: membership drive, try to negotiate time allowances for officers etc.' (Barry, 1975).

This was elaborated into a four-point programme, of which 150 copies were distributed; the programme is reproduced in Box 4.2. In retrospect, Hayward comments: 'What strikes me about our programme was its moderation (electoral calculation?) but it did break the logjam after earlier failures' (Personal communication, 3 August 2009). On the first day of the conference the insurgents met at Brian Barry's room in Nuffield, moving on to the Welsh Pony at the bottom of George Street, to concert strategy.

Box 4.2:   The Manifesto of the Insurgents

Statement on behalf of I. Budge, R. E. Dowse, J. E. S. Hayward, D. M. Hill, D. Kavanagh, G. Parry, L. J. Sharpe, J. Stanyer, candidates for the committee, R. A. W. Rhodes, candidate for the secretaryship.

'The elections for the PSA executive committee are being contested by a group of people who have not stood before but offer themselves this year in the belief that the PSA needs a change of management. While they span a wide range of fields and methodological outlooks, they are united by the desire to make the PSA a more effective body, better adapted to meeting the needs of a large and scattered membership.

Among the ideas so far suggested by people in this group are:

(i)   The committee should take a more active role in planning the annual conference. There should be a variety of convenors but no return to the illogical and deadening fourfold division of recent years [political theory; UK politics; comparative politics; international relations]. In other words, the committee should actually exert itself to think of subjects for the conference.

(ii)   The journal should be used to carry association news and provide a forum for the discussion of matters of professional and disciplinary concern, as well as a place for publishing learned articles.

(iii) The committee should take the lead in setting up a variety of meetings at which faculty and graduate students with common research interests can get together, either on a regional or a national basis. The ECPR workshops provide one (though only one) model but obviously cannot involve more than a fraction of PSA members at a time. Much more is needed.

(iv)   On the basis of offering a real service to members (including a lively and interesting journal) it should be possible to mount a campaign to bring in the many university and polytechnic teachers who have not in the past joined the PSA. This would strengthen the resource base of the association and enable it to do a better job. Members should also have the opportunity to vote on an amendment to the constitution opening the PSA to all who subscribe to its objects, whatever their institution.

Above all the members of the group pledge themselves to bring more imagination and energy to the conduct of the association's affairs and on that basis ask for your vote.'

Rather than just getting two or three candidates elected as a 'ginger group' on the committee as they thought might happen, Barry and his associates saw their whole committee slate elected. The secretary in office, Peter Woodward, defeated Rod Rhodes, but resigned immediately and Rhodes was co-opted on to the committee as secretary. Given their forecasts of their likely performance, they had not thought about a new chair of the association and Jack Hayward was selected as he was the only professor among those elected.

There was a tie for last elected place on the ballot between Tony Birch, the outgoing chair, and Fred Ridley, the editor of *Political Studies*. Birch (2009) recalls:

> We naturally had a quiet chat about this at which I proposed to withdraw my name as he was editor of *Political Studies* and he probably ought to be on the EC. Ridley demurred, saying that as I was involved in the organisation of the forthcoming World Congress and was acting as liaison between the PSA and IPSA (of which I was the British member of the Executive Committee) it was more important that I should remain on the EC.

After this inconclusive bout of 'after you' they both decided to withdraw and the place went to the next person in the order of voting, Frank Castles.

Barry's central role was demonstrated by an incident the author experienced during the conference. Dr Phillip Giddings had not been opposed as treasurer, but resigned once the election results were announced. At the dinner afterwards, I was somewhat disconcerted to notice the formidable Brian Barry staring at me while someone whispered in his ear. At the age of 28, I was subsequently appointed to the post of treasurer, taking over from Phillip Giddings in the summer. Giddings was a person of high integrity who had discharged the role of treasurer with conscientiousness and efficiency and the transition was a very smooth one thanks to his good organisation and helpfulness. Having Grant on the committee also brought in someone from Warwick. Sharpe (1990, p. 144) defined 'Wyn Grant' in his lexicon as 'A technique common among some British political scientists for dressing up a proposed research project so as to make it appear to be making a decisive contribution to industry in order to appeal to the instrumental philistinism of research funding agencies'.

As outgoing chair Birch 'told the AGM with complete sincerity that I welcomed the changes because I thought it had been a bit unhealthy for EC members to have been re-elected year after year with no opposition, and I wished the new members of the EC every good luck in their efforts to improve the association' (Birch, 2009). At a brief business meeting of the new Executive Committee immediately after the annual general meeting, Birch was asked if he would serve as a co-opted member until the 1976 IPSA Congress was held and was pleased to agree.

Not all of the 'old guard' accepted these events with as much equanimity as Tony Birch. Norman Chester 'muttered darkly' that the revolution would not have succeeded 'had he been present – and the darkness of his utterance convinced me that he was probably correct' (Goodin, 2009, p. 43). One senior member of the discipline approached Jack Hayward waving the four-point plan and said: 'Jack, I am going to hold you to this'. Hayward responded: 'Don't worry, I will do more' and, as he commented, 'We did', allowing him to stand down as chair after two years with Hugh Berrington from Newcastle University taking his place. It has not been possible to establish exactly what Sammy Finer said, but it was apparently vigorous in its expression and outspoken in its content, one informant describing it as 'outrageous'.

> After the vote was announced at the AGM, the head of the Electoral Reform Society, Enid Lakeman, rose to express the hope that there would be no more talk of 'slates' and 'contested elections' in the PSA ever again. From the back of the hall, Ian Budge offered the observation, 'Some of us spend a lot of our time on elections and think they are pretty good things on the whole' (Goodin, 2009, p. 43).

These developments were not without their costs. Some senior people simply stopped attending the annual conference. Three years later Ivor Crewe noted in a memorandum reflecting on the 1978 conference:

> Like Jim Sharpe I was a little disturbed at the absence of the professoriat. I suggest that Geoff [*sic*] Stanyer [the organiser for 1979] makes a point of asking at least some of the established senior professors to organise panels. They will then almost certainly invite their kith to present papers (LSE, 1978b, PSA/17).

One informant said that the stance of Norman Chester reflected the loss of respect for the PSA of heavyweight academics. One view that was put forward by another informant was that the Politics Section of the British Academy, to which entry is restricted and follows a careful scrutiny of the candidate's academic record and standing, had come to serve as a forum for the leadership of the discipline rather than the PSA. An alternative view offered was that '[The] British Academy matters only to those who aren't in it, [it's] not an intellectual power house'.

It is evident from the archive and also from the author's participation that the new EC got down to their work with considerable enthusiasm and energy with much more buzz in EC meetings. After the first full EC meeting, Jim Sharpe wrote to Rod Rhodes, commenting: 'I was very pleased with way the committee went yesterday and I hope we can keep up the momentum' (LSE, 1975a, PSA/16). The new EC issued another statement at the Nottingham conference in 1976 at which they emphasised their recruitment campaign, the changes made in the editorship of *Political Studies*, the introduction of a regular newsletter edited by Jeff Stanyer and the work done on specialist groups. The financial commitment to IPSA was emphasised as a constraint, but 'we regard maintaining and increasing the new momentum of the PSA as the main task of the PSA Executive. It is in that spirit that we ask for your support in the current election to the Executive' (LSE, 1976a, PSA/16). In these elections, Jack Hayward and Jim Sharpe topped the poll with 101 votes each and two members from polytechnics joined the committee, David Donald (Glasgow College of Technology) and Roy May (Lanchester).

A similar document was issued in 1977 which referred to the proposed constitutional changes that would admit graduate members and also a new category of corporate membership, which was seen as a way of raising additional funds. The success of the IPSA Congress in Edinburgh was celebrated and reference made to the work of specialist groups, improvements in the annual conference and the journal (LSE, 1977a, PSA/16). Bob Dowse topped the poll, but Joni Lovenduski, a member of the newly formed Women's group, was unsuccessful.

If a statement was issued in 1978, it has not been preserved in the archives. The last year in which a 'Manifesto' was apparently issued is 1979. It opened with the statement: 'During the past year, the Committee have continued with a vigorous programme of initiatives, and have maintained the services already instituted'. Drawing attention to the annual two-day policy review meetings that the new EC had initiated, it commented: 'Some of these proposals may, for lack of resources, or for other reasons outside the control of the Association, prove to be stillborn and there may be some delay before others bear fruit, but the Committee have tried hard to maintain the momentum established earlier' (LSE, 1979a, PSA/18). The main headings covered in the manifesto were: services to members; women in political studies; postgraduates; relations with outside bodies and individuals; resources; and recruitment drive. All members of the slate named at the end of the manifesto were nominated by Jeff Stanyer and seconded by Jim Sharpe, and all of them were elected with Jim Sharpe topping the poll. Bernard Crick, nominated by Graham Moodie, was also elected although he was not on the slate.

Political Studies

The future of *Political Studies* was one of the key questions that faced the new EC. It had been at the top of Brian Barry's list of priorities. A special general meeting was convened on the second evening of the Oxford conference and comments about the journal took up around a page of the minutes; it was clearly the issue that most pre-occupied those members that attended. For example, it was argued that the journal should invite controversy and a full refereeing system should be introduced.

Jack Hayward contacted the Clarendon Press about the arrangements for appointing the editor of the journal. 'He was informed that the Executive Committee of the Association recommended an editor to the Clarendon Press who would approve or veto the recommendation. The initiative over the appointment, and the tenure of the editor thus lay with the Committee'. At its April meeting the EC agreed that editors should henceforth be appointed for a three-year term with the possibility of a renewal for a further but final three years. An editorial board would be established (Brian Barry had submitted a paper to the EC outlining the functions of such a board). It was agreed that Professor Ridley should be asked to continue for one more year, giving him a tenure of six years in line with the new arrangements. This would give the committee time to find a new editor to whom manuscripts should be directed from 1 January 1976. Professor Ridley would not be involved in the constitution of the new editorial board. He was then invited to join the meeting:

> Professor Ridley pointed out that he had received many critical comments about the journal apart from those made at the General Meeting. In general he found these

comments unhelpful and only rarely were they constructive. It was difficult to determine which comments should be taken seriously. Moreover, he felt that the criticisms
should be placed in the context of both editorial policy and the constraints under
which the editor had to operate.

In particular, 'The journal had to be relevant not only to all members of the PSA
but to all readers of the journal. As a result, a range of articles was accepted for
publication in an attempt to cover all schools of political science'. Responding to
the criticism that there was too much emphasis on political theory, Professor Ridley
argued: 'If anything, there was probably a slight bias to empirical political science
because relatively few articles of this type were received'. As far as the quality of
articles published was concerned, this 'was a difficult question to assess. Nearly
everyone disagreed on the merits of any given contribution'. It was emphasised that
all articles were refereed although the final decision remained, as it should, with the
editor. 'Ultimately, the standard of the journal reflected the standards in the profession at large. The journal received relatively few submissions from senior members'.
He also dealt with the difficulty of getting book reviewers and their tardiness in
responding, insufficient secretarial assistance and the backlog of articles.
    Professor Hayward:

> thanked Professor Ridley for his services to date and expressed the unanimous feeling
> of the Committee that he had been the best editor to date. In making these changes
> the Committee was striving to establish some impersonal principles governing the
> editorship of the journal and the changes should not be interpreted as in any way a
> criticism of Professor Ridley's undoubted contribution to improving the journal (LSE,
> 1975b, PSA/16).

Nevertheless, Professor Ridley subsequently resigned and Professor Hayward had
to write to him about a letter he had sent to Clarendon Press about the sum paid
by PSA members for the journal. Professor Ridley subsequently served as chair of
the PSA's curriculum development sub-committee. A distinguished academic, he
also became editor of *Parliamentary Affairs*, where he had been review editor since
1968, in the year he relinquished his editorship of *Political Studies* and he served in
that capacity for 30 years.
    A search committee was established to find a new editor for the journal. Chaired
by Dennis Kavanagh, it included Jack Hayward, Geraint Parry and Bob Dowse, but
also Brian Barry. This shows the continuing influence of Barry, while Parry, a future
chair of the association, was probably included because it was thought desirable to
include another political theorist. Kavanagh set out an interesting set of reflections
about the role of an association journal and the dilemmas that *Political Studies* faced
which have continuing relevance:

> There are many different views about the role of the journal. There is Fred Ridley's
> view that it should be representative of all areas in the discipline, but also be aware
> that many readers are not political scientists. Historians of political thought feel their

work is excluded from history ('too political') and philosophy ('not enough philosophy') journals. Should it aim to be distinctive from BJPS? Should it aim to carry the best articles on British politics as the APSR does for American politics? It could be distinctive, I suppose, by simply getting the best articles written by the British – of the 24 major articles in the last six issues of BJPS only 5 were authored by British academics. Or should it be committed to outstanding scholarship regardless of subject area? I consider the last is probably the safest and most desirable (LSE, 1975c, PSA/16).

The search committee started with a list of fifteen names and reduced this to five, one of whom was a future editor of the journal, Jack Lively, described by Sharpe (1990, p. 70) in his lexicon as 'A very old seafaring term for the most ebullient, zestful and boisterous member of the lower deck'.

Jim Sharpe, who had been one of the original insurgents, was selected as editor. Although he was known for his work on local government and politics, having directed the research work of the Redcliffe-Maud Commission on local government reform, he developed a much broader interest in public policy. As editor, 'Jumbo' Sharpe displayed his usual enthusiasm and energy for ideas and their debate. He was not well enough to interview for this volume and passed away in 2010.

Sharpe seems to have found the volume of work greater than he anticipated, so as well as recruiting Steven Lukes as review editor, he appointed Patrick Dunleavy as editorial assistant. Dunleavy was then a research fellow at Nuffield but was already perceived as a rising star in British political science. At the October 1975 meeting of the EC, Sharpe set out his policy for the journal:

> The journal should be enlivened by the inclusion of high quality review articles. If such articles were included in the journal, the case for conventional book reviews became weak. They might be dropped altogether, although book notes (particularly on British politics) might be included. The Editor considered that there should be fewer articles on political theory; there would be a conscious attempt to encourage people to 'chance their arm' with articles which might not stand the test of time but would advance the subject in new directions (LSE, 1975d, PSA/16).

Sharpe subsequently emphasised that the changes he was introducing did not mean that traditional political theory would be cut out. He was striving for a better balance of articles.

In 1978 Sharpe was reappointed for a three-year term. There had been some production delays at the end of 1977 and the beginning of 1978, according to the editor partly caused by a change of printer and other changes at OUP and partly by him trying to include more material than he was allowed. However, from 1979 OUP had agreed to make 40 more pages available at no increase in price. In his report on his first three years, Sharpe seemed somewhat tentative about whether there had been an improvement in the quality of the journal, although this was more difficult to measure in the absence of impact scores and other data that are available today:

There . . . seems to have been an increase in the number of articles submitted, I receive between three and four a week. There may have also been an increase in quality, for I now have more articles in the 'firm acceptances' file than ever before . . . The content of the journal has also changed – I hope for the better – and although we still publish a fairly high proportion of Hobbes, Locke and Mill etc. we have published more articles on modern analysis and more on empirical research (LSE, 1978c, PSA/17).

Expanding the Membership

One of the key objectives of the new committee was to expand the membership of the PSA, not just to make it more representative of the discipline, but also to engage a more active membership in its work. A key part of this effort was the building of a new relationship with political scientists in the polytechnics, which was largely successful and is discussed in more depth in the next section. However, it was also important to build membership in the universities. Ian Budge, who led the recruit-ment drive, sent round a memorandum to academic and research staff and PhD students in the Department of Government at Essex. This document has a wider interest than Essex because it reflects the approach that Budge was adopting in his energetic drive to gain new members. He outlines the key objectives of the new EC and emphasises that 'most of these plans depend on the support and interest of British political scientists . . . The Executive Committee can do a certain amount but it depends very much on suggestions and participation of an expanded mem-bership' (LSE, 1975e, PSA/15).

The search for the Olsonian holy grail

What is apparent from these and other documents is that the EC was very aware of the free-rider problem in organisations and of selective incentives as a means of overcoming it as set out in Mancur Olson's (1965) seminal work on collective action. Budge explains that 'Under its new Executive Committee the PSA is broad-ening its activities to become much more of a service organisation for its members'. Budge then uses a solidaristic appeal, stating: 'If you are interested in seeing these developments seriously pursued, the only way to ensure that they are is to join the Association'. However, he does not rely on solidarity too much, stating in the next sentence that 'This is self-interest really since you will benefit personally from an improved professional Association' (LSE, 1975e, PSA/15).

Bob Dowse was much influenced at the time by Olson's book, which he saw as explaining the need for state action, and in particular by the idea of selective incen-tives (Author's personal knowledge). In an early paper for the new EC, Dowse reflected:

The problem about the selective benefits is that we need a considerably larger mem-bership in order to induce manufacturers, retailers and more to the point, publishers to consider it worthwhile entering into some sort of an arrangement with us. Both the British Psychological [sic] and the [B]SA have at least three times our membership and, incidentally much higher fees and a full-time office staff (LSE, 1975f, PSA/15).

Dowse had thus identified the central problem of how resource constrained the PSA was, although presumably when he was talking about retailers he did not mean discounts for members at Boots but at, for example, bookshops. Dowse, something of a larger-than-life character, subsequently took a post at the University of Western Australia, later moving to Tasmania.

In his memorandum Dowse set out six ideas for expanding the Association's publications. He thought that four were probably not feasible: expanding the size of *Political Studies*; establishing a second journal devoted primarily to political thought; a yearbook; and a newsletter. More feasible he thought was establishing a cyclostyled journal, that is, using the now virtually extinct technology of stencils and duplicating machines, one that would appear twice a year or a series of occasional papers. One practical consequence of these discussions was the establishment of a regular newsletter edited and produced by Jeff Stanyer which was distributed with *Political Studies*, something that caused problems with time-sensitive items if the production of the journal was delayed. In the 1950s and 1960s, news items about the PSA had been published in *Political Studies* but this new format was more flexible and gave members a more regular and systematic stream of information. It was the forerunner of the contemporary *PSA News* which is an important mechanism for two-way communication between the PSA and members. However, Stanyer's newsletter was duplicated, admittedly on paper of different colours and with special conference editions handed out at registration. As Stanyer told the policy review meeting in 1977, 'the present format and methods of production was as much as he could manage easily' (LSE, 1977b, PSA/16).

It is arguable that the discussion of selective incentives is an example of academics becoming too influenced by their own intellectual categories and that the idea restricted discussion rather than broadening it. In subsequent years there were repeated attempts to locate the key selective incentives that would influence membership decisions. Although there was no research on this during this period, probably the journal was the most important selective incentive, but many academics simply felt a sense of obligation to belong to their disciplinary association. Others did not, or did not even think of themselves as being in the politics discipline, and no amount of selective incentives would have changed that mindset. Indeed, when the PSA gave out mugs to mark its 50th anniversary, this attracted criticism from some members, particularly from one who had felt it necessary to have the package X-rayed as potentially suspicious.

Many of the specific attempts to construct selective incentives in this period eventually proved to be not worth the effort that was made. Considerable effort was made to obtain discounts of other journals for PSA members, but some publishers were not interested, while others were prepared to offer only very small discounts. Ken Newton, who was by then responsible for this initiative, had to report that 'after all the effort entailed in arranging the journals concessions for PSA members take up of these benefits had been disappointingly small; so far, only 9 people had applied for a total of 13 journals under the scheme. It agreed that the Committee had at the least learned that the initiative was not worth repeating' (LSE, 1981a, PSA/18).

The EC's efforts had some effect as membership increased from 600 in 1975 to 703 at the end of 1976, reaching 770 by 1979. It should be remembered that this was at a time when public expenditure constraints meant that higher education was growing far more slowly than it had in the 1960s so that the pool of new entrants was much smaller. Nevertheless, there were clearly still many people who were eligible who had not joined. In 1979 Ian Budge reported that he was sending out 500 letters to individual political scientists who were not yet members of the PSA.

Two new categories of membership were created by constitutional amendment in 1977, corporate members and graduate members. The idea of corporate membership had emerged from the 1976 heads of department conference. It was explained at the 1977 annual general meeting that the money raised would be used to support the graduate conference, the conference of heads of department and meetings on curriculum development. Nevertheless, it was a less popular idea than graduate membership and the motion was approved by 53 votes to 10 with 13 abstentions while that on graduate membership was approved by 79 to 3 (LSE, 1977c, PSA/16). By the end of 1977, twenty departments had applied to take up corporate membership, including three polytechnics, realising £500. Four declined, one explaining that this was not permitted by university budgetary policy. One university attempted to join at a reduced fee of £10 because of budgetary constraints, but this plea was rejected by the EC. The idea never really developed either as a means of raising funds or linking the PSA with departments and was undermined by public expenditure cuts in the 1980s.

By the end of 1977, twenty postgraduate students had joined. However, it was a trickle rather than a flood and when Joni Lovenduski joined the committee she 'expressed concern at the still low rate of graduate recruitment and relayed the comment of the PSA Women and Political Studies Group that graduates seemed unaware that they were eligible to join specialist groups' (LSE, 1979b, PSA/17). Although it is questionable whether this was compatible with the Association's charitable status, it was initially decided to exclude the Count de Grandy from membership but he did eventually join (see Box 4.3).

Integrating the Polytechnics

This was a significant area of activity during this period, partly because the new EC genuinely wanted to integrate polytechnics into the PSA's work and partly because it was seen as a particularly promising field for recruitment of new members. The new EC seems to have been particularly successful in its membership drive in polytechnics. By 1976 13.5 per cent (95) of the members were drawn from polytechnics

Box 4.3: Count Lysander de Grandy, 1930–2007

The Count de Grandy, also known as the Duke of Vallonbrosa, was a familiar figure at PSA conferences. He was known for his positive interventions at annual general meetings, but also for the unfathomable questions he asked visiting speakers. In 1976 he was reading philosophy and theology at Southampton University as a mature student. At the time it was suggested that his title was a courtesy one from the Channel Islands, probably Guernsey. He died in December 2007 from multiple injuries after being mown down by an articulated lorry on a motorway slip road in Hampshire where he was apparently hitch-hiking. The *Daily Mail* headlined its story: 'Police Probe Death of Mysterious Aristocrat'. He was also involved in a number of church history societies, one of whose members said: 'He liked to travel around lots of meetings and didn't appear to have much money' (http://www.dailymail.co.uk/news/article-502291/Police-probe-death-mysterious-aristocrat-body-motorway-slip-road.html [accessed 23 April 2010]). After the extensive press reporting of his death, many readers provided tributes to this likeable eccentric.

with Lanchester (Coventry) having the largest number of members of any polytechnic (seven) and by 1979 18 per cent (138) of the members were polytechnic teachers. Even so, there were fears of a breakaway group which might reduce PSA membership. In October 1975 Ian Budge reported to the committee that 'It . . . appeared that an Association of Politics Teachers in Polytechnics might be formed, although this was not an immediate threat' (LSE, 1975g, PSA/16). There does seem to have been some basis to this as Mick Ryan of Thames Polytechnic responded somewhat cryptically to an invitation to attend a PSA EC:

> [At] this stage I think it would be a little more than difficult for me to commit myself to attending – if for no other reason than it could so easily be said that I was only out to enlarge my own circle of Polytechnic contacts with a view to later using them as a nucleus of some breakaway association. However, I can assure you that the situation remains fluid and I will be in touch with my colleagues here at Thames and also at other Polytechnics about what the PSA has decided to do as a start (LSE, 1975h, PSA/16).

The underlying issue here was how the polytechnics fitted into the system of higher education and whether they were simply universities set up in another way. The meeting of eight polytechnic lecturers with the Executive Committee in 1976 took the view that 'The needs and interests of political scientists in both universities and the polys were very similar. Future relations of the polys with the PSA should be based on the assumption of common interests and concerns and not on any perceived differences: it was also stressed that improving the relationship was a two way process' (LSE, 1976b, PSA/16).

The question of the nature of the relationship was also taken up in a paper by Ian Henderson of Lanchester Polytechnic which was a response to a paper written by Malcolm Keir in June 1975, of which no copy survives. Henderson challenged 'Keir's assumption that no significant research in politics is likely to take place in the polytechnics' as 'unnecessarily defeatist, and likely to import an undesirable binary structure into PSA membership' (LSE, 1976c, PSA/16). In any case, as David Donald pointed out, the comparisons made were often inappropriate: 'University staff members are NOT all engaged in funded projects with a consequent flow of professional papers and books. It seems likely that many polytechnic staff compare themselves not to the average university lecturer but to the much more visible and exceptional "high producers"'. He emphasised the 'separate but equal' idea that had guided government policy towards the binary system. The difference was not so much in resources, but in the emphasis on education that was relevant to life and work (LSE, 1976d, PSA/16).

This was not to say that polytechnic staff did not face distinctive challenges, although some of them were exaggerated. Henderson pointed out some of the difficulties that polytechnic staff faced which might explain why they were not more research active. Politics was only taught in about half of them, often as part of a social science or modern studies degree, and there were rarely politics departments as such. It was only possible to major in politics at Birmingham, Central London, Liverpool and Portsmouth. As Donald noted, 'The development of Political Science in the Colleges has been very uneven and there can be little doubt that the subject is not as highly valued and does not have the almost automatic acceptance and inclusion of teaching programmes of e.g., Economics, Sociology and Psychology' (LSE, 1977d, PSA/16). This was, however, perceived to be a challenge outside the polytechnics as well.

Although Henderson considered that staff–student ratios were comparable with universities, heavy teaching loads did occur, particularly for more junior staff. The 'difficulty about research in the polytechnics is not lack of time, but rather lack of stimulus, aggravated by the ambivalent attitude of some polytechnics towards the whole activity of research' (LSE, 1976c, PSA/16). Henderson argued that instead of having a separate panel for polytechnic lecturers, they should be encouraged to stand for the EC. Donald noted that the British Sociological Association (BSA) policy of treating polytechnic lecturers as a distinct group with special problems was not liked by polytechnic teachers who would 'rather be identified as sociologists than as "polytechnic teachers"' (LSE, 1976d, PSA/16).

In 1976 at the request of the EC David Donald carried out a study of politics teachers in polytechnics. A questionnaire was sent to 40 institutions but not colleges of education. 'The population of teachers is still indeterminate but is likely to lie between 200 and 300'. Of the 112 respondents to the questionnaire, 75 per cent (84) described themselves as research active. Publications were claimed by 44 per cent of those who replied, but about half of these 'were classified as only minor articles'. Reflecting the vocational emphasis in polytechnic work, 21 per cent described themselves as teachers of public administration. Just under half of respondents were PSA members. Average teaching loads were between eleven and fifteen hours a week (LSE, 1976e, PSA/16).

Having recruited more polytechnic members, the PSA tried to make sure that it retained them by addressing issues of particular concern to them. Donald presented a paper on the PSA and the Council for National Academic Awards (CNAA) at the 1977 policy review meeting. He noted that the polytechnics and colleges 'differ from the Universities in having a central organisation which attempts to evaluate and monitor the standard of work undertaken in political science' (LSE, 1977d, PSA/16). He identified three matters as being of prime concern which were taken up in a letter to the CNAA: 'First, the classification of political science under humanities. Second, the allocation of political science and public administration to separate boards. Third, the fact that political science had only a panel instead of a full board considering the subject' (LSE, 1977e, PSA/16).

The Formation of BISA

The formation of a separate association for international studies also represented a potential challenge to PSA membership figures, although in practice many individuals belong to both associations as is reflected in their joint membership directory. The emergence of BISA did require some clarification of relations in the 1970s, although in general the PSA EC appears to have devoted very little attention to the topic. However, in 1979 Geraint Parry, as academic convenor of the 1980 PSA conference, had reported that he had asked John Simpson to serve as convenor of the International Politics panel. He had replied 'asking whether the academic community could support both the PSA panel and the BISA conference at Christmas'. One point made in the ensuing EC discussion was that 'political scientists whose interests range over many specialist areas cannot attend all the specialist conferences'. The use of the word 'specialist' in this context is interesting as it says something about the PSA's perception of BISA at this time. It was agreed that there was 'no need to see the issue as requiring reassessment of the PSA's relations with BISA' (LSE, 1979c, PSA/18) and indeed John Simpson ran two panels on international politics at the 1980 conference.

The development of international studies as a sub-discipline had profound implications for political science which are returned to in the concluding chapter. It is important to note the distinction between international *relations* and international *studies*. International relations, often approached within a realist paradigm, could be seen as an extension of political science as it was concerned with what happened when nation states, either peacefully or through armed conflict, interacted with each other. This approach always only captured one part of international reality, even if it was extended to international organisations. There was a growing awareness of the importance of other international actors such as multinational companies, criminal organisations and non-governmental bodies of various kinds. More recently, the study of terrorism has become an important sub-field.

Lucian Ashworth (2009, p. 23) maintains that 'IR's capture by political science in the 1950s' stunted its intellectual development. Part of his complaint is the dominance of the realist paradigm, in part as Jack Spence points out 'a reaction to the idealism of the 1920s' (LSE, 1978a, PSA/17) which led to 'decades of realist isolation' (Ashworth, 2009, p. 20), and the other part is that the links between international relations and other subjects were cut off by political science. 'IR was an essentially transdisciplinary subject with only very limited attachments to political science' (Ashworth, 2009, p. 23). It may be questioned whether international relations has ever achieved trans-disciplinarity, which implies rising above specific disciplinary roots, and in any case if anything political science in the 1950s was beset by too great an openness to other disciplines. It might also be argued that the exercise of power, even if it is not confined to nation states, remains an important aspect of international relations and this provides a link to debates in political science. However, as Lawrence Freedman argues (2006, p. 698), the problem with the political science approach was that 'Power was evaluated only in its surface manifestations – to be judged only who won or lost when an issue got to the fore rather than its underlying structures'.

Freedman (2006) argues that the formation of BISA halfway between the Second World War and the present was propitious and not entirely accidental. It was possible at that time to detect the first signs of the end of the Cold War. Détente was on the agenda, and the prospect of a hot war was receding, leading eventually to an entirely new international climate. Freedman argues (2006, p. 696) that one also saw 'the exhaustion of the left after the heady days of the student revolutions and the general militancy of the early 1970s'. Libertarian currents were leading to challenges to racism, homophobia and sexism, while human rights were increasingly becoming an agenda item. Paradigm change was in the air, but not in political science:

> Critics charged that political science had become political silence, as it had passed quickly by the civil rights movement and paid scant attention to economic inequalities. It had become a way of failing to achieve science while avoiding that dangerous subject politics. It had limited itself by dealing only with the conspicuous and measurable. Perhaps it was possible to say some interesting things about why people with certain opinions behave, for example in elections, but not so much about why they hold these opinions (Freedman, 2006, p. 698).

BISA was preceded by the Bailey Conference or the British Coordinating Committee for International Studies. As Chris Brown insists (2006, p. 677), 'The key point is that BISA didn't emerge out of nowhere, or as an offshoot of PSA as some in that organisation would have it – it was the legitimate offspring of a pre-existing quasi-organisation and inherited quite a lot from the latter'. The formation of BISA was proposed by the British Coordinating Committee for International Studies (BCCIS) in 1973, following much debate about creating a multidisciplinary forum for the study of international affairs. The group who formed BISA, including Alastair Buchan, Peter Lyon and Jack Spence,

> was concerned that a growing interest in international studies did not have an institutional or scholarly 'home' that served its interests. The *Political Studies Association*, for example, was concerned, naturally enough, with particular aspects of the study of the international but was predominantly taken with the promotion of domestic, comparative politics and of course public policy issues (Kennedy-Pipe and Rengger, 2006, p. 665).

In January 1974 an inaugural meeting was held at the 14th Bailey Conference on International Studies at the University of Surrey, and at that time a draft interim constitution was agreed. If these developments had attracted the attention of the PSA, there is no mention of them in the minutes.

A key figure in BISA's development was its first treasurer, Susan Strange (see Box 4.4). In particular, she had developed the new sub-field of international political economy. She was impressed by the International Studies Association in the USA and wanted to start something similar in the UK. 'I wrote to every vice-chancellor in the country asking for the modest sum of £2 as start-up funds for a British ISA' (Strange, 2002, p. 24). Caroline Kennedy-Pipe and Nicholas Rengger (2006, p. 675) chart the achievements of British international relations and of BISA and proclaim 'that British International Studies thirty years after BISA's founding, is in a healthy state'. However, Susan Strange was disappointed with the progress of her brainchild:

> Unfortunately, I think both ISA and BISA have failed to live up to their names. They are not associations of people engaged in international *studies* but of people engaged in international *relations*. A few historians, a few lawyers, a few sociologists have joined in from time to time – indeed the International Political Science Association could hardly function without its IR participants (Strange, 2002, pp. 24–5, emphases in original).

Indeed, the University Association for Contemporary European Studies (UACES) has probably been more successful in attracting an interdisciplinary membership or certainly articles, particularly from economists, to the *Journal of Common Market Studies*. The UACES was established in 1968 and, despite its interdisciplinary character, most of its members are political scientists. It is another example of potential PSA members feeling they need an intellectual home elsewhere.

A Voluntary Model

One of the limitations of the PSA during this period was that for much of the time it was largely dependent on voluntary effort. For example, as treasurer the author

Box 4.4:   Susan Strange, 1923–98

Susan Strange was the daughter of Colonel Louis Strange, DSO, DFC, a legendary First World War flying ace. She is generally credited with pioneering the study of international political economy in Britain and she was the principal instigator of BISA. She took a first in economics from the LSE in 1943 from where she joined *The Economist*. 'In many ways Susan Strange's career was a particular personal odyssey. She never liked to be called an academic, regarding her early career as a journalist an integral element in the development of her approach to the study of the global system' (Tooze and May, 2002, p. 17). She then became Washington correspondent of the *Observer* where she was the youngest White House correspondent of her time before going to New York as UN correspondent. Returning to Britain, she continued to write for the *Observer*, but also took an academic appointment teaching international relations at University College, London from 1949 to 1964. In 1965 she moved to Chatham House as research fellow and then Director of the highly successful and important Transnational Relations project. In 1978 she accepted the Montague Burton chair of international relations at the LSE. After her retirement at the statutory age in 1988 she went to Florence as the foundation chair of international political economy at the European University Institute. After five years in Florence, she accepted a post-retirement Professorship in International Political Economy at Warwick University. In 1995 she became the second non-American to be President of the US-based International Studies Association in the near half-century history of that organisation. She wrote extensively on international political economy, but her best-known books include *States and Markets* and *Casino Capitalism*. While she was not anti-theoretical or a-theoretical, she had little time for what she saw as 'theorising for its own sake'. She could be outspoken which did not endear her to everybody. A person of great personal energy, she was the mother of six children. While she was at Warwick, the then vice-chancellor funded a particular research trip. He was surprised but pleased to receive a postcard declaring 'You're a brick, Vice-Chancellor'. Susan Strange was herself a foundation stone of the analysis of international political economy, which has become a key part of the study of politics and international relations.

used to keep details of members on a card index system in his bedroom. This was a contrast with the BSA which had a near full-time administrative secretary. However, it appeared that the BSA received a subsidy from the LSE in terms of premises and staff, while subscriptions were much higher. They were calculated on a sliding scale related to income, but there was thought to be some resistance by those paying the highest rate of £20. The UACES also had a full-time administrative secretary, although grant aid from the Foreign Office and the European Commission had expired, but it was thought that sharing offices with the Federal Trust might involve some cross-subsidy. Possible models for the PSA were seen as a relationship with a politics department (which is what eventually happened) or someone working from home.

This discussion has been stimulated by a paper by Rod Rhodes who had remained on the committee on an *ex officio* basis for six months after his term as secretary had come to an end. Rhodes was largely concerned with the reallocation of tasks among committee members, but also supported the appointment of a part-time administrator. However, a memorandum by the treasurer, Alastair Thomas, showed that the cost of employing an administrative secretary would be £1,800 per year, apart from any capital costs or overheads, and the PSA was generating a surplus of between £800 and £900 a year. Hence, membership subscriptions would have to be substantially increased.

Using contacts in the Royal Society and elsewhere, Alastair Thomas carried out a considerable amount of research on the options that were available. He located offices in Reading called Harvest House which serviced a number of disciplinary associations such as the Society for General Microbiology. He visited the offices and was impressed by what he saw. Paid staff serviced a number of associations on a model found in trade associations, but shared the work among them so that there was cover if someone was away. He recommended to the EC that they should contract with Harvest House to provide administrative services to the PSA. 'It was agreed that the service offered by Harvest House appeared to be remarkably good value for money and that A. Thomas should proceed with negotiations, preferably for an initial trial year' (LSE, 1979c, PSA/18). Harvest House subsequently turned the PSA down. Quite why this was the case is unclear; it may be that they were more used to dealing with natural science associations.

What was evident from all these discussions is that a new source of income would be needed if the PSA was to cope with its greatly expanded workload. Ken Newton recalls:

I was in Jim [Sharpe's] room at Nuffield with him and Pat Dunleavy when we started to talk over morning coffee about the journal and stumbled across the idea that OUP was [not treating] the Association [generously] over royalties, which led to a steep rise in royalties paid to the PSA, and then to Blackwell [as new publishers] (Personal communication, 16 June 2009).

How this developed is treated in later chapters.

Conclusions: Status Anxiety

Political science in Britain was afflicted by an understandable anxiety about its standing relative to other disciplines during this period. In a paper for the EC Ian

Budge drew attention to 'the lack of any professional recognition for political science outside the Universities and colleges. The obvious contrast is with economists and sociologists. Both of the disciplines, economics obviously more than sociology, are on the way to conferring the same professional status on their graduates as medicine or law' (LSE, 1977f, PSA/16). There was trouble ahead for sociology in the 1980s, but that could not be anticipated in 1978.

The subject was doing well at undergraduate level. It lacked a strong base in schools, but many students switched into politics at the end of their first year and these numbers might increase as economics became more mathematical. '[T]he number of candidates taking Single Honours Politics degrees or their equivalent, had risen since 1974 by considerably more than the average for all other subjects, though . . . this increase was from a small base' (LSE, 1978d, PSA/17).

The discipline needed further strengthening at graduate level, which required a more effective relationship with the SSRC and it also needed to review its links with the practice of politics. Building up the PSA's specialist groups was a key aim of the new EC. These and other initiatives are reviewed in Chapter 5. What is evident is that the Oxford insurgency had reinvigorated the PSA and had given the discipline a more effective Association which was trying to think systematically about the challenges it faced and how they might be met.

Figure 1: Professor William Robson, a key figure in the formation of the PSA. *Source: National Portrait Gallery, London.*

Figure 2: Professor Sammy Finer, giving a typically ebullient lecture at Keele where he built up the politics department.
Source: Special Collections and Archives, Keele University.

Figure 3: Sir Norman Chester, Warden of Nuffield College, Oxford and a key figure in the formation of the PSA.
Source: International Political Science Association.

Figure 4: Professor W. J. M. Mackenzie at the PSA conference in 1996. He was a leading figure in the foundation of British political science and PSA chair from 1960 to 1962.

Figure 5: Professor Sir Bernard Crick at a PSA awards ceremony.

Figure 6: Professor Sammy Finer (left) and Professor Jean Laponce at the IPSA conference in Edinburgh, 1976.
Source: International Political Science Association.

Figure 7: Delegates to the IPSA conference in 1976 wait in the courtyard of Edinburgh Castle for the reception.
Source: International Political Science Association.

Figure 8: Elizabeth Meehan presents the Sir Isaiah Berlin prize for lifetime achievement in political science to Professor Lord Parekh in 2003.

Figure 9: The PSA has used its annual awards ceremony to develop links with practitioners. Here Elizabeth Meehan, the first woman to be chair of the PSA, makes a presentation to Shirley Williams.

Figure 10: From left to right, Jack Hayward, William Paterson and Patrick Dunleavy. Jack Hayward became chair of the PSA at the time of the Oxford insurgency. William Paterson is a leading figure in German and EU studies and Patrick Dunleavy has made many contributions to the PSA for over 30 years.

Figure 11: From left to right, John Benyon, Jon Tonge and David Denver. John Benyon has been treasurer of the PSA since 1992, Jon Tonge was chair from 2005 to 2008 and David Denver has been a prominent member of EPOP and served on the PSA EC.

Figure 12: Rod Rhodes, secretary of the PSA after the Oxford-led insurgency and chair from 1999 to 2002.

Figure 13: Paul Whiteley has been a prominent member of the PSA and is a member of the EC in 2010. He is one of the current generation of political scientists who started his career in a polytechnic.

Figure 14: Patrick Dunleavy has been a key figure in the history of the PSA, including a period as general editor of *Political Studies*.

Figure 15: Wyn Grant, treasurer of the PSA after the Oxford-led insurgency, chair from 2002 to 2005 and author of this book.

Figure 16: Jon Tonge, chair of the PSA from 2005 to 2008.

Figure 17: Signing of the new contract for Political Studies journals, April 2007. From left to right (seated), John Benyon; Rachel Smith (Wiley-Blackwell); Jon Tonge; (standing), David Denver, then chair of the PSA Publications Committee; Martin Smith, editor of *Political Studies.*

Figure 18: Vicky Randall, chair of the PSA in 2010.

Figure 19: John Benyon with Charlie Jeffery (left), organiser of the 60th anniversary conference in 2010 in Edinburgh.

Figure 20: Joni Lovenduski played a leading role in the formation of the PSA Women's group but has also made an important contribution to the wider work of the PSA.
Source for Figures 4–5 and 8–20: Political Studies Association Archive.

Figure 21: Alex Salmond, First Minister of Scotland, addresses the 60th anniversary dinner of the Political Studies Association in Edinburgh, March 2010.

Figure 22: Electoral expert Professor John Curtice at the Political Studies Association reception at the 60th anniversary conference in Edinburgh, 2010.

Figure 23: Delegates at the 60th anniversary dinner of the Political Studies Association, Edinburgh 2010.

Figure 24: Alex Salmond presents Professor Frank Bealey with an award for his lifetime contribution to political science at the Political Studies Association 60th anniversary dinner, Edinburgh 2010.

Chapter 5

An Activist and Expanding PSA:
1975–79

This chapter examines the efforts of the PSA Executive to expand the Association's activities in a number of key areas after 1975 so as to create a more innovative disciplinary body that would play a more central role in the professional lives of its members. The reinvigoration of the conference and the creation of more varied and active specialist groups were central to this academic programme. However, it was also recognised that a healthy postgraduate population was of central importance to the future of the discipline, so the development of relationships with the SSRC was given a high priority. By 1979, however, the ability of the SSRC to sustain the discipline was being called into question by public expenditure reductions, and, as these cuts intensified across higher education as a whole, the availability of academic posts for these postgraduates was called into question. Hence, this chapter generally stops in 1979, except where the completion of the narrative requires explanation of the final outcome of initiatives begun in the 1975–79 period. One of the motives for the 1975 insurgency had been concerns about the staging of the 1976 IPSA conference in Edinburgh and this chapter considers how that was eventually achieved in the face of some official scepticism about the value of political science.

Conferences

A key objective of the new EC was to enliven the PSA conference. The idea emerged of having 'bloc convenors' as a means of achieving this objective. The key features of this proposal as set out in a letter by Bob Dowse to eight prospective bloc convenors were:

- 'I think it is probably best if the initial paper of each bloc is produced as a combination of the state of the sub-discipline, major problems and orientations, growth points and an indication of the major literature.

- The other two or three papers could then easily be research reports, flag flying or individuals' ideas about current work.
- You have, of course, total discretion about how you approach, who you approach and what you ask 'em to do within the general ambit of your bloc' (LSE, 1975i, PSA/16).

This was quite an ambitious plan and it was never fully realised, but it enabled the PSA formally to end the traditional four-fold basis of conference organisation. At the 1977 conference in Liverpool, for example, although the traditional categories of British Politics, International Relations, Political Theory and West European Politics persisted (and were no doubt popular), there were also sessions on Public Order, Policy Studies, New States, Local Politics and Communist Politics. Even so, there were still substantial criticisms made of the format, which was seen as still being organised along traditional lines.

An early decision of the EC was to end formally the traditional rotation between London, Oxford and the 'provinces', which had never been strictly adhered to in any case, and it was planned to hold the 1978 conference at Lanchester Polytechnic in Coventry, which would have been the first meeting at a polytechnic. However, the charges proposed were regarded as excessive and the conference was switched at a relatively late date to Warwick University. Approximately 200 participants attended and 50 papers were delivered at 18 panels. A papers room was instituted for the first time: the arrangements for making papers available were to occupy a lot of EC time over the next few years and a satisfactory resolution was not really found; this problem was only resolved with the advent of electronic technology and the provision of papers online. A new feature was a series of linked panels under the general title 'Politics of the Third World' covering Latin America, Africa, South Asia and Communist Politics. Panels with titles like 'Latin American Politics: Capital Accumulation and the State' were a new departure for the PSA.

The graduate conference continued on an annual basis throughout this period and received financial support from the SSRC from 1975. The 1977 conference attracted 50 students, 80 per cent of whom were working for a research degree. Oxford, the LSE and other London colleges and Essex accounted for just over a third of those attending, but then less fashionable institutions such as Brunel, Paisley College of Technology and Salford were also represented.

An important innovation was the introduction of a heads of department conference. The first of these was held in Birmingham in May 1976 with 32 participants, of whom seven were from polytechnics, and it focused on four broad topics:

- the state of the discipline and the possibility of permanent cooperative arrangements between politics heads of department;
- graduate training and graduate awards;
- the funding of research and the role of the SSRC; and
- the teaching of politics and curriculum development for undergraduates.

According to a report at the next annual general meeting, 'the participants, although many were sceptical at the outset, found it of value' (LSE, 1977c, PSA/16). A second conference was held in 1978 with the intention that it would become a biennial event. Attendance increased to 40, of which just over a quarter were from polytechnics or equivalent institutions.

Specialist and Regional Groups

The encouragement of specialist groups represented a key part of the new EC's work. Dilys Hill, who was allocated the specialist groups portfolio in 1975, explained the strategy in retrospect:

> The work of the PSA in the 1970s was to encourage the expansion of these groups, which not only brought members into contact with each other and the work of the PSA, but helped to 'delegate' roles to the group convenors. This was important in encouraging the improved organisation of the annual conferences, as much of a conference's activities centred on providing for, and encouraging, the groups' presentations as well as the plenary sessions and guest speakers (Personal communication, 12 May 2009).

The number of specialist groups that were active in the sense of having a workshop or conference did start to show a substantial increase. By June 1979 there were thirteen established groups and thirteen new ones (see Box 5.1); although it could be a challenge to sustain existing groups as well as forming new ones. For example, the Political Sociology group could trace its origins back to the 1950s, but by early 1979 it was reported: 'Used to be fairly active but nobody willing to be convenor at present. Temporarily defunct'. Later in the year, a new convenor was found (Roger King, later to be a university vice-chancellor) and a weekend conference was planned and held. The extent of activity undertaken by specialist groups was often impressive. For example, the Local (later Urban) Politics group had 100 members, its own newsletter and had held three meetings in 1978, plus one with the SSRC Research Panel on Central/Local Government Relations. Greek Political Thought had 50 members, although many of these were from classics or philosophy departments. The Anglo–German Political Theory group had held a five-day conference while the new Political Communication group was headed by a practitioner, Robert Worcester of Market and Opinion Research International (MORI). The Political Theory group, in which Bernard Crick was active, was seen as problematic: 'Annual conference. Rumours about starting a journal. Not really a PSA group' (LSE, 1979d, PSA/17).

There were different views within the EC about the contribution that regional groups might make to the PSA's work. They had been mentioned in Brian Barry's original set of priorities. It could be argued that PSA members would be prepared to travel some distance to attend a meeting related to their research or teaching interests, but would be less enthusiastic about travelling a shorter distance to a

Box 5.1:   Specialist Groups in June 1979

Active groups holding workshops
American Politics
Anglo–German Political Theory
Arts, Politics and Society
Association for the Study of German Politics
Communist Politics
Contemporary British Politics
Greek Political Thought
Local Politics (re-named Urban Politics)
Political Sociology
Political Theory
Scandinavian Politics
UK Politics (Richard Rose)
Women and Politics
New groups
Administrative History
British Hegel Society
Cinema and Politics
Ethnic Minorities
Law and Politics
Nationalism
Political Communication
Political Economy
Political History
Politics, Education and Society
Public Policy
Scottish Political Studies
Utopianism and Political Thought
No reported activities
African Politics
Association for Franco–British Studies

regional meeting that was in effect a mini-PSA conference but with a smaller and often less distinguished number of participants. Dilys Hill's initial view was that:

> Clearly, it would be a good idea to see if there is a demand for regional groups in Scotland, but I doubt if there would be sustained interest for permanent regional groups in England, and my recent experience with regional groups of the Royal Institute of Public Administration leads me to think they might not be viable (LSE, 1975j, PSA/16).

Ian Budge, however, saw a role for regional groups in building links with the polytechnics and as a means of stirring up activity:

> I use the word 'stir up' advisedly because I think if we sit back and wait for people they probably won't – at least that is the experience with the ECPR. What we need is an evangelical crusade to convert people to the idea that they really gain from discussion (LSE, 1975k, PSA/16).

The idea of English regional groups never got off the ground, other than in terms of *ad hoc* arrangements between departments, but the question of Scotland was more difficult, given that the PSA was always concerned about breakaways, whether regional, from the polytechnics or by political theorists. This was not so surprising given the formation of BISA in 1975. A grouping apparently called the Scottish Political Studies Association was based on 'a reasoned recognition there were reasons for people in Glasgow/Edinburgh/Aberdeen to form a larger mass than alone. But the interest was limited and it evaporated' (Personal communication, Richard Rose, 31 July 2009).

However, this development had alarmed Tony Birch who was concerned that the Scottish association would one day break away and affiliate to IPSA (IPSA does allow sub-national associations such as that in Quebec to join). 'As this situation has explosive possibilities (however latent) I think it would be wise to tread very carefully' (LSE, 1975l, PSA/16). The issue flared up again in 1978 when the EC received an approach from Jack Brand who that year published *The National Movement in Scotland*. This was considered at the 1978 EC policy review meeting where it was evident that there was concern about anything that might be interpreted as a tartan breakaway:

> J. Brand [had asked] for support for a Scottish Political Studies Association which would not have its own journal but would have an annual conference. It was agreed that I. Crewe reply that the PSA would support it financially on the understanding that all PSA members could attend its meetings. He would also suggest that it be called a group, not an association (LSE, 1978c, PSA/17).

What eventually emerged was a Scottish Political Studies group within the PSA.

Relations with the SSRC: Another Self-Perpetuating Oligarchy?

There was considerable disquiet during this period that politics was less successful in getting a share of the funding pot than other social science disciplines. This was raised at the first heads of department meeting in 1976 where 'There was some speculation as to the reasons why the Politics Committee spent substantially less than the Economics or Sociology Committee? Was the Politics Committee less generous? Were political scientists less ambitious?' (LSE, 1976f, PSA/16) One of the difficulties in the PSA's relations with the SSRC during this period was that it often felt it was making progress but misinterpreted a polite and conciliatory response from the SSRC for a substantive change of policy.

In a paper for the policy review meeting, Ian Budge discussed the problem of 'distant' relations between the PSA and the Political Science Committee of the SSRC. While SSRC funds had been a major dynamic behind the growth of research and the development of professional self-consciousness,

> [the Political Science Committee's] operation still conforms to the model of the old Executive Committee of the PSA rather than the new, i.e. it is rather oligarchic and self-perpetuating; secretive in operation; and is suspected of not pushing political science as hard within the SSRC as it could. Perhaps these perceptions are wrong but they are widely believed (LSE, 1977f, PSA/16).

In 1977 Hugh Berrington as chair wrote to complain about a recent policy review undertaken by the Area Studies Panel. There had been a lack of consultation with the PSA, although it was unclear whether this was confined to the PSA or had been extended to other bodies.

> We are also most concerned at the Panel's conclusion that it feels that its primary responsibilities lie with the second and third world countries. We are unable to see the reasons for this discrimination against Europe and North America. I was particularly asked to point out that a number of Politics Departments have developed postgraduate courses in European and American Studies and that the Panel's views on its priorities could have serious consequences for Departments which have developed courses of this kind (LSE, 1977g, PSA/16).

While waiting for a reply to this letter, Hugh Berrington got an emollient and speedy reply from the chair of the Political Science Committee, Saul Rose, about a hasty consultation over the Triennial Review, admitting that while the information gathered had been very useful and necessary, the notice given had been too short (LSE, 1977h, PSA/16). The Area Studies Committee reply, when it came, was a robust response to the attempt of political scientists to trespass on their turf: 'The Panel is responsible for *interdisciplinary* studies related to geographical areas. Our Policy Review related to these alone, and said nothing about the activities of Political Science or any other subject committee' (emphasis in original). The letter delivered a final blow by commenting: 'we failed to grasp the meaning of your final sentence' (LSE, 1977i, PSA/16).

In December the chair 'reported that he had made informal contact with the SSRC to discuss the Executive Committee's views. He had been greatly encouraged by the response and felt there was no need to convene a special sub-committee' (LSE, 1977b, PSA/16). This led to a meeting between Hugh Berrington and Jim Sharpe and the Political Science Committee of the SSRC in May 1978. The PSA pairing was an interesting one. Berrington had an acute mind and was the model of courtesy. He was conservative by temperament: if a meeting should be held on a Sunday, arrangements invariably had to be made to transport him to Holy

Communion. Sharpe (1990, p. 65) described 'Hugh of Berrington' as 'One of the founders of the early English Church . . . Renowned for his command of the Holy Scripture he was . . . what would now be called a psephologist and his pessimism was also the source of his profound asceticism'. Berrington, who had an emollient personality, wished to achieve reconciliation between the old and the new. Sharpe's role was a continuation of the 1975 thrust for change. Sharpe was very much an extrovert and sometimes got a little carried away in his enthusiasm for progress in the discipline. Nevertheless, his presence at the meeting with the chair was evidence of how his influence in the committee extended beyond editing the journal, which has been the sole focus of more recent editors.

This meeting was thought to have been a great success at the time, but subsequently transpired to be less so. The report to the PSA EC which covered four closely typed pages said that 'The discussion was throughout, friendly, stimulating and highly fruitful'. However, a close reading of the PSA report shows that the chair, Professor Dennis Austin, a very wily individual, and like his predecessor Saul Rose a Third World specialist, responded to most suggestions by saying that they would receive 'sympathetic consideration'. In other words, we hear what you say, but don't expect us to do anything.

The Political Science Committee, given that it was responsible for spending public funds, may have been less sympathetic towards a statement by Jim Sharpe at the end of the meeting when he got on to his favourite theme of taking risks:

> Mr Sharp [sic] expressed appreciation of the meeting and said there might be a tendency for the Political Science Committee to be over-critical in its appraisal of research projects. Political scientists were by temperament cautious and conservative and this may explain why research in the subject had lagged behind. It seemed as though political science did not obtain as big a share of resources for research as did economics and sociology. One way of meeting this problem would be for the committee to be prepared to take a chance rather more even at the risk of funding some work which turned out to be of poor quality (LSE, 1978e, PSA/17).

Sharpe was being prescient, as this was a theme taken up by the benchmarking review of the profession in 2007: 'Although there is truly outstanding research in the UK profession, a little more of it could be more ambitious and innovative; and funders could assist greatly in promoting that by emphasizing that they are anxious to fund risky, innovative research in addition to safe research with immediate policy applications' (ESRC, 2007, p. 5).

The importance of a good relationship with the SSRC was reflected in an extensive discussion at the next EC meeting. In an RAE/REF context, their expressed preferences might seem unusual, but it has to be remembered that at this time research outputs were not measured while postgraduate students were seen as essential to the future success of the discipline. It was agreed that the chair:

> should raise with the Political Science Committee Chairman the question of postgraduate studentships, and in particular should suggest:

(1)   that resources be diverted from research grants to additional studentships;
(2)   that, if the SSRC favoured a policy of coordinating resources within particular institutions, this could at least be on a regional rather than a national basis;
(3)   that more studentships be awarded to postgraduates (LSE, 1978f, PSA/17).

When the PSA received the official SSRC report of its meeting with the Political Science Committee it differed significantly from their own account. 'In particular, it was unenthusiastic about the proposal that the SSRC make some very small grants for "one-off" projects' (LSE, 1978c, PSA/17). This response was perhaps not so surprising given the transaction costs involved for the SSRC in making very small grants and the consideration that the Nuffield Foundation had at the time its own small grants scheme which was used quite extensively by political scientists.

In 1979, before the general election of that year, there were substantial cuts in postgraduate awards and Hugh Berrington was invited to the May meeting of the SSRC Political Science Committee, by that time chaired by Jack Lively. Berrington made it clear that 'The treatment of political science by the Council had caused great ill-feeling. This ill-feeling was directed both against the cuts themselves and against the apparent discrimination towards the subject and the philosophy which appeared to lie behind that discrimination'. Jack Lively replied 'that it was not altogether clear what philosophy did lie behind the SSRC's decisions. The philosophy seemed to be vague and inarticulate, and he and his colleagues hoped to get a clearer impression when they met the Chairman of the SSRC that evening'. This rather lame reply does not give a very positive impression about relationships between the SSRC and its subject committees at that time. However, to be fair to the SSRC, it may have simply been required to make cuts very quickly and had directed them at the subjects that appeared to have less clout in terms of the politics of higher education.

That this might be the case became apparent in response to the next issue raised. Professor Berrington expressed his concern about the small percentage of the total SSRC budget spent on political science, although he admitted that this might in part be the result of a smaller number of applications. It is interesting that in response the SSRC official serving as secretary pointed out that the figure for political science at 7 per cent of the total budget was very similar to that of sociology, at 8 per cent; it was economics that had the lion's share. About half the total SSRC budget was spent by two subject committees: Economics and Sociology.

Professor Berrington pointed out that 'If the number of "spontaneous" applications was relatively small, the question was should the Committee take a more initiatory role'. He pointed to the success of the central–local relations panel. Professor Lively suggested that the specialist groups of the PSA could play an important role in identifying areas for research and developing applications. However, he warned that 'Very often, however, considerable preliminary structuring of the research proposals was needed. A bright, but rather general idea was not enough' (LSE, 1979e, PSA/18). This was perhaps a hint that political science applications relied too much on inspiration and not enough on the thorough development of a proposal. In time the SSRC and its successor, the ESRC, became much more proactive in identifying areas for research which could be met through programmes that had a research director, or research centres, but there is a view that this has crowded out money for response-mode work which may be less tied to prevalent fashionable orthodoxies.

The PSA Executive was very unhappy about the SSRC's cutbacks but was impotent to do very much about it. Moreover, they presaged even bigger cutbacks to come. The EC was told by Professor Berrington that 'There was little hope . . . of restoring the studentships that had already been cut'. He was asked to write to the chair of the SSRC, 'regretting the disproportionate cuts in politics studentships and expressing the fear that they reflected the inadequate representation of political science in the higher decision-making bodies of the SSRC' (LSE, 1979f, PSA/18).

This may well have been so, but one needs to ask why it was the case. The PSA EC had put a sustained effort into developing a dialogue with the SSRC Political Science Committee, but the outcome of these discussions was often shaped by decisions taken at a higher level which the PSA could not easily influence.

Relationships with Practitioners

A systematic attempt was made during this period to engage more effectively with practitioners of politics. One form of link was with political scientists who had become MPs and the most prominent of these at the time was John Mackintosh, who died prematurely (see Box 5.2). Other MPs with a political science background included Alan Beith, a Liberal, and two other Labour MPs, John Mendelson (1917–78) who had been a Sheffield extramural politics lecturer, and Robert Kilroy-Silk, also a former politics lecturer, but evidently not well known as he was confused in the PSA records with a member of staff at Leicester with a similar but different name. Kilroy-Silk later became a Eurosceptic Member of the European Parliament (MEP) and founded his own political party, Veritas, which was not conspicuously successful.

The systematic approach taken by the new EC to the relationship with practitioners involved three dimensions:

- internships for graduates and academic staff in governmental and political institutions;
- relations with the civil service; and
- the recruitment to the PSA either as honorary fellows or members of 'notables' or 'influentials'.

The first dimension was pursued by Ivor Crewe in the form of 'internships' for graduates and academic staff in governmental and political institutions, although for understandable practical reasons the effort quickly became focused primarily on postgraduates. Crewe was a key member of the committee in the period that Hugh Berrington was chair, in part because they had a good working relationship, reflected in regular telephone conversations on a Sunday evening (Personal

Box 5.2:   John Mackintosh, 1929–78

John Mackintosh was the outstanding example of someone who combined a career in the study and teaching of politics with an involvement in its practice. His premature death was a great loss and he would undoubtedly have contributed to the ongoing debate on devolution of which he was a powerful advocate, not on nationalist grounds, but in terms of arguments about democratic control. He did not live to see his vision come to fruition. Mackintosh was educated at Edinburgh University, Balliol College Oxford and Princeton. He did not enjoy Oxford and this may have influenced his later views and conduct towards the metropolitan establishment. After lecturing at Edinburgh University from 1954 to 1961, a post at the University of Ibadan from 1961 to 1963 gave him an interest in Nigerian politics on which he wrote a book, but he was best known among contemporary students for his account of *The Government and Politics of Britain*. However, probably his most important work was *The British Cabinet* which initiated the debate about prime ministerial power. Mackintosh was an outstanding lecturer and 'arguably the most compellingly persuasive parliamentary orator of his generation' (Dalyell, 2009, p. 1). The author still remembers a lecture he gave in the late 1960s. Referring to the resources (including bombing by the RAF) that had been deployed in the Scilly Isles, the site of Harold Wilson's holiday home, to try and cope with the sinking of the *Torrey Canyon* oil tanker, Mackintosh claimed that a similar event in Scotland would have led to the dispatch of a pigeon with a box of washing powder tied to its leg. On his return to Scotland, Mackintosh became a professor at Strathclyde. He had already stood unsuccessfully for parliament in 1959 and 1964, but in 1966 he was elected MP for Berwick and East Lothian. Despite being an assiduous constituency MP he lost the seat against the national trend in February 1974, but regained it in October 1974. He never achieved ministerial office. He might have done in 1964 if he had accepted an invitation to stand for a safe seat at Paisley in 1960, but he went to Nigeria instead. However, he also had a 'malicious tongue' and a 'rather too obvious and impatient ambition, dangerously allied with an incapacity to suffer fools gladly' (Dalyell, 2009, p. 1). A man of considerable energy, he combined his duties as an MP with being chair and Professor of Politics at Edinburgh University. He was chair of the Hansard Society from 1974 to 1978. In relation to the two lectures he gave at the IPSA congress in 1976 the author wrote as acting secretary on behalf of the PSA EC 'to express its warm thanks for the considerable contribution you made to the success of two of the PSA sessions at the IPSA Congress in Edinburgh' (LSE, 1976g, PSA/16).

recollection). In an action-oriented four-page paper that he produced for the 1977 policy review meeting, Crewe noted:

> British political scientists are often criticised, with some justification in my view, of being too happy to stick to the library and too self-effacing to push their way into the corridors of power (think of the number of first-time revelatory works by North Americans, e.g. McKenzie on the parties, Goldstein on the TGWU, Wilson on the commercial broadcasting lobby, Wildavsky and Heclo on the Treasury) (LSE, 1977j, PSA/16).

The EC strongly supported the idea of internships and decided to undertake pilot studies of the House of Commons and local government, Jeff Stanyer being given the latter task. The EC subsequently decided to see how the parliamentary scheme fared before pursuing the local government assistantship scheme, which eventually did not result in any tangible outcome, although Stanyer reminded the committee of the paper on it when he eventually stood down from the EC. Crewe's work, assisted by Michael Rush and Malcolm Shaw from Exeter, developed into a one-year pilot scheme for seven parliamentary assistantships for graduates on which he reported to the committee in June 1978. The development of the scheme was interrupted by the 1979 general election, but it faced a lack of interest both from MPs and from university departments. Ivor Crewe submitted an understandably rather despairing paper to the EC in 1980, commenting: 'Our "scheme" is very small beer, and in a sense scant return for all the correspondence and to-ing and fro-ing of the last two years. But at least it has taught me – and thus indirectly the Executive – something about the opportunities and facilities for studentships in the Commons'.

Crewe reported that 'After long and frustrating delays, it is now clear that the Whips' Office, at least of the two main parties, would not want to be involved, although they have not expressed hostility to such a scheme'. The scheme therefore came to depend on informal arrangements with back-benchers, of whom a small number from four parties, including the Scottish National party, were prepared to help. An informal arrangement for a student was eventually made with Labour MP Bruce George who had taken an MA in Politics at Warwick. Crewe was very well aware of the limitations of what was on offer: 'I am aware that the "Parliamentary Assistantship Scheme" is a dignified label for what amounts to no more than the informal making of introductions. Unlike the internship schemes that exist in the United States and Canada, the PSA is offering no stipend and no programme of training'.

What evidently particularly frustrated Crewe was 'the low level of even initial interest shown by British students and teachers. The various notices in the Newsletter and announcements at the annual conference have produced only seven letters of enquiry' (LSE, 1980a, PSA/18). In the longer run, the way forward in this area was through schemes run by individual departments which they could use as a means to attract students. At Hull, Philip Norton, who had been an undergraduate student of Crick's at Sheffield University, set up a British Politics and Legislative Studies degree which includes one year in placement in parliament before he later became a peer himself; there is also the option of a semester with an MEP. The BA in Politics and Parliamentary Studies at Leeds also offers one year at Westminster or the possibility of spending one semester in Canada or Washington DC, and a one-semester internship at Westminster is also available as part of its MA in British Politics.

Parliament was only one part of the overall picture and in an important overview paper Ian Budge argued that political scientists should be more ambitious in their efforts to develop relations with government, bearing in mind the professional recognition that was offered to economists and, to a lesser extent, sociology, but particularly those interested in social work and administration:

> It is my contention that political scientists should lift their sights a bit and seek the same kind of recognition at governmental and business levels. In fact much of the work done by economists as part of their specialised remit e.g. in the Economic Advisory Unit in the Home Office is of a kind for which our graduates (particularly those in public administration and/or with a quantitative training) are better equipped . . . By increasing the demand for the skills of our graduates we should be enhancing their career prospects. However we should be broadening and diffusing the interest of our subject by giving political scientists the opportunity to circulate freely between academic and teaching departments and the outside world, without demanding that they change their outlook and preoccupations between the two.

Budge thought that most political scientists would welcome such initiatives,

> though there are some who see such vocational careers as detracting from the academic purity of the subject. Generally however the main question is practical: how to get such recognition which would certainly not be accorded easily. This may be where my concerns tie in with those relating to influentials and the desirability of getting powerful patrons for the PSA.

Budge did not think that the creation of a separate political science grade in the civil service would be feasible, but thought that the economist grade could be broadened to an economic and political grade for which a political science degree would be recognised as a valid qualification.

The difficulty in a generalist civil service with an elite system of recruitment was that the civil servants regarded themselves as the experts on how to operate the machinery of government with knowledge being handed down from one generation to the next through informal socialisation and on the job training. An example of this approach is the career of Sir Derek Mitchell (1922–2009) who served as private secretary to Sir Edwin Bridges, the then head of the Treasury and of the Civil Service early in his career, and sought to apply Sir Edwin's values later in his professional life (*The Times*, 21 August 2009). Budge was aware that 'the Civil Service wants to keep away outsiders, particularly informed outsiders', although civil servants may have disputed how informed political scientists were. Budge thought that 'The best point of pressure might not be the British government and Civil Service, but the

European Commission which has probably less of a closed mind on the subject (since economics, sociology, political science and law often interpenetrate in Continental degrees)' (LSE, 1977f, PSA/16).

Budge's paper was discussed at the 1977 strategy meeting of the EC which considered: 'the problem of getting the discipline recognised as a profession by the Civil Service and by local government . . . there was a general difficulty of finding a plausible story about the nature of the discipline and thus gaining the sort of recognition achieved by economists, psychologists and sociologists in central government' (LSE, 1977e, PSA/16). The EC tried to pursue the question, but not surprisingly received little encouragement from the civil service. As a former senior civil servant, William Plowden, the director-general of RIPA, might have seemed to offer a bridge between the two worlds. However, he informed Hugh Berrington that while 'there was a need to change the attitude of civil servants to the social sciences as a whole, [he] preferred not to be involved in a campaign specifically on behalf of political science and public administration' (LSE, 1979b, PSA/17).

William Plowden did eventually become involved in a joint PSA/RIPA conference on government and political science held in 1980 and this is discussed in Chapter 6. However, while there were some secondments of academics into the civil service during this period (although at least one ended up teaching in the Civil Service College rather than in a department), they were few and far between; one exception, politics academic Peter Fletcher from Exeter, became a lifelong civil servant through the late entry scheme and responded sympathetically to PSA inquiries. What was really needed was a complete change of culture which came about when the civil service became far more open to late entry recruitment and more transparent in its operations. Rod Rhodes was then able to engage in intensive participant observation of ministers and their officials, Philip Cowley spent a substantial period on secondment in the Treasury in 2008–09 as part of an ESRC scheme and the author spent a period working as a civil servant in Defra in 2009 as part of a Research Councils work shadowing scheme.

The recruitment of practitioners as honorary fellows of the PSA encountered particular resistance from the membership. This strategy originated with a paper written by Jim Sharpe for the 1977 policy review meeting of the EC. Sharpe complained that 'Political science lacks status as an academic discipline. For this reason we enjoy less esteem in government circles and are less able to attain contact with and access to the political world than many other disciplines'. Sharpe pointed out that wartime secondments to Whitehall had provided contacts, but this generation had retired or was about to do so.

> To some extent our isolation is even greater that it need be because many of the successors to the retiring, well-connected old guard, seem to be positively against having any contact with the world of politics at all. I am perplexed to know how this last hurdle can ever be surmounted, since its origins touch on all sorts of motivations from Marxist and reactionary quietism, to exalted interpretations of the role of the academic and the nature of scholarship (LSE, 1977k, PSA/16).

In fact Sharpe was touching something of a raw nerve here, for it is evident that there has always been a range of opinions in the discipline about how much contact with the political class is necessary or desirable. As Hayward notes (1999, p. 2), 'political zoologists became separated from the denizens of the political zoo . . . the specifically academic study of politics parted company from its subject matter, a self-conscious detachment that has imposed costs as well as affording benefits that have often not been detected, still less evaluated'. Legitimate reasons for limiting that contact can be a desire to preserve autonomy of thought and judgement, and possibly a concern about being associated with what is regarded by the general public, and increasingly so, as a rather tawdry activity.

In its discussion of the Sharpe paper, the EC drew a distinction that was to shape its work over the next few years in this area:

> It was decided that the committee would draw a distinction between those influentials it wished to encourage to become ordinary members of the PSA and those it wished to recognise as Honorary Fellows. Whilst both categories were important, the committee would wish to be highly selective over those individuals invited to be honorary fellows. Moreover, such individuals should not only command intellectual respect but they should also be in a position to assist the PSA in its relations with government (LSE, 1977e, PSA/16).

It was agreed that members of the committee would be tasked to produce lists of potential members and honorary fellows in the following areas: MPs; the media; local government; public corporations; and 'academic' civil servants. At the 1978 policy review meeting, it was reported that 65 letters had been sent out to 'influentials' inviting them to become members and a few had asked to join, all but one of them journalists. A constitutional amendment was put by the EC at the 1979 annual general meeting providing that 'Persons of special distinction may be invited by the Committee to serve as honorary fellows on terms determined by the Committee or the Annual General Meeting'. Although the motion was approved by 39 votes to 24, it failed to achieve the necessary two-thirds majority and was therefore dropped.

This was the first time that the new EC had encountered serious opposition to its plans at an annual general meeting and the arguments that were put forward are of more general interest in terms of the relationship between political scientists and practitioners:

> Members objected both to the vesting of the choice of Honorary Fellows in the Committee and to what were seen as the elitist implications of the proposal as a whole. It was further objected that there was a danger that the PSA would lose its independence from practitioners of politics. In defence of the proposal, it was argued that the profession of political science did not carry much weight with important national bodies, so that influential associates would be useful, for instance in raising funds for specific activities. Also contact with practitioners of politics was necessary if political scientists were adequately to study the profession of politics (LSE, 1979g, PSA/18).

The Relationship with Teachers in Schools and Colleges

After Bernard Crick joined the committee, a considerable amount of effort was devoted to developing relationships with the Politics Association (PA). Crick saw himself as 'having a special responsibility for relations with the Political Studies Association'. Whether this effort delivered a proportionate result is another matter. There may have been unrealistic expectations on the part of the PA about what either the PSA or individual politics departments could practically deliver. For his part Crick, having pointed out that 64 university and polytechnic teachers were members of the Politics Association, expressed his concern 'that the [PSA] does not begin a recruiting campaign among non-degree teaching staff in FE and Techs and colleges or departments of Education'. What aroused this concern is not clear as there is no archival evidence that the PSA ever contemplated such a campaign.

In 1976 Crick had produced a three-page memorandum on possible mutual help between the two associations. This mostly seemed to be about what higher education could do for secondary education, so the reciprocal element was quite limited, but quite reasonably he pointed out that 'the [PA] can help the [PSA] by interesting people in the subject who are likely to go into higher education'. He also drew attention to the particular challenges that politics teachers faced in schools (many of them, of course, also taught other subjects such as history, having taken a joint degree in the two subjects): 'ordinarily someone teaching Brit. Con. [British Constitution] or Politics in school or in FE is very isolated, usually on his own, has no department, little or none of the professional support that our colleagues in History and Geography give to schools at FE'. It should be noted that at this period many schools did not teach politics at all, even in the less controversial and implicitly celebratory form of British Constitution. University departments of politics were therefore used to accepting candidates who had no prior systematic training in the subject; indeed such students may well have been in the majority.

Crick's main request was that university and polytechnic departments should be asked to organise one or two day schools as refresher courses for school pupils and staff. However, he then made what he underlined as an important reservation, emphasising that political education was for all the nation's children, anticipating his later work on citizenship. He made it clear that the PA did not like it 'when universities only lay on schools or conferences which are flagrantly and solely recruiting and which ignore the needs of teachers of non-GCE streams, those teaching politics as part of the General or Liberal or Social Studies lower down the school, or simply as non-examination subjects in the last two years in school'. But, of course, one of the incentives for a university to use up resources and time in this kind of provision was the possibility that it might improve the quantity and quality of the recruits to their degree programmes. Crick also called for more interest by higher education in what were the often outdated syllabuses for politics examinations in secondary education and urged university and polytechnic staff to become involved in the examination process at this level (LSE, 1976h, PSA/16).

The Crick memorandum was recirculated to the EC in 1979 after he had been elected to the EC and made responsible for relations with the Politics Association. The PSA did then send out a circular on day schools, but Crick reported that the response to it 'had been somewhat disappointing' (LSE, 1979h, PSA/18). This was in spite of the fact that the PSA offered to assist in the expenses of such events up to a limit of £150. During this period the EC saw the immediate concerns of their own members as a greater priority and it may be that Crick's somewhat abrasive personality hindered rather than helped matters. The way in which something is said can sometimes undermine a message, particularly if people are told they are not doing enough about something.

The IPSA Conference in Edinburgh

It is more difficult to raise the funds to stage a triennial congress of IPSA in Britain than in most other countries. For example, the 2009 conference in Santiago received generous support from private sources in Chile and from the Chilean government. The holding of the congress in Chile was seen as a major event and a boost to the country's prestige. President Michelle Bachelet addressed the congress and gave the IPSA executive and the local organising committee a reception and a personal tour of the presidential palace. The author was asked whether the Queen would do something similar if the congress was held in Britain (the King of the Belgians did give a reception when the congress was held in Brussels, although the dignity of the occasion was not enhanced by one participant from Britain passing out at his feet and having to be carried away after indulging in too much alcohol).

The PSA tried to stage the triennial congress in 1967 and 1970, but to its embarrassment was unable to raise sufficient funds. As the then chair of the PSA, Graham Moodie, commented in a letter to the Foreign and Commonwealth Office (FCO), 'Private organisations are reluctant to help if the government refuses, and it is difficult to explain to other countries the British government's apparent inability to find the resources corresponding to those which have enabled even a German Land and a Canadian Province to make substantial contributions to their national associations' (NA, 1971a, p. 1).

In 1967 Norman Chester had tried to use his personal contacts to produce a change of government policy. He had met George Brown, the then foreign secretary, at Wembley, presumably at a football match. He subsequently wrote a three-page letter to the foreign secretary, drawing attention to the absence of international academic congresses in Britain:

> The reason is either that HMG is too mean, or has not yet caught up with the great developments in international academic cooperation, or is not interested in London as an international centre. I do not think you personally are guilty of any of these, and my great hope is when you are apprised of the problem you will see something is done about it (NA, 1967, p. 1).

Chester complained: 'British scholars are always put in the ignominious position of listening to invitations from this or that poorer and smaller country to hold a meeting there, knowing that they cannot extend a similar invitation because the small sum involved cannot be raised from the British Government' (NA, 1967, p. 2). Someone from the FCO wrote a note in the margin questioning whether Belgium or Germany, where the 1967 and 1970 congresses were held, fell into the category of poorer and smaller countries.

Chester's efforts to butter up George Brown were undermined when he resigned from the government and was replaced by Michael Stewart. Chester had proposed that £6,000 to £7,000 be made available towards the cost of holding an IPSA congress in 1970 and also requested the establishment of an annual fund of £50,000 a year for such congresses. His attention was drawn to a 1956 Treasury ruling, reiterated in 1965, that:

'for reasons of administration and Parliamentary supervision of expenditure, any financial support for such expenditure should be undertaken by the Department in closest touch with the Conference concerned'. In the light of this ruling it was explained that the idea of a general fund could not be entertained and he was advised to approach the Department of Education and Science (NA, 1971b, p. 1).

Chester was not put off by this piece of bureaucratic buck passing and questioned the reply. In 1968 he 'was received by Mr Michael Stewart who made no commitment to have the position further examined' (NA, 1971b, p. 1). In other words, he got a polite brush off. Meanwhile, two other initiatives were being undertaken which suggests that the whole PSA effort was not very well coordinated. Another unidentified 'member of the UK association separately approached Mr Harold Lever [financial secretary to the Treasury, but more influential than his mere title implied] asking for Treasury support for a 1970 Congress' (NA, 1971b, p. 1). He was also told that the DES was the responsible department. Harold Lever did offer to put in a personal word with the Wolfson Foundation, but nothing seems to have come of this.

In early 1969 Professor Beloff approached the British Council who offered to make £1,000 available for an IPSA congress, subsequently increased to £6,000–£7,000 after discussions with the FCO, provided that it was given additional funds in its budget. However, by this time it was too late to make a bid to stage the congress in 1970. These discussions did lead the FCO to consider whether it should establish a general fund to assist international congresses held in the UK. However, it was thought that this would mean a battle with the Treasury and it would also be inconvenient for the FCO 'since we should then be faced with having to discriminate between applicants for assistance whose number would inevitably greatly exceed whatever provision was made'. The existing system avoided embarrassment of this kind, while it allowed the FCO to back 'particular conferences of special value to them in the light of foreign policy considerations' (NA, 1971b, p. 2). The example given in the files was the London conference of the Council of European

Municipalities which no doubt provided many opportunities to exert influence on behalf of British foreign policy.

Professor Beloff wrote another letter about IPSA in February 1971 and this provoked some discussion within the FCO about what sort of organisation it was. The initial assumption was that 'It is presumably respectable if Professor Beloff is involved'. This provoked a handwritten query: 'Would you tell me, or find out urgently, about the Association?' (NA, 1971c) It should be remembered that at this time the Cold War was still very much in progress. The following assessment was provided:

> As one might expect from such a body not all the officers are respectable. One of the Vice-presidents is (or was in 1968) Viktor Tchikvadze (USSR) a member of the World Council of Peace. He is however balanced by the Ugandan member of the Executive Committee, Ali Mazrui, who holds extreme Right-wing views. None of the other officials have adverse records in this department (NA, 1971d).

A handwritten note confirmed this assessment (questionable in the case of Mazrui): 'This is a mainly "western" organisation about which we have no adverse information. Its only communist members are from the USSR, Poland, Czechoslovakia and Yugoslavia' (NA, 1971d).

Having passed the respectability test, the way was now open for the PSA to make a formal approach to the FCO. Professor Moodie did so in September 1971, pointing out that apart from the reputational advantages, 'international conferences are very good business: in our case, a fairly modest outlay would result in the visit of at least 800 and probably over 1,000 delegates and their wives, each of them staying for a week' (NA, 1971e). This approach provoked a division of opinion within the FCO. From the Cultural Relations Department, it was argued that 'the field is one . . . of concern to us, particularly in the light of the interest we are now having to take in facilities for study of comparative government and administration in Europe and the need to promote closer links between British and European universities and other institutions' (NA, 1971f, p. 2). However, from the Information Administration Department, Mr Fyjis-Walker took a different view:

(1) 'I am sorry I do not much like this submission.
(2) If it is so academic why are the British Council not being approached this time as they were in the past?
(3) If the Office decided that the Association's Congress is really "political" and fit for support for Overseas Information expenditure, i.e., we are hoping to influence people who will be politically useful to us in their own countries, we shall have to go at it by way of a request to the Treasury for authority, probably in the form of a Grant-in-Aid. For this we shall need a convincing argument plus estimates of private support the Association could hope for' (NA, 1971g).

Professors Moodie and Birch, who were 'effectively a sub-committee of the PSA EC' dealing with the IPSA congress, met in October 1971 with Sir Stanley ('Tommy')

Tomlinson, then the deputy under-secretary of state who 'had a remarkable physical similarity to [the film star] Clark Gable' (Miall, 1994) and Mr Shawyer of the Cultural Relations Department at the FCO. Birch (2009) recalls: 'Graeme [Moodie] made a splendid contact at the Foreign Office, whom we both went to see and who promised the FO would sponsor the Congress'. The official record notes that 'Sir S. Tomlinson emphasised that he could make no promises but that the Department would look sympathetically into the possibilities of securing authority to give some help to the Association' (NA, 1971h, p. 2). Translated out of bureaucratic jargon, this means that the FCO was prepared to take on the Treasury on this issue. In fact, the archives show that the subsequent path was not as smooth as the outcome of the meeting might suggest.

Moodie and Birch certainly seem to have made an effective case using a variety of arguments ranging from reputation to broader political considerations. They argued that 'If the UK Association could not issue an invitation, after the two previous disappointments, it would be placed in an uncomfortable situation in relation to other Associations, particularly those who had already acted as hosts and who had succeeded in obtaining official support for the purpose, and its influence would be diminished' (NA, 1971e, p. 1). They also drew attention to the rivalry between the Americans and Russians: 'The Western European delegations strove to maintain the Association's neutrality in such matters. Consequently they would not welcome the holding of the 1976 Congress in either the USA or USSR, which was the probable alternative if the United Kingdom could not act as host' (NA, 1971e, p. 2).

Lengthy discussions with the Treasury followed. Putting its case in March 1972, the FCO argued that both IPSA and the PSA are 'well regarded here, and we should very much like to help if we can'. Elaborating its case, the FCO said:

> The Congress though perhaps academic in character would be very directly concerned with political problems. The members of the British branch (the Political Studies Association) include a number of leading figures in political studies and it is through people like these that we depend a good deal to influence similar moulders of opinion and thought in other countries and thereby help create a climate favourable to understanding of this country's thinking and the political objectives of HM Government. This seems in fact to be a good opportunity, at little cost, to cooperate with the PSA in a wide ranging information project (NA, 1972b).

In response the Treasury insisted that 'we must stick to the doctrine' of such requests being referred to the appropriate department, in this case the DES, which, of course, had no budget for such purposes. As far as the argument that support could be construed as an information project went, the Treasury was dismissive:

> I'm afraid I find it very hard either to accept that the value of this congress being held in the UK could be anything but minimal and indirect from the overseas information viewpoint, or to see how you would draw a tenable line of distinction between this organisation's meeting and those of the many others to which the same very broad reasoning might be applied (NA, 1972c).

The battle continued, but eventually the Treasury gave 'grudging approval' (NA, 1972d) to the proposal for financial assistance for the congress provided that it did not exceed £5,000. The Treasury still posed the question: 'should HMG assist at all? The general doctrine on Exchequer help for meetings in this country of international non-governmental organisations is essentially restrictive' (NA, 1972e). It also remained 'very doubtful' whether the funding should come from the FCO vote. However,

> perhaps we should give the FCO the benefit of the doubt, taking also into account that no doubt it is useful for the FCO in its contacts with British academics to be helpful to the UK Association, and that many of those attending from overseas will (I hope) be the sort of 'moulders of opinion' whom the FCO and its posts overseas are aiming at in the normal course of the overseas information effort (NA, 1972e).

Securing this money, and a government reception at Edinburgh Castle where the Soviet delegation was very insistent on seeing the Scottish crown jewels, was not the end of the challenges the organisers faced. The author recalls a tense meeting of the PSA Executive on 23 January 1976 in which Professor Moodie and the very capable local organiser (Sarah Kilbey, now the Reverend Sarah Kilbey MBE) asked for a further standby credit in addition to the original grant of £1,000. Although calling up this money would have seriously depleted the PSA's reserves, the author as treasurer backed making the money available at the next EC and £3,500 was set aside. In the event, it was not required, in part because the congress attracted 1,081 delegates, slightly more than the 800–1,000 that had been forecast earlier. The net cost to the PSA was only £317.30. Moreover, PSA financial liability was contained when Jack Hayward told the French that if they wanted simultaneous translation for more than the opening plenary session they would have to pay for it. Hayward recalls: 'This kept down costs appreciably' (Personal communication, 2 September 2009).

Despite the success of the congress, the question of whether the PSA should remain in IPSA was debated over the next few years. This was partly a question of financial considerations and partly a reflection of dissatisfaction with the operation of IPSA. Because of the PSA financial contribution to the Edinburgh congress, IPSA reduced the British subscription by 50 per cent in 1977, using its Equalisation Fund which was intended to help poorer countries, and this arrangement was extended. As John Trent, the IPSA secretary-general pointed out in a letter to the PSA, IPSA was itself facing financial difficulties because of the reduction of UNESCO funding after the USA had withdrawn from the organisation following its discontinuation of funds for Israel.

Tony Birch, who by this time had taken a post in Canada, mounted a robust defence of IPSA against criticisms from the PSA:

> The allegation that IPSA is a cliquish body is one that is made against all organisations of this kind from time to time. It is in the nature of things that academic associations should be run by a small group of volunteers, and it is easy to describe them as a

clique. When I was on the PSA Executive its members were sometimes described as a clique and I have heard exactly the same term used about the present Executive Committee (LSE, 1978g, PSA/17).

These letters were considered at the EC meeting in September 1978 and 'Most Executive Committee members felt that these letters indicated that the IPSA Executive was trying to meet PSA's criticisms'. It was agreed that Hugh Berrington should write to John Trent stating that 'the PSA would continue its collective membership for the time being but that if subscription costs rose sharply such membership might be too expensive to continue' (LSE, 1978h, PSA/17). Considerable time was also taken up during this period discussing the IPSA congress to be held in Moscow in 1979, which raised a number of difficult issues about academic freedom that caused some controversy within the PSA and APSA.

Conclusions

The period from 1975 to 1979 released a new energy within the PSA. Considerable progress was made with both the Association's representative and service functions, although there were still many political scientists who felt they did not need to be members. There was still much work to be done on the conference, which will always pose challenges, but the development of a more diverse range of specialist groups was one of the most important legacies for the future as they were a means of responding to increasing specialisation within the discipline and thus became the foundation of a much more academically vigorous disciplinary association. A new emphasis was placed on external relations, particularly with the SSRC and with practitioners. This did not immediately bear fruit, but pointed in a direction that became important in the contemporary PSA. After the 1979 annual general meeting, only two of those elected in 1975 remained on the EC. This was sensible: as Benjamin Barber notes (1984, p. 239) of transitional leadership, 'like founding leadership it must fade away. Leaders who linger on into the operational period have failed: to be successful is to make oneself superfluous'. Despite these departures the EC was again being seen as a self-perpetuating group, leading to a challenge from a 'counter slate' in 1980. However, of far greater significance were the cutbacks that higher education was to face in the 1980s. The rapid expansion of the discipline in the 1960s and the slower expansion in the 1970s gave way to a period of retrenchment, but the momentum that the PSA had developed was maintained in more adverse circumstances.

Chapter 6

Political Science in a Cold Climate: 1979–92

The 1980s were a difficult time for political science in the UK. Public expenditure on higher education, particularly the social sciences, was cut back and the SSRC placed in jeopardy. Many departments made no new appointments during this period or, at best, one 'new blood' appointment under a special funding scheme. The result was a 'lost generation' of recruits to political science. By the late 1980s, there had been a cumulative loss of nearly one in ten political scientists. This was not a favourable background for the development of the activities of the PSA. Membership began to stabilise: in 1980 it was 832 (145, 17 per cent in polytechnics) but in 1981 it was 825 despite a membership drive. The 1980 heads of department conference had as its theme 'Political Science in an Era of Retrenchment' and the dinner held at the Reform Club to mark the PSA's 30th anniversary was a somewhat muted celebration. Nevertheless, a number of important initiatives did take place as a result of the energy displayed by chairs of the Association and individual members of the EC.

The funding crisis in higher education was the central theme of an alternative slate of three candidates who offered themselves in the 1980 EC elections, although only one of those nominated, Patrick Dunleavy, was elected. They stated that 'Our major theme . . . is that in a period of Government cut-backs there is a clear need for the development of new channels of professional self help in order to maintain the growth and health of political studies in Britain'. They considered that 'the organisation should be more active in promoting and protecting the interests of the profession in general and underprivileged sections of the profession in particular'. They complained that there was 'a tendency for the present executive to act as a self-perpetuating elite, selecting its successors to the "Executive Slate". This means that the policies adopted by the Executive are rarely innovative or radical' (LSE, 1980b, PSA/18).

The Crisis in Higher Education

When the Conservatives under Margaret Thatcher had come into office in 1979 they had proclaimed a policy of 'level funding' for higher education, but this policy was abandoned in December 1980. The public spending round of 1980–81 led to cuts in planned expenditure of 8 per cent with cuts in real terms over each of the next two years. Cuts of this scale in recurrent funding of higher education were unprecedented.

In November 1982, as the politics member of the Social Studies sub-committee of the UGC, Professor Peter Campbell reported on the condition of departments in the discipline. He reported growing anxieties about 'the long-term possibilities of developing the discipline if there are to be hardly any new recruits and if libraries are to suffer permanently'. The cutbacks had not been distributed equally and 'in five institutions the current situation and/or the prospects for the next 2–3 sessions are particularly grim: Aberdeen, Bradford, Brunel, Keele and Salford'. In the longer run, the recruitment of overseas students was to provide a new revenue stream for departments, but in the short run 'the recruitment of considerable numbers of overseas postgraduates entails heavy costs in publicity and will cause academic problems, e.g., by making it necessary to provide sub-master's diploma courses for overseas students' (NA, 1982a).

Campbell reported that, apart from cutting back travel funds, library budgets (especially for periodicals) and non-academic support staff, departments were relying on natural wastage and voluntary retirement to contain costs. The distortions that this could lead to are illustrated by the case of Lancaster, which had been the subject of a visit by the Social Studies committee in November 1981. 'The department is a centre of strength in relation to other departments within the university, and to the study of politics, and particularly international relations, in the United Kingdom as a whole . . . It has a flourishing graduate school which has for many years received SSRC quota awards and continues to do so'. However, one of its professors had become vice-chancellor of the university and another had retired, leading to a situation in which the department had no professor (NA, 1982b). An attempt was made to secure restructuring funds to appoint a professor, but the members of the Social Studies sub-committee did not feel that this was a legitimate use of restructuring funds.

Peter Campbell sought to make the case for politics as a discipline, drawing attention to its areas of strength and in particular where its work might be relevant to policy makers. First, he drew attention to the way in which the study of North–South relations had developed in the discipline. 'Academics concerned with this field could contribute a great deal to policy-makers' appreciation of the *political* as well as the economic and social circumstances of areas of vital trading and strategic interest to the United Kingdom and could help policy-makers to avoid costly errors' (emphasis in original). Citing a specific example, he pointed out that both the Foreign Office and businessmen 'very conspicuously failed to appreciate the political impact of "modernisation" in Iran and therefore failed to focus on the dangers of encouraging the Shah to proceed with his modernisation policies which contributed markedly to the political destabilisation of Iran, with major economic and strategic consequences for the West'.

His second point was about the development of new methods and approaches in the study of international relations. He noted that:

> new conceptual frameworks have appeared and interdisciplinary studies (particularly in regard to the political economy of international relations) seem to have advanced more effectively than elsewhere in Politics and I get the impression that there may be a greater gap between the over-45 age group and the under-35 age group in this sector than in the other sectors.

This was relevant to policy makers in terms of 'the interconnection of "political" policies and "economic" ones' in both East–West and North–South relations.

Third, he drew attention to advances in the study of public policy. Political economy approaches were popular with younger scholars and there was more emphasis on the interconnection of political and administrative structures. The whole subject area had been modernised:

> Public administration and local government studies have traditionally been concerned in a rather dreary way with the machinery of government; in recent years there have been cheering developments in the study of the relationship between governmental structures and policies in such sectors as Inner-city problems in general or the administration of housing and health as particular points (NA, 1982c).

The general view taken of politics by the Social Studies sub-committee was that 'Politics grew greatly in the 1960s so it has a low retirement rate; some staff could teach in other subjects. It seems to be a medium-demand subject, with increasing popularity of single-subject courses'. The committee considered that 'Some weak university departments are in the same area as strong polytechnic departments; concentration of resources should, therefore, be across the binary line' (NA, 1982d).

In some respects politics benefited from being a relatively low-profile subject as it escaped the obloquy heaped on sociology at this time. The Rothschild committee set up to review the future of the SSRC made a specific recommendation that the SSRC should not help to establish new departments or sub-departments of sociology (not that doing so was in the SSRC's remit) or finance those departments considered to be sub-standard. When the matter was discussed in the Social Studies sub-committee, Professor Pahl approvingly quoted Professor Halsey of Oxford who said: 'there is a whole chapter about Sociology as well as scattered remarks, and they are mostly unfriendly in the received establishment style'. Professor Pahl commented of the report: 'The lay reader will gain the impression that Sociology is a pretentious mistake, now discredited and replaced by more sensible, less ambitious and better established disciplines which are the heirs to the grander claims of Sociology – for example Human Geography, [Social] Psychology, and

Social Anthropology' (NA, 1982e). In discussions in the civil service it was suggested that 'It would be important . . . to get other potentially superfluous departments into the frame along with the sociologists' (NA, 1982f).

There had been justified fears that the Rothschild Report might lead to the closure of the SSRC. However, there was a considerable rallying of support in internal discussions in the civil service. Sir Robert Armstrong, the Cabinet Secretary, commented: 'There is a virtually unanimous view, which I share, that it would be pointless to liquidate the SSRC, which some people think the Secretary of State would like to do'. He argued: 'Clearly the SSRC should not be further punished. Social Science in the UK has a few outstanding people in it and many problems to illuminate (not in general to solve) – and ones of great importance to the nation' (NA, 1982g). As far as the allegation of political bias or at any rate lack of sympathy for the government was concerned, a civil servant in the Department of Health and Social Security (DHSS) commented:

> I do not doubt there are some left-wing social scientists on SSRC committees and that some left-wing social scientists get research grants. But I have absolutely no sense of the SSRC itself being left-wing: indeed the Council and both Boards seem to me to be conservative bodies which put a high premium on such old-fashioned virtues as academic excellence and public service (NA, 1982f).

Political science was very much the dog that did not bark in the night as far as discussions within the civil service about the Rothschild Report were concerned. Sociology and social policy had something of a sponsor in the DHSS which was concerned about SSRC funds being concentrated on economics. Political science lacked a specific interlocutor in government.

In the event, a change of name had to be agreed to so the SSRC became the Economic and Social Research Council (ESRC). As the chair of the Council at the time, Michael Posner, commented, 'he would have been happy for it to have been renamed "the White Fish Authority" as long as it was allowed to continue funding high quality social science research' (Gaber et al., n.d., p. 16). However, survival came at a price in terms of financial cutbacks. Sir Keith Joseph, the Secretary of State for Education and Science, explained: 'The Government believes that within the Science Vote relatively higher priority should be given to work in the natural sciences – particularly to sustain a flow of the best research talent – and relatively lower priority to work in social studies' (Hansard, 1982). Spending was cut by £6 million or 30 per cent between 1983 and 1986. One consequence was that there were doubts that the survey-based study of the 1983 general election could be funded, ending a series of studies that spanned seven general elections. In the event it could not be fully funded by the ESRC, but relied on a joint funding arrangement involving Robert Maxwell of Pergamon Press.

This particular initiative aside, it was evident that politics was often not well placed to obtain its share of the diminished funds available. Peter Nailor, as chair of the Politics committee, wrote to the PSA complaining that:

> Far too many of the applications are badly presented . . . It seems clear to me that some applicants either do not think through clearly enough what they want to do or don't get enough help in setting out their proposals clearly . . . I even venture to suggest that some of the proposals do not seem to be very good.

Nailor explained that the committee system of review was not deliberately obstructive and wanted to give a fair wind to a good idea, but it had a strong interest in quality and 'has to serve a critical review function which, ideally, one might hope departments would provide' (LSE, 1980c, PSA/18).

There was recognition that in these difficult circumstances the PSA needed to do what it could to help the discipline. One small step in this direction was the funding of a secretary's salary at Manchester University, where the chair was then based, for one day a week to deal with PSA business. Lynn Dignan was appointed to this position in 1981. In 1985 Ian Forbes, later to chair the Association, became part-time executive director, a post he held until 1989.

Longer-term impact of the cuts

In 1986–07 the PSA conducted a number of surveys of heads of department, individuals and degree courses which were designed to estimate the longer-term impact of the cuts in higher education spending. Despite positive trends in student demand, the overall picture was a bleak one. Some departments were identified as having experienced particularly severe staffing cuts, but the general picture was also discouraging:

> Most departments face problems which are less dramatic but equally serious in the long-term. These problems are the gradual but continuous reduction in the number of academic staff, the lack of new blood appointments, the shift from permanent to temporary positions, the increased teaching loads, the minimal opportunities for promotion, the lack of mobility for transfer between institutions, leading to long-term decline of morale within the profession. The evidence suggests that if the reductions in staffing continue at the rate experienced since 1981 then by the end of the decade the profession will have experienced the loss of one in seven political scientists (Berrington and Norris, 1988).

The 1988 survey provides detailed information on those who left the profession permanently in 1987–88, 62 in all. Of these, about one-third or twenty took early retirement, ten accepted academic jobs overseas, five moved to non-politics departments and the rest took retirement at the traditional age or for reasons of illness, or moved to non-academic employment or further education (Norris, 1988, p. 5).

In 1989, however, after seven years of positions being lost there was a turning of the tide, although by that year there had been a cumulative loss of about one in ten political scientists:

The results for the last academic year (October 1988–89) indicate that on balance there has been a relatively high level of job mobility and a slight expansion of staff, with 104 appointments leading to a net gain of 16 posts, or 1.5 per cent of the profession. Polytechnics made slightly more gains than universities, indicating that departments in this sector are responding to the substantial growth in student numbers. In addition many who came into the profession entered directly from full-time postgraduate training, bringing a much needed transfusion of new blood (Norris, 1989, p. 1).

This momentum was maintained in 1990. On the one hand, there was a sharp decline in the number of retirements, from 23 in 1988–89 to just seven in 1989–90. Moreover, there were 127 appointments, producing a net gain of 52 posts or 4.4 per cent of the profession, although in this academic year the expansion was largely in universities rather than in politics. The major driver appears to have been the continued popularity of the subject among undergraduate and postgraduate students. 'According to the University Statistical Record during the last decade the number of full-time politics university undergraduates expanded by 23 per cent, compared with 12 per cent growth across all subject areas. The number of full-time politics postgraduates expanded by 15 per cent' (Norris, 1990, p. 1). Staff–student ratios had deteriorated sharply, but this could not be allowed to continue indefinitely. In particular if politics departments had worse staff–student ratios than other comparable departments, this would show up in internal resource allocation calculations and allow a case to be made for extra staff. Of course, the growth in 1989–90 simply restored the political science profession to approximately the position it had been in 1984–85 (Norris, 1990, p. 1). Nevertheless, simply ending the period of stagnation in which some departments had made no new appointments for a decade was of itself significant for morale and the academic health of the discipline.

Journals

This was the aspect of the PSA's activities in which perhaps the greatest progress was made during this period. A new journal was added to *Political Studies* in the form of *Politics*, which published shorter articles, contained material that was more usable for teaching purposes and offered opportunities for younger staff and postgraduates to gain experience of publication. This was very much the brainchild of Patrick Dunleavy who had explained:

> [It] would seem to me likely that PSA members as a whole would derive benefit from, and be much more interested in, an extension of the Association's publications towards a short article/report journal . . . *New Society* currently publishes articles closest to the form I have in mind. But the political/policy content of *New Society* is very sporadic, and their interest in academic topics very largely restricted to currently fashionable topics (LSE, 1979i, PSA/18).

Dunleavy submitted a proposal for a PSA short-article journal to the EC, noting that it was 'a logical and attractive extension of the Association's publishing activities, offering a valuable extra service to members of the profession of direct relevance to both their research and teaching activities'. The EC discussion anticipated various difficulties:

> On the one hand, it was suggested that demand for the journal might be insufficient, unless it competed with *Political Studies*, an option that would not be acceptable to OUP. On the other hand, an adequate supply of suitable material for inclusion might not be forthcoming, though it was conceded that the new opportunity could create a new supply (LSE, 1980d, PSA/18).

Despite these misgivings, the EC allocated £1,000 for up to two trial issues in 1981–82. In the event, only one issue could be produced in time. It was admitted that the typing and proofreading of the first issue were below an acceptable standard, but the fact that a niche existed for a publication of this kind had been established and it became an important part of what eventually became a PSA family of journals.

At its strategy review meeting in 1980, the EC considered the expansion of *Political Studies*, which was suffering from a backlog in the publication of book notes. Drawing attention to the central strategic issue, Jim Sharpe pointed out that '[Even] if quite dramatic increases [in membership] were achieved neither is likely to generate enough income. We need something else and it's my view that there remains only one other source of additional revenue that we can tap without raising subscriptions dramatically and that is the journal' (LSE, 1980e, PSA/18).

Sharpe had examined the experience of the British Sociological Association in producing *Sociology* itself, but this had not worked out as well as had been hoped, suggesting that the collaboration of a professional publisher was required:

> Evidently they are making a smaller surplus than they anticipated. This is for two reasons; first, there seems to be some ganging up on them by other publishers over advertising and the revenue from that source is much less than they hoped. Second, the overhead costs of distribution and maintaining an accurate subscription list, dealing with queries etc. is much higher than they anticipated (LSE, 1980e, PSA/18).

Sharpe had therefore approached Martin Robertson and Company, a sister company of B. H. Blackwell, and asked them for estimates of the cost of the PSA producing the journal. As a consequence, their 'appetite was whetted . . . and they therefore made a proposal to take us over. My strong impression is that [Martin Robertson's] would be better all round than OUP' (LSE, 1980e, PSA/18). The finance director of Martin Robertson wrote setting out financial proposals that 'reflect our belief that the Association as a whole should share directly in the commercial success of the Journal' (LSE, 1980f, PSA/18). They envisaged an annual payment to the PSA of £5,000 which would include the costs of the editorial team. They also set out detailed proposals on how subscriptions might be increased.

The Martin Robertson proposal was not acted on but under the chairmanship of Geraint Parry (who had topped the poll in the EC elections in 1980 and 1981) the journal was moved to Butterworth in 1983, which he rightly terms 'the most important development during my watch'. Parry recalls: 'We approached OUP (through Jim Sharpe I think) about the possibility of their paying some form of royalty. OUP rejected this as financially impossible. So we decided to sound out alternatives'. Parry is uncertain how Butterworth emerged as a possibility, but thinks it may have been suggested by law colleagues.

The negotiations with Butterworth were conducted by Parry, Alastair Thomas as treasurer and Joni Lovenduski. However, they also brought in an outsider, John Whittaker, a lecturer in accountancy and business at Loughborough University, 'with some business negotiating experience (which none of us possessed)'. The crucial meeting with Butterworth was held at a restaurant in Manchester: 'Butterworth made us an offer which we in our naivety thought very attractive only to hear Whittaker dismiss it out of hand. By the end of the meal Whittaker had almost doubled it. Belatedly OUP made an offer to pay a royalty, having found it financially possible after all!' As Parry concluded, 'The significance of this move was that it transformed PSA finances. For the first time there was a major source of income apart from membership subscriptions. It allowed more support for such ventures as specialist groups etc.' (Parry, 2009).

In 1988 the contract was coming up for renewal and Colin Rallings 'got my accountant in Plymouth to advise on this during the 1988 conference. This was an important input in moving publication to Blackwells and significantly upping the Association's income' (Personal communication, 22 July 2009). Blackwell became the publisher of *Political Studies* from 1989. From 1988 to 1993 it funded annual meetings of the editorial board at its Oxford offices. Discussions in the board led to the introduction of an annual special issue preceded by a workshop and increased pagination for the journal.

Conferences

The graduate conference had performed an important function for many years, but by 1980 the numbers attending were dropping with only 32 present at that year's event. It was noted that:

> Manchester, Keele and universities with only one or two awards were strongly repre-
> sented – Essex, Oxford and the LSE were much less so . . . it suggests that the confer-
> ence was relatively more attractive to students where other possibilities for interaction
> within the discipline were more limited. If this is true, then it is clear that the confer-
> ence has had a socialising as well as a purely academic function (LSE, 1980g, PSA/18).

In any case the ESRC, with its funds diminishing and being switched from graduate training to research, had concluded that the graduate conference had outlived its useful purpose: 'It has come to the view that its resources might be better allocated to specialist conferences for students researching in particular areas of the discipline rather than for some more general type of conference' (LSE, 1980h, PSA/18). Patrick Dunleavy wrote a paper for the EC reviewing the functions of the graduate conference and making suggestions that subsequently became routine parts of PSA provision such as a special reception for graduate students and financial provision from PSA funds for 'hardship' cases. The EC decided to adopt Dunleavy's suggestion of a one-day graduate conference preceding the main conference with a maximum of 50 graduate places at the main event (LSE, 1981a, PSA/18). This is a formula that has persisted until today, but it has not been without its critics, who consider that the postgraduate element in the main conference has become too large.

The 1980 annual conference was held at Exeter and it was feared at one stage that members of the EC would have to serve drinks at the opening reception as an economy measure, but a generous contribution by the city council overcame this problem. This conference attracted 23 panels and 78 papers and at times there were as many as eight panels running simultaneously. In his report on the conference, the academic convenor, Geraint Parry, reflected: 'Have we gone too far in the number of panels organised at the same time? Should the convenor attempt to pull the profession together by drawing up a restricted number of general themes for discussion?' What was 'at least as encouraging as the size of attendance at Exeter was the fact that nearly one in three of those present was actively involved in the Conference by way of giving a paper or organising a panel' (LSE, 1980i, PSA/18). There was an underlying tension between the growing specialisation of the discipline and the risks of fragmentation associated with this trend. Specialisation boosted attendances, but it raised questions about the coherence and unity of the discipline.

Inviting keynote speakers to conferences was an uncertain art. In 1982 the philosopher Bernard Williams was invited to address the conference dinner at the University of Kent at Canterbury. Geraint Parry had invited him:

> on the basis that he was one of the best and wittiest speakers I have ever known. The top table was up on a dais high above the diners with the floodlit cathedral behind. Throughout dinner Bernard was at his wittiest with side-splitting anecdotes. Then he got up and delivered this dry speech saying that there was no such discipline as political science. It was all either history or philosophy (Parry, 2009).

Needless to say, this was not a popular message with the audience and Parry recalls 'barracking'. The author recalls that someone set off a musical box that played *The Internationale* and the local organiser strode up and down the rows of diners looking for the culprit, who was not identified. Richard Rose then got up and provided a critique of what Williams had said, but the diners were not in the mood for a debate.

In 1988 the conference was held at Plymouth Polytechnic, the first and only time it was held at a 'poly': it has subsequently been held at a post-1992 university

(Lincoln). Colin Rallings recalls: 'The conference went well and made some money – an unusual and unlooked for bonus in those days, but attendance was a little lower than normal. Not sure whether that was the physical or academic location – or both!' (Personal communication, 22 July 2009) For all the effort that was made on conferences when Michael Goldsmith became chair in 1989 he saw 'improving the quality of format of the annual conference' as one of his priorities (Goldsmith, 2009).

Relationships with Practitioners

William Wallace, eventually to become one of a small but significant group of political scientists in the House of Lords, wrote an important review paper on this topic in 1980. He provided a succinct summary of the problems that arose in relationships between political science and government:

> The problem is that the Civil Service has no *general* view of 'political science' as a whole, even if various sections of Whitehall have a favourable or unfavourable image of their parallel areas of academic expertise. There are a number of barriers to improving the situation: official secrecy (so that academics are often unaware of what is going on), the unscientific bias and lack of rigour in Civil Service training, the ethos of the 'insider' as someone who knows so much about the intricacies of official business that the 'outsider' has nothing much to offer, the unavoidable problem that most civil servants are in London and most academics are a long way outside London, and to be honest the resistance of many academics to any closer involvement in Whitehall and advice to government (emphasis in original).

Wallace argued that what the PSA should want from the civil service was:

(1)   'more information of all sorts . . . It is a characteristic of British government that these things tend to be organised on the old-boy network rather than on a more open basis';
(2)   'more organised exchanges between Whitehall and political science';
(3)   'greater recognition within the Civil Service for the contribution which political science has to offer'.

Wallace recognised that the times were not propitious for constructing a new relationship between political science and the civil service:

> Apart from the resistance of the Whitehall ethos to structured thinking in administrative and political areas and, in many instances, to the academic world as a whole, the tone of the current government is unsympathetic to social science and to policy research as a whole. The public expenditure cuts have fallen heavily on all forms of government support for policy research and social science; it is widely appreciated that the Prime Minister herself is unimpressed with social science, and considers most of its practitioners to be biased towards other parties.

Wallace also recognised that there were limits to what could reasonably be requested:

There are severe limits to how far we can go in getting the Civil Service to accept political science as a specialised subject comparable to its acceptance of economics and statistics in the early 1960s. That took place as part of a general recognition of the inadequacy of government thinking about economic management; for better or worse, no general appreciation of the inadequacy of government handling of political and administrative matters exists (LSE, 1981c, PSA/18).

Wallace made a number of practical suggestions such as developing a closer relationship with the Civil Service Department, in particular with the Civil Service College and the Machinery of Government division. Civil servants could be invited to the annual conference as speakers and as participants. As a result of the paper, the EC decided to organise an exploratory conference 'with the aim of clarifying the contribution that political scientists could make and of considering why economists have a greater impact'. This was organised by David Steel and William Wallace in conjunction with William Plowden, the Director-General of RIPA in December 1980. The programme is reproduced in Box 6.1.

Of the 30 people present, 20 were classified as 'outsiders' (of whom at least 10 had inside experience) and 10 'insiders'. The intention had been to have equal numbers, 'but the acceptance rate of outsiders to the first wave of invitations was higher than anticipated'. This perhaps suggests that political scientists were more interested in developing relationships with civil servants than the other way round. This tendency is also reflected in the balance of paper givers.

Box 6.1:   Conference on Government and Political Science,
12 December 1980

Session 1: Social science and government
Speaker: L. J. Sharpe (Nuffield College, Oxford)
Discussant: T. B. Rees (Home Office Research Unit)
Session 2: The contribution (in terms of concepts and techniques) that political science can offer to government
Speaker: A. Barker (University of Essex)
Discussant: Dr Helen Wallace (Civil Service College)
Session 3: The use of political scientists as advisers and temporary civil servants
Speakers: Dr W. J. L. Plowden (Royal Institute of Public Administration), J. M. Lee (Birkbeck College, London)
Session 4: The status of political science in the recruitment and training of generalist administrators
Speaker: Professor P. Nailor (Royal Naval College, Greenwich)
Discussant: J. R. Wakely (Civil Service College)

Three general points emerged from the discussion in terms of the role that political scientists could play:

(1) 'That it was necessary to distinguish between different aspects of this question (the contribution of political science to policy analysis, its role in the training of generalist administrators and the contribution of political scientists as special advisers and temporary civil servants) as to some extent different considerations arose in each case'.

(2) 'That it was important not to consider the position of political science in isolation from the other social sciences'.

(3) 'That it would be mistaken to focus attention exclusively upon central government (particularly as the present status of political science in local government is rather more favourable)'.

It was also acknowledged that many of the difficulties arose from the attitudes of political scientists who either did not think through sufficiently clearly what they wanted from a relationship with government or did not want a relationship at all. 'It was felt that political scientists had generally not paid sufficient attention to promoting themselves and their subject to government. Nor had they always been clear exactly what they sought from government and, in designing research projects, they had assumed too readily government's reputation for impenetrability'. It was also admitted 'that there are many academics, including colleagues in political science departments, who resist the idea that greater involvement in government is a proper or desirable part of an academic's work or that political science as a discipline has any direct relevance to the practical skills of government' (LSE, 1981b, PSA/18). Some thought that if the discipline was going to be a science, its researchers should be at least at arm's length from those engaged in the activity.

It was argued that these views should be refuted, but those who held them did have a coherent case to make. There was a view that the study of politics represented one form of a general humanities education in which intellectual growth, including the development of rigorous analytical skills, was what was offered rather than specific pieces of knowledge or techniques that could be deployed in a particular occupation. Academics had in any case decided to follow an academic career rather than an administrative one. There was also a suspicion of the possibility of those whose contacts with government were too close becoming 'inside dopesters' who could reproduce the latest gossip, but gained knowledge that was essentially ephemeral in its content.

Subsequent developments included, as Colin Rallings recalls, 'meetings with journalists and politicians to talk about areas of "mutual interest". Philip Norton was closely involved and very keen on that development' (Personal communication, 22 July 2009). Nevertheless, by the time that Michael Goldsmith became chair, relationships with practitioners and other outside bodies remained a challenge:

[There] was the whole question of how we dealt with outside bodies. In practice we at best were reactive to events rather than trying to shape them. As political scientists we did not practise what we preached about organised groups and lobbying. We had poor relations with the press . . . whilst government departments largely did not want to know about political scientists (Goldsmith, 2009).

The Emergence of the RAE

The development of research selectivity has been one of the most controversial subjects in British higher education policy. It has certainly had a profound effect on the way in which research is conducted and careers are structured. Some question the principle of research selectivity, while rather more have questioned the way in which it has been put into practice and in particular its impact on the discipline of politics. It has certainly provided a challenge for successive leaderships of the PSA.

It is perhaps too easy to assume that there was once a 'golden age' of unfettered scholarship in which academics had the time to develop their work free of external pressures. Before the RAE, it was possible for members of a politics department to be undertaking no research at all. What is more, research-inactive members of a department were not only receiving research support and not making use of it, but they often acted as a block to younger research-active members whose work was seen as a form of 'rate busting'. Research activity in departments was scrutinised by occasional visitations from the UGC; however, their judgements that a particular department was 'very sound' might reflect its reputation but had little in the way of an evidence base to support them.

The 1981 cuts had been implemented selectively with some suggestion that there was an arbitrary bias in favour of the older universities and against the younger, particularly technological, universities. This led to pressure for a more systematic approach to allocating research money and the first Research Selectivity Exercise was conducted in 1986. It was repeated in 1989 and 1992 and became more systematic and with greater implications for funding. The PSA had minimal links with the UGC and then with the Higher Education Funding Council for England (HEFCE). Michael Goldsmith as chair 'had to deal with the fallout after the 1989 exercise and with the 1992 one. The 1989 exercise was patently unfair and inconsistent in the way it treated different disciplines with politics coming out badly' (Goldsmith, 2009). Box 6.2 gives Goldsmith's recollections of the campaign he subsequently organised.

Elizabeth Meehan recalls that 'quite a lot of suggestions made by the PSA were taken on board by HEFCE'. Among the subjects discussed were the relative consideration of articles and chapters, what to do about interdisciplinary research, and the protection of younger researchers against being left out because they necessarily had fewer publications. Meehan is convinced that one of the best initiatives the PSA took was the establishment of the shadow panel:

Box 6.2: Campaigning on the RAE

Michael Goldsmith recalls: 'We organised a campaign – getting some coverage in the HE press – which culminated in a private meeting with the then UGC chair, Peter Swinnerton-Dyer. I was lucky in that one of his close members of staff was someone I had known from working with ESRC: I was virtually told that if we did not give him too hard a time, Swinnerton-Dyer would not take note and instruct UGC to listen carefully to the arguments we were making. I had lined up three of the great and the good to rough S.-D. up a little – and they did give him quite a hard time. He conceded most of our points and agreed that further discussion should take place at officer level. They did, we got our way on almost everything we wanted (including the number of publications to be taken into account and the right to nominate members to the panel), with the result that the 1992 exercise worked better, even if one might take the view that the panel was still harder on political science than was the case elsewhere. At that time we ran shadow exercises, with our own panel making an assessment based on each department's return: I can only say that the 1992 shadow panel was harder on the departments than the UGC/HEFCE one' (Personal communication).

The real panel consented to let the shadow panel (with the consent of the departments) have a copy of the submissions. This had several benefits for all concerned. The PSA was able both to monitor and learn from the real panel. To the extent that the shadow ratings matched those of the real ones, some confidence was engendered in the integrity of the RAE itself. It also meant that the shadow panel could assist departments in reflecting upon their results. If I remember correctly, there were only about two or three cases per exercise where the shadow panel and real panel diverged in their assessments and, where this did happen, this then became part of the decision about what to look out for in the next round of discussions (Meehan, 2009).

The other dimension of research funding was the ESRC and Goldsmith admits that links were 'minimal'. The PSA set up meetings with Howard Newby when he was chief executive 'but we were not able to deter him from pursuing initiatives as against responding to research bids' (Goldsmith, 2009). Successive PSA leaderships seem to have favoured response mode bids over programmes, although many political scientists have benefited from the latter. It may be, however, that they are seen as too directive in terms of favouring some aspects of the discipline over others.

Goldsmith also had to deal with the increasing interest of the HEFCE in teaching quality and standards. He recalls: 'The first assessments of history and English were appallingly bad, with the historians in uproar. We supported their case publicly and privately with the agency – one result was that politics and IR was relegated almost to the end of the TQA exercise, by which time nobody in high places was particularly worried about how politics did' (Goldsmith, 2009). Important changes in higher education policy were taking place from the end of the 1980s and it was evident that the PSA was seeking systematically to influence policies that affected its members in a way that it had not done before.

Making the PSA more Professional

This had been a constant concern of the PSA's leadership since 1975, but Colin Rallings, who was secretary from 1983 to 1986, remembers 'the EC as far less professional in those days – no real administrative support except informally from members' departments and little concern except publishing *Political Studies* and arranging the annual conference'. For Rallings, based in Plymouth, it was fortuitous that his period in office largely coincided with that of Maurice Goldsmith at Exeter, so 'we used to discuss meetings on the train to London and I was able to visit his secretary when necessary re agenda/papers etc.' (Personal communication, 22 July 2009).

Nevertheless, a number of important developments took place during this period. Trevor Smith as chair considered that, compared with other disciplines, political studies lacked prizes that recognised important books or successful theses which he saw as a useful means of boosting the PSA's profile. Colin Rallings recalls that 'at the time this was met with typical academic scepticism' (Personal communication, 22 July 2009). By 1987 the W. J. M. Mackenzie book prize was established for the best book in political science published in each calendar year. This was followed by the Lord Bryce prize, first awarded in 1989 for the best dissertation in comparative and international politics and the Sir Ernest Barker prize for the best dissertation in political theory, also first awarded in 1989. The Walter Bagehot prize for the best dissertation in government and public administration was first awarded in 1990 and the range of prizes has been expanded since then.

Michael Goldsmith recalls that 'My time as chair of the PSA was largely concerned with trying to make the organisation more professional in the way it worked and in its dealings with outside bodies'. As well as ensuring that the PSA was on a secure financial foundation, he:

> wanted the organisation to be more professional in the way it dealt with members and the services it delivered to them. This meant improving the way in which we responded to requests for information from members . . . ensuring that the various subject groups were organised and achieving something and not just receiving a small grant, and improving what we did for departments – hence introducing regular HoD meetings (Goldsmith, 2009).

Heads of department meetings had been an innovation of the late 1970s, but had not been continued beyond 1980, in part reflecting a more stringent financial environment (the PSA lost £1,000 on the 1980 meeting).

Goldsmith rebuilt links with IPSA, inviting its executive to an annual conference at Leicester. He also sought to ensure that Britain was represented on the ECPR executive, standing as a candidate with Ivor Crewe. He recalls:

> The campaign was successful, the British representatives toed the party line, and we have had two representatives for most of the time since. I do remember at one point somebody simply saying 'don't bother Mike just tell us who we are voting for' rather different from the 'We'll vote for who the hell we like – bugger off' I met with origi- nally (Goldsmith, 2009).

The leadership of the PSA tried to move the organisation forward and develop new initiatives, but it was limited in what it could do by the resources available. The general condition of the discipline also affected the vigour of the PSA. Although there were plenty of analyses of Thatcherism on offer, the 1980s was not a decade in which there was significant new paradigm development in the UK. The concept of 'policy communities' developed by Jeremy Richardson and Grant Jordan (1979) was influential and in the US the seminal article by James March and Johann Olsen (1984) heralded the arrival of the 'new institutionalism'.

Specialist Groups: The Formation of Elections, Parties and Opinion Polls (EPOP)

The modern PSA has many highly successful specialist groups, but on many criteria the most successful is that dealing with Elections, Parties and Opinion Polls (EPOP). Following its foundation in 1990, its membership reached 121 in 1992, peaking at 202 in 2002 (the inclusion of a journal subscription since then has reduced mem- bership somewhat). Its annual conference regularly attracts over 100 people for a three-day event which secures considerable media publicity. EPOP published a yearbook from 1992 and in 2005 this became the highly regarded *Journal of Elections, Public Opinion and Parties*. EPOP always ensures that some of its members stand for the PSA EC and achieves a high rate of success in securing their election, which is not always the case when political scientists attempt to apply their work in prac- tice. The group also benefits from having a specific government agency that is highly relevant to its work and interested in its research, the Electoral Commission.

For many years there had been a very successful University of Essex conference following each general election organised by Ivor Crewe, Martin Harrop and Bob Worcester from MORI. In the early 1990s, Pippa Norris, who was actively engaged in elections research, suggested to Ivor Crewe that rather than meeting every four to five years it would be a good idea to have a regular conference to present work on electoral studies. 'He thought, quite rightly, that the topic would be slightly too narrow to attract a critical mass of participants but that an annual conference held around the broader theme of Election, Parties and Public Opinion could attract a good crowd, including practitioners as well as scholars' (Personal communication, 23 March 2009).

Ivor Crewe and Pippa Norris were convenors from 1990 to 1993 and when Norris left for Harvard, she was replaced by David Denver who had been involved from the beginning and remained a convenor until 2001, and was also an active member of the PSA EC. Others involved as convenors were Colin Rallings (a former PSA secretary), Justin Fisher (a long-time EC member) and Jon Tonge (chair of the PSA from 2005 to 2008). Philip Cowley and Rosie Campbell were the convenors from 2007.

Why was the group so successful? Pippa Norris explained (personal communication, 23 March 2009):

In part because from the get-go we set high expectations that the meeting would present written conference papers which would be edited into a collective publication; the annual yearbook raised the bar. Moreover the collective leadership meant that there were always 3–4 colleagues who were editing the yearbook and were invested in co-organising the events and sustaining the group. We made sure that the group also had international links to related groups and colleagues elsewhere. The size of the annual meeting – not too small, not too big – also helped. Lastly, the collective nature of electoral studies, requiring teams of colleagues for major data collection projects across related areas of expertise, with the teams at Essex, Oxford, Sheffield and so on, also provided a solid collaborative and institutional foundation for the meeting.

Philip Cowley noted: 'One thing that distinguishes EPOP from some, though not all specialist groups is that we are well run financially. We have been very well stewarded by all convenors, and there is a good record of going out and getting sponsorship and additional revenue'. EPOP has also been very successful at developing links with practitioners, something that has bedevilled the PSA, as has been apparent from discussions in this and earlier chapters. Philip Cowley points out:

I was struck that the first four of the winners of the PSA's Communicator of the Year award all went to EPOP members. This is partly because of the sort of areas they work in, but it's also to do with a mindset amongst almost all in the group which is outward facing and believes in engaging with politics as it is actually practised (Personal communication, 24 March 2009).

More generally, it reflected the strength of sub-disciplines within British political science.

Conclusions: Survival through Adversity

The 1980s was undoubtedly the most difficult decade that the study of politics in Britain has encountered since its formation as a discipline. The cuts in higher education expenditure had a substantial impact on recruitment, retention, mobility and general morale. Faced with deteriorating staff–student ratios, it was all too easy to concentrate on getting the teaching done and to neglect research. The appropriate response was not, however, despondency or lethargy, but professional self-help and this is what the PSA tried to stimulate. Its impact was limited by the resources at its disposal and there was clearly still much to be done at the end of the decade in terms of making the PSA more professional so that it could offer better support to its members. The formation of EPOP was an indicator of continuing vitality within the discipline, while at a professional level the PSA responded effectively to the challenges presented by the RAE and teaching quality.

The subject remained popular with students and, as the decade ended, the number of academic staff teaching politics began to increase again. The PSA needed more funds to serve its members effectively and it was decided to put the publishing contract up for auction. Changes in the structure of higher education were also imminent. The final phase of the professional development of the PSA was about to begin. Up until then the post of treasurer of the Association had not been a key one, but this was about to change.

Chapter 7

A Work in Progress: 1993–2009

The period since 1993 has been one of vigorous growth both for the study of politics in the UK and for the PSA. The year 1992 saw the end of the binary divide in higher education and the conversion of polytechnics and other institutions of higher education into what were known for a time as post-1992 universities but are now more often referred to as 'modern' or 'mainstream' universities. A number of them have flourishing politics teams and their growth has contributed to the growth of staff numbers in the discipline as a whole. This has been underpinned by growing student numbers at both undergraduate and postgraduate level from home and overseas. Applications to the university admissions system have overtaken those for sociology and 'The discipline is . . . in conspicuously good health in terms of student numbers' (ESRC, 2007, p. 19).

This was also a period in which the discipline showed resurgent intellectual vitality. New paradigms such as governance, multi-level governance (especially in relation to the EU) and path dependency emerged. Path dependency became a central construct in policy studies and the varieties of capitalism debate predominated in comparative political economy. Rational choice and new institutionalist approaches competed for influence and eventually led to the emergence of rational choice institutionalism. Social constructivist approaches became more widely used resulting in an interest in how issues were 'framed' and discourse analysis. The study of international political economy was stimulated by the contested phenomenon of globalisation. Security studies, and subsequently critical terrorist studies, received a boost after 9/11, while nuclear proliferation was revived as a key issue. The collapse of the Soviet Union and its satellites, and of military regimes in the global South, encouraged studies of democratisation. Depoliticisation and the regulatory state became central themes in the study of British politics. Development studies were popular with students and charted new areas such as the role of NGOs both in influencing policy and in delivering aid. Political theory, electoral studies and feminist studies remained areas of strength in UK political science, while fields such as the media and politics acquired a new vigour, later reinforced by the analysis of the role of the Internet in politics.

The PSA has undergone an equivalent transformation. In large part this has been made possible by a substantially increased income from an ever-increasing family of journals, soon to grow to five. The additional resources made available to the PSA have allowed it to employ a full-time staff, permitting a substantial expansion in its range of activities. Throughout this period John Benyon has been the treasurer of the PSA. When the author was treasurer of the PSA in the 1970s, it was essentially a clerical function requiring bookkeeping duties and some responsibility for warning the EC if it looked as if funds were running down to a dangerous level. John Benyon has in effect converted the post into that of a chief financial officer for the PSA, seeking out new sources of revenue and tax exemptions. The PSA registered for VAT in 1995 and this made an increasingly important contribution to finances, amounting to some £30,000 a year in 2008. John Benyon also ensured that money was spent in a way that delivered most benefit to members, while being aware of the PSA's public service obligations as a charity. He is often referred to as 'Mr PSA'.

The Association now stages an annual awards ceremony and lunch in London which receives considerable media coverage and has greatly improved links with practitioners. The initial awards ceremony, held to celebrate the Association's 50th anniversary, 'was a controversial proposal' but proved to be 'a great success' (PSA, 2000). One concern was that it would be a drain on the Association's resources but the event attracted £28,500 in sponsorship and broke even. Members' evaluation of what has become an annual event has improved over time. In 2003 27.3 per cent agreed with the statement that 'The PSA Awards Ceremonies are a success at promoting the profession', but this had increased to 42.3 per cent in the 2006 survey of the profession with only 18.2 per cent disagreeing with the statement. Although particular awards to politicians have attracted controversy, the awards ceremony has become established as an event that brings together academics and practitioners, overcoming a lack of contact that proved difficult to address in the earlier history of the PSA.

During this period, under the guidance of its dedicated webmaster, Richard Topf, the PSA had to respond to the revolution in information technology and it has established a highly effective Web presence including a portal which helps to meet the public benefit test that all charities have to fulfil. The internal organisation of the PSA has been strengthened with the development of a system of subcommittees working to the EC and a management group reviewing progress between EC members. The EC holds regular strategy meetings to set the future direction for the organisation.

The beneficial effects of expansion could already be seen in the early to mid-1990s. After a period when it had been relatively static, membership increased from 920 in 1992 to 948 in 1993 and 1,094 in 1994. Conference attendances were also increasing. There were 442 at the 1994 conference, which saw the innovation of publishing conference papers in volumes under the title of *Contemporary Political*

Studies (*CPS*). In 1995 at York there were 574 delegates (25 per cent or 142 were women). In 1996 at Glasgow there were over 600 delegates and 140 panels.

The most marked improvement was seen in the state of the Association's finances. This was not a result of the membership increase as 'more members resulted in a smaller income for the PSA as most of the new members were graduates' (PSA, 1995a). PSA expenditure tripled from £33,494 in 1991 to £99,053 in 1995. Over the same period income went up from £41,938 to £110,560 and growing surpluses meant that the PSA's reserves doubled over this period. Of the income in 1995 over two-thirds (68.5 per cent, £75,771) came from Blackwell for the PSA's journals, *Politics* forming part of the publishing package from 1994. This meant that the journal appeared in a more professional format and was indexed in ABC POL SCI. Ian Forbes explained the broader significance of this development:

> We had been trying for years to increase the subscriptions for *Politics*, but had very little success. This led to the suggestion to Blackwells that they package *Political Studies* and *Politics* together. This enabled them to place *Politics* in all libraries already taking *Political Studies*, and to increase the package price at the same time. This completely transformed the finances of the Association because it generated in one swoop an additional 1,000 subscriptions for *Politics*. It meant that, from then on, membership services could be provided at an effective loss to the Association, while services and activities could be increased in quantity and standard (Personal communication, 14 September 2009).

The Challenges of the Mid-1990s: A Strategic Response

Most of these were not, of course, new challenges, but in some cases the changed financial situation of the PSA offered new opportunities to respond to them with innovative solutions. In 1995 the PSA held a major strategy meeting at Chester which reviewed the tasks facing the Association and led to a number of changes in practice that shaped its work over the next decade.

One group looked at the conference: it is almost impossible to find a formula that satisfies everyone. It was reported that the 'York questionnaire showed there was mild dissatisfaction with format, too many panels, not enough discussion, too big for itself'. The group 'considered a number of options including scrapping the conference altogether and handing it over to individual specialist groups, but this was too radical'. It shows that there were limits to the disintegration of the discipline into sub-disciplines: there was still a wish to meet once a year as a discipline. The PSA has not yet gone as far as the German Political Science Association which holds a conference only once every three years, while its equivalent of specialist groups meet every six months. The 'Second radical option is to relocate and reorganise and hand it over to professional conference organisers. Cheapest option would work out at around £85 per day (Blackpool). Therefore no good' (PSA, 1995b, p. 1). (It is not quite clear whether this was because of the location or the cost.) What the PSA eventually did, but not for over ten years, was to appoint its own in-house conference organiser and end the system whereby the academic convenor was drawn from the host university.

The research group considered a number of topics. On the RAE it had 'little to say. Could not see how it could be done better. This was a success for organisation'. The picture was less encouraging in relation to the ESRC: 'We haven't done our job very well with them in terms of monitoring and working with ESRC. We understand that it is an organisation in continuing crisis but there is an opportunity here'. Reporting back to the full EC, the group convenor, Joni Lovenduski, 'stressed that this was an issue of great importance and particularly important to research interests. She said that the fact we were not doing it well was doing us harm' (PSA, 1995b, p. 2). Progress made in this relationship is discussed later in the chapter.

Michael Moran showed no hesitation in pointing out the limitations revealed by his group on teaching and services. As far as PSA services were concerned, they were a 'most heterogeneous collection of items, symptomatic of lack of clarity in PSA' (PSA, 1995b, pp. 2–3). In relation to teaching he was even more critical:

> M. M. said that in his group it had been the view that both the profession and the PSA had a pretty undistinguished record and the Association in particular. This reflected the wider attitude in the profession and universities generally. There were some horror stories especially about the situation regarding teaching by graduate students and part-timers. The code of conduct [on part-time teachers] was being disregarded and we needed to do something about that. It was felt that teaching was held in low esteem. People were rewarded by being given less teaching (PSA, 1995b, p. 2).

One practical suggestion was a prize for teaching: the Sir Bernard Crick prize, in the form of a main prize and a separate award for new entrants, was first awarded in 1996. The suggestion of in-service and weekend courses was not followed up and the PSA has no equivalent of the annual teaching and learning conference of APSA. However, the benchmarking review found that the discipline was 'very healthy in terms of teaching quality . . . Of the 51 departments on which information is available, 63 per cent of them scored either 23 or a top mark of 24' (ESRC, 2007, p. 19).

Throughout this volume it has been noted that relationships with practitioners have been a recurring challenge for the PSA. The external relations group led by John Benyon found that 'The Association has not been terribly successful in external relations, outside profession it has low visibility'. Outlining the idea of what eventually became the highly successful annual awards ceremony, the group suggested that there were 'strong arguments in favour of [a] ceremony in London, to give out awards and invite politicians' (PSA, 1995b, p. 4). The group also favoured an annual lecture which eventually came to fruition in conjunction with the Hansard Society.

The strategy review also proposed a number of changes in the internal organisation of the PSA which were of considerable significance for its operational effectiveness. The working group on administration established by the Chester strategy meeting found that 'The rationale for an overhaul of strategy on policy and administration is given by the expanding scope of the PSA organisation and activities'. Although the principle of a central office was now well established, operated in 1995 by Lynn Corken at Queen's University Belfast, and the EC had become much more professional in its approach, 'One suspects . . . that our administrative structures are becoming increasingly stretched, especially in the growing burdens placed on Exec members' time, even at our current level of activity . . . Our current administrative structures would not seem capable of dealing effectively with a significant expansion of activity' (PSA, 1995c, p. 1).

A three-fold action strategy was proposed to respond to these challenges. First, it was proposed to have an expanded central office in a fixed location. This was eventually established at Newcastle University in 2000 after Rod Rhodes became chair, with Jack Arthurs as company secretary, joined by Sandra McDonagh as membership secretary and later by Sue Forster as conferences officer. Second, 'The current portfolio structure is uneven in the burdens it imposes on individual Exec members and fragments responsibilities in closely related areas, hindering coordination'. There had already been some *ad hoc* committees such as those dealing with conferences and publications and 'the working groups set up by the Strategy Meeting are seen by some as a move to a more consistently applied sub-committee structure' (PSA, 1995c, p. 3). However, it was felt that a systematic and comprehensive sub-committee structure was needed and this was initially set up in 1996. Although modified from time to time in response to changing needs, it has become a central part of how the EC works. Third, the PSA became a company limited by guarantee from January 1999. This might seem to be a rather technical change, but it protected members from the possibility of unlimited liability. It also represented a final quashing of the 'tendency to behave as if we are a private club looking after our members' interests and generally minding our own business. That has to change, and we have to develop appropriate standards and practices' (PSA, 1995c, p. 6).

One area in which change was necessary was information technology as use of the Internet became more widespread. Richard Topf presented a review document to the January 1996 EC, urging a strategic approach rather than making policy 'on the hoof'. He pointed out that 'the PSA www site was passive. It provided basic information about the Association and worked as a good map but there was no information on primary materials and the PSA was being overtaken by APSA and IPSA, who offered resources in a structured annotated form' (PSA, 1996a, p. 1). Subsequent developments ensured that the PSA had a highly effective Web presence.

Sustaining the level of membership has been a continuous challenge for the PSA. Graduate membership has been particularly liable to fluctuation, depending on how well the graduate network is working. Total membership in June 1998 was 797 compared with 905 in June 1997, but much of this net decline was due to a fall in the number of graduate members, full UK members showing a net decline of 33. The maintenance of membership levels in this period was probably not helped by a number of changes in the administration of membership subscriptions from Blackwell to the Charities Aid Foundation and then to the PSA office, which has retained the responsibility. The EC decided to set up a working party on membership recruitment and membership subscriptions were up by 11 per cent in 1999 compared with a roughly equivalent period in 1998. However, 17.7 per cent of those joining were new members and retaining members remained a challenge. There was an overall fall in members (excluding graduate membership) from 869 in 1996 to 791 in 1999. The 2003 survey of the profession included an analysis of non-members which gave them two suggested reasons for not joining the PSA. The two most important seemed to be that the PSA did not adequately represent their research area and they preferred to be a member of another professional organisation. In other words, they did not regard themselves as a mainstream political scientist which raises again the question of disciplinary identity referred to at various points in this book.

Journals: Expansion and Change

The PSA journals represent one of the most important services the Association provides to members and are at the core of its financial model. During this period the flagship journal, *Political Studies*, underwent important changes and two new journals were launched, *Political Studies Review* and *The British Journal of Politics & International Relations*. In 2010 the PSA announced plans for a new journal, *Political Insight*, to be launched in connection with its 60th anniversary celebrations. It is printed in full colour in a magazine-style format and aims to present research in politics and international studies to a broad audience. Paul Whiteley, the chair of the PSA's publications sub-committee, explained the thinking behind the new publication:

> The Association has got a lot better at presenting the profession to the outside world in recent years. The awards ceremony in particular has been an important event on the calendar which brings the Association's work to public attention and raises our profile in the wider world. Yet there has been a gap in all of this, namely the absence of a journal which explains research and debates in academic politics for the benefit of a wider readership (Whiteley, 2009, p. 17).

Following a very successful editorship by Michael Moran at Manchester, a team from the LSE led by Patrick Dunleavy took over running *Political Studies* in the summer of 1999. Running the journal was now becoming a major task and it was perhaps significant that the flagship journals in sociology and economics were also located at the LSE at that time. Some members of the EC were concerned about the lack of competition for the journal, noting that there had been four major bids when Manchester took responsibility for the journal (PSA, 1999a). However, when the LSE team was replaced by a team led by Martin Smith at Sheffield in 2006, this was the outcome of just two shortlisted bids. Although financial assistance is provided to run the journal, it is not an activity that every department or university can undertake.

The LSE team took a proactive approach to a number of aspects of the journal. First, they reorganised the structure of the journal team. As general editor, Patrick Dunleavy took strategic responsibility for the overall development of the journal and the management of journal policy. Responsibility for processing all manuscripts and making final decisions on acceptance and rejection fell to the executive editor, Paul Kelly. The new team was 'profoundly unhappy with the current image and appearance of *Political Studies*, and the development of "electronic" modes of reading the journal poses some considerable problems for the current format'. In conjunction with Blackwell they developed a new cover and colour scheme, and a complete redesign of internal pages. 'The new page format is larger, the margins are bigger, and the emphasis is on a modern, clean design which will be more attractive to international authors and readers. Footnotes are scrapped in favour of Harvard referencing' (PSA, 1998a).

The new team noted that the journal office received about 1,200 books a year, of which only about 450 were covered in published reviews. The existing systems did not 'permit "real time reviewing". Most books coverage comes out at least 18–24 months after a book has been published, while most sales take place in the first year of books' lives' (PSA, 1998a). The new team therefore moved to a system of giving brief factual information on new titles and to publication of book reviews on the Web immediately and in print thereafter. This was achieved through a new website at www.politicalstudies.org.

A strategy of promoting the journal at APSA and the ECPR, as well as at conferences never previously covered by the journal such as those of the Mid-Western Political Science Association and the Public Choice Society, increased submissions to the journal substantially. These doubled from 99 in 1999 to 199 in 2003 with a particularly marked increase between 2000 and 2001 which is just the point when one would have expected the strategy of the new editors to have an impact. Although political theory submissions fell off after 2001, this reflected 'the emphasis the editors have put on publishing papers across the full range of political science' (PSA, 2003a) and what they saw as an over-representation of political theory. Indeed, there had been some concern on the EC about 'the LSE bid which seemed to be moving [*Political Studies*] towards a behavioural journal and away from a theoretical stance' (PSA, 1999a). Given the editor's stated priorities, it is remarkable what a large proportion of total submissions political theory articles accounted for over the 1999–2003 period (see Table 7.1). Forty-one per cent of submissions were of political theory articles, suggesting that *Political Studies* was still seen as a journal of first resort for such articles. Another 22 per cent were British politics articles, so that nearly two-thirds of total submissions were accounted for by these two categories.

When they submitted a paper as part of the mid-term review of their tenure, the editors noted that 'In the past there has been a tendency for . . . editors completing their second 3 year term to be markedly less activist and innovative than they had been in their first term, leading to a recurrent pattern of "second term stagnation" of the journal's style and a certain atrophication of its contents' (PSA, 2004a). As a

Table 7.1: Submissions to *Political Studies* by Category,
1999–2003

Political Theory	292	41%
Britain	156	22%
Europe	100	14%
Other Areas	76	11%
Comparative	52	7%
International Relations	35	5%
North America	25	4%
Asia-Pacific	22	3%

Source: Calculated from PSA, 2003a.

new initiative, the editors proposed the creation of *Political Studies Review*. This would pull together the current books coverage of *Political Studies*, but also contain an average of three review articles per issue on broad-ranging and topical issues. They considered that this change would give *Political Studies* 'a much clearer image as a wide-ranging political science research journal at the cutting edge of scholarly work in the discipline'. It was also pointed out that the *American Political Science Review* was separating out its books coverage to a new journal to be called *Perspectives on Politics*. The first issue of *Political Studies Review* appeared in 2003, the editors making it clear that, while they were always willing to discuss proposals for review articles, a commissioning model was being followed.

Political Studies Review was the fourth component of the PSA family of journals, as *The British Journal of Politics & International Relations* had already been established in 1999 under the editorship of David Marsh. The *Political Studies* editors considered that 'The new division of labour with *BJPIR* has been helpful to us in broadening our coverage' (PSA, 2004a). In 1996 the PSA had been considering four proposals for a new journal which need not have been one with a British focus. The successful bid was 'not intended to be *Political Studies 2*. Rather, the aim of the *BJPIR* is to deepen and broaden our understanding of British politics' (Editors, 1999, p. 1). In particular, 'the first concern of this journal is to encourage theoretically informed studies of British politics' (Editors, 1999, p. 3). The initial editorial was also critical of what it saw as a dominant pluralist view of British politics. The journal became successfully established, although in time more attention had to be given to attracting articles that reflected the international relations portion of its title.

In Table 7.2 some data are provided on members' evaluations of the journals in a survey in 2003. It is evident that *Political Studies* came out top in terms of perceived utility, quality and the regularity with which it was read, but it has to be remembered that it had by then been established for over 50 years with strong name recognition. *Politics* was performing a rather different function to the other three journals, in particular providing publication opportunities to new entrants.

Table 7.2: Members' Ratings of PSA Journals, 2003

Journal	High quality	Articles read regularly
Political Studies	43.6%	52.0%
The British Journal of Politics & International Relations	18.5%	34.7%
Politics	9.6%	31.4%

Source: PSA Survey of Profession, 2003 (PSA, 2004b).

The 2006 survey of the profession produced broadly similar results, although the percentage giving a high quality rating to *The British Journal of Politics & International Relations* had increased to 26.6 per cent from 18.5 per cent in 2003. *PSA News*, which keeps members informed about developments in the Association and wider profession, received a high rating for usefulness in both surveys, although 57 per cent of respondents rating it as very useful or useful in 2003 declined to 46.3 per cent in 2006.

Conferences

Alongside the journal, the annual conference was the most important product provided by the PSA for its members. As Patrick Dunleavy commented, 'The Conference is a key means of creating and sustaining a political science "community", and hence the ways it operates resonate throughout the whole profession and the rest of the year, far beyond the three days when the Conference is actually in session' (Dunleavy, 1994, p. vi). Understandably, a considerable proportion of the time of the EC was spent discussing both conference strategy and the detailed arrangements for conferences. Many of the problems were long-running ones and no formula was going to satisfy all members. Surveys of the profession carried out in 2002 and 2003 found that 'The specialist Group conferences were seen as the most useful conference by quite a large margin' (PSA, 2004b); 67.9 per cent of members rated them as very useful or useful in 2003 while 55.8 per cent of members gave a similar rating to the annual PSA conference. However, this does not necessarily suggest that the annual conference was not being organised in the right way, but could equally reflect a growing sub-disciplinary orientation in the discipline.

One of the perennial problems surrounding the organisation of the conference once it became a large event was the provision of papers. For a time a system was operated where paper givers had to provide 200 copies to the local organiser by mid-January and when someone registered for the conference they would be sent a complete set of papers. This system had a number of deficiencies: papers were often not ready by mid-January, or a hastily prepared and poorly presented effort was submitted; some individuals found it difficult to get 200 copies printed at a time of stringent university budgets; and members did not want all the papers anyway. Thus, a system of paper rooms was introduced where papers were photo-copied by the local organisers in a somewhat frenetic atmosphere and sold, which meant that:

> those attending could easily spend £25 if they were interested in four or five of the panels – and still not get the paper they wanted. My 'representative' or 'composite' memory of recent panel meetings is of being handed a paper of more than twenty pages, with half-a-dozen tables and a chart depicting the wiring of a power station – at 9.02 a.m. on the Thursday for a session starting at 9.05 a.m.' (Stanyer, 1994, p. viii).

The solution that the committee devised was the publication of all available papers in the *CPS* volumes edited by Jeff Stanyer. As Dunleavy explained, 'The two under-lying aims were to encourage the best possible standards of paper writing at PSA by offering the chance of immediate publication, and to provide for the dissemina-tion of papers to libraries and the wider profession in an accessible and convenient way' (Dunleavy, 1994, p. vi). What was also a consideration was that papers pub-lished in this way might count as contributions to an edited book for the RAE. The downside was that the quality of the papers remained variable as they had not been subject to a refereeing process.

In 1998 the EC considered a working party report on the future of *CPS* which recommended a more selective post-conference volume combined with the avail-ability of all papers on the PSA website. There was a wide-ranging discussion in which it was argued that the establishment of *CPS* had led to a considerable improve-ment in the quality and availability of papers. An alternative to a selective volume could be a special issue of one of the journals. Eventually the working party recom-mendations were approved by thirteen votes to one, but no special volume or issue ever appeared and papers are made available on the PSA website.

A recurrent problem was the composition of those who attended. The local organiser for the 1999 conference held at Nottingham reported:

> A depressing aspect of the conference for the local organisers was the poor showing by senior members of the profession, particularly after our efforts to improve the academic quality of the conference, and also because we were led to believe that part of the logic of holding the conference in purpose-built facilities was to attract/appease those colleagues. It was noticeable how few attended from what might be regarded as the leading departments in the country. Very few came from any of the London col-leges . . . Oxford, Strathclyde, Essex, Manchester, etc., leaving the new universities and postgraduates as easily the largest 'user group' (PSA, 1999b).

Of course, there may have been an element of self-reinforcement here. The more the conference became dominated by postgraduates and junior academics, the less attractive it may have become to senior members of the discipline. The local organ-iser commented that 'As a reluctant attender of PSA conferences myself, I don't think that it is very difficult to see that the PSA conference is still too expensive relative to the quality of the academic offering' (PSA, 1999b). Perhaps as a consequence, the registration fee for the conference at the LSE in 2000 was reduced and this was the biggest event to date, attracting 700 participants and more panels than ever before.

At the 2004 strategy meeting it was agreed 'that a key area for further action for the Association was the future of the annual conference. It is clear that some members regard the present format as insufficiently professional and may be discouraged from attending as a result' (PSA, 2005). However, evidence from a membership survey suggested that members were broadly satisfied with the existing format. The innovation that attracted the greatest support was some form of quality control over papers. However, the view was expressed 'that quality control would inhibit attendance. The primary purpose of the Annual conference appears to be bringing like-minded people together' (PSA, 2006a).

In both the 2003 and 2006 surveys, 'organising conferences' was rated fourth among tasks rated as a 'first priority' for the PSA, behind research promotion, representing the profession to policy makers and publishing journals. Between 2003 and 2006 there was a slight decline in the percentage of survey respondents classifying the annual conference as 'very useful' or 'useful' (from 55.8 per cent to 53 per cent) and a slight increase in those rating it 'not at all useful' (from 4.2 per cent to 5.8 per cent). Although these were marginal shifts, they were enough to stimulate further thinking in the EC about the conference format.

In a paper submitted to the EC, Richard Topf commented: 'Despite, or maybe because of, their longevity, Annual Conferences lack a clear vision as to their purpose, are literally amateur in their administration, and amateurish in their management in practice. The appointment of a permanent PSA Conference Organiser should be seized as the opportunity to review the Annual Conference from first principles'. Topf identified three conceptually distinct purposes for a PSA annual conference:

(1) 'an annual gathering of Association members, aimed to be as all-encompassing as possible with the presentation of papers as the formal reason for the meeting, but with social and collegiate activities as the well-recognised informal justification;

(2) a large, all-comers event, aimed at members and non-members alike, with no conference theme, no evaluation of the quality of paper proposals, and success measured by overall attendance levels;

(3) a themed conference, with well-controlled standards for acceptance of panels, predetermined numbers of panels, and papers per panel, with the expectation that it will attract high-status presentations [by] leading members of the profession'.

Topf observed that 'Current practice lies somewhere between (1) and (2), and our market research shows that this no longer appeals. I would argue for (3) and the necessary infrastructure to effect this option'.

Topf pointed out that the role of conference convenor had become outmoded and anomalous:

> It may be that, historically, an invitation to serve as a PSA Conference Convenor was perceived as an honour as well as an opportunity to mould an important event in the professional, academic calendar. I do not believe that this is any longer the case. On the contrary, my impression is the Convenors see the task as a chore, often simply imposed on them by their Head of Department. In any case, nowadays, Convenors have very little scope to stamp their mould on the proceedings, beyond, perhaps the choice of plenary or after-dinner speakers. I recommend that the PSA no longer links the choice of Convenor to that of the conference venue. Conference convenors should be chosen on their academic merit, linked to a genuine conference theme decided by the Conferences Sub-Ctte.

Conference organisation 'should be solely and fully the responsibility of the PSA Conference Organiser and removed from the hands of the local academic staff altogether' (PSA, 2006b).

Viewed in retrospect, successive ECs had been tactical rather than strategic in their approach to the conference. Much of their energy had been taken up with finding a location and appointing a convenor, not always straightforward tasks as the volume of work associated with staging an annual conference increased. They then focused on the details of conference organisation, understandably concerned that these should work smoothly from the perspective of participating members. Questions of academic quality were given insufficient attention. The conference had perhaps lagged behind other aspects of the PSA's work in being professionalised.

The EC agreed to implement the recommendations outlined in the Topf paper from the 2009 conference held in Manchester. They agreed that there would be a 'predetermined standard plan of the conference with fixed numbers of sessions, panels etc'. The link between the convenor and the conference venue would be broken with convenors chosen on their academic merit, linked to a conference theme. There would be 'some peer-reviewed tracks of papers running through the conference' and conference organisation would be the responsibility of the PSA conference officer (PSA, 2007).

Specialist Groups

These remained of central importance to the work of the PSA, both in terms of providing the spine of panels at the annual conference and in terms of their activities between conferences. In 2009, the PSA had over 40 specialist groups, of which fifteen dealt with the politics of particular countries or regions of the world; eleven were concerned with political theory or thought; and thirteen were thematic in the sense that they dealt with particular areas of the discipline such as executive or legislative politics or particular intellectual approaches such as interpretive political science. Two groups were more generic in character: the Women's group and the

Teaching and Learning group. The PSA increased by six times the amount it spent on supporting the work of its specialist groups between 2000 and 2006, a total of nearly £28,000 in 2008.

Over time new groups appear and older ones go out of existence as the impetus behind them diminishes. An example of a successful new group formed in this period is the Media and Politics group established in 1999, whose range of interest extends to new information technologies. This group has a strong interdisciplinary character with members coming from a variety of backgrounds including politics, sociology, communications and media, history and management. It has also promoted involvement with practitioners in the media. As an example of its activities, it held a two-day conference in 2008 on media, security and religion which included paper givers from Russia and Switzerland and a keynote address by a journalist from *The Observer*.

New specialist groups have to be approved by the EC, but the process is made as straightforward as possible to encourage their formation. Keeping track of the groups and their activities can be a time-consuming task. There has been some controversy about whether specialist group members should also be PSA members, but that would be difficult to enforce and the current view is that this should only apply to convenors. In 2009 the PSA developed a code of conduct for specialist groups which should help to ensure that they meet some basic standards in their work.

The Importance of Research Income: Relations with the ESRC

Research income became of even more importance during this period. It was used as one measure of research activity and success in the RAE. The shift to full economic costing (FEC) from September 2005 also increased the pressure to obtain research grants as from that point onwards universities recouped a considerable sum of money from them to contribute towards their infrastructure costs. Yet, as in earlier periods, there was evidence that the discipline was not being as successful as it ought to be in obtaining research funds and this placed a strain on the relationship with the ESRC, although the fault often did not rest with the Research Council but with political scientists themselves.

The underlying problems were discussed at a meeting of the EC in September 1996. It was reported 'that the ESRC Responsive Mode competition produced a very low number of applications for Politics (58), in contrast to the figures for Sociology and Psychology, which were approximately 120 for each subject'. Political scientists had not recognised the importance of the ESRC's thematic priorities. 'The PSA's problem was that political science appeared to the ESRC to be twenty years behind; that it was not listening to the new reality; it was not responding; and that colleagues were not thinking about what they wanted from a centrally-funded agency'. Ian Forbes said 'that the PSA had to ask why political scientists were not punching their weight in the ESRC competition'. Michael Moran noted that 'Politics was particularly under-represented in the small grants competition'. As far as research grants for postgraduates were concerned, 'the politics outcome was way below average for giving awards to alpha-rated students. Politics applications had a success rate of 42 per cent; Economics, 92 per cent; Business Studies, 100 per cent; Sociology, 60 per cent. This result caused great anger among colleagues and contributed to negative reactions to the ESRC' (PSA, 1996b).

New liaison arrangements were set up with the ESRC and these improved communications with the PSA. In 1998 the EC noted the successful bids for ESRC funds for new programmes by Ed Page and Paul Whiteley. It was felt that securing these programmes was 'of direct relevance to political scientists, reflecting the greater effectiveness of the PSA in its interaction with the ESRC and that the Politics Liaison Group is also working effectively' (PSA, 1998b). When the author was chair of the PSA, Ian Diamond, as chief executive of the ESRC, maintained a regular dialogue with the Association, including face-to-face meetings and a presentation at the heads of department conference, and was willing to listen and respond to the views expressed.

For all the importance of Research Council funding, research money received from the funding councils remained of greater importance. Following the 2001 RAE, funding arrangements were changed in a way that substantially cut funds for departments with a 4 rating and eliminated them altogether for those with a lower rating. The PSA arranged for a delegation to meet the then higher education minister, Alan Johnson. In a paper sent in advance they pointed out:

> Departments made fine judgements about the inclusion of staff in order to maximise their chances of achieving the desired grade . . . There is ample evidence to support the concern that the removal of funding from Departments related below 5 will damage not only the quality of academic research, but also the ability of some researchers to produce policy relevant research.

The delegation found that 'The Minister was receptive to our arguments and it was apparent that we were alerting him to some difficulties of which he was previously unaware' (PSA, 2003b). Although this meeting did not lead to any specific changes in policy, it was symptomatic of a more systematic PSA engagement with higher education policy and policy makers.

Internal Organisation and the Role of the Chair

As the work of the PSA expanded in range and depth, the structure of the organisation became a more important topic in ensuring that the Association was effective both in serving the discipline and promoting it externally. In particular, additional demands were placed on the chair of the PSA as its most visible public representative. The position of the chair was somewhat anomalous as the constitution only referred to a chair of meetings of the EC which was just one of the roles that the chair carried out. The chair was elected from the EC for a three-year period, but in practice a chair often had to be recruited from outside the EC which is what happened in the cases of Rhodes (1999) and Grant (2002). In both these cases, a rather convoluted procedure was followed: 'the "problem" of what to do was first discussed informally among what might be called "senior" committee members and possible external candidates were then sounded out – again informally. Some sort of more formal discussion then took place as part of EC business and eventually there was majority agreement that a particular colleague would be suitable' (PSA, 2004c). The selected individual then had to seek election and, if successful, was appointed at the EC meeting following the elections. It was admitted that 'The actual sequence of events may be a little more messy than described' (PSA, 2004c). The author's recollection is that he had heard a rumour that he was being considered, but thought nothing more of it until he arrived at the conference at Aberdeen, was taken aside and ushered into a buffet lunch of the EC and introduced as the new chair.

There were some clear difficulties with this procedure which were reviewed in a report by a working party. It was noted that 'Initial informal discussions look suspiciously like an elite trying to organise the succession. To put it positively, it is more a case of "senior members" trying to ensure an appropriate new Chair but, even so, the informality – and even secrecy – involved could look like plotting'. There was also no mechanism whereby existing members of the EC could express an interest in the position, other than informally, so that existing members might feel they had been overlooked. 'It is always possible that the person who is effectively the EC's nomination could be defeated in an election and the executive would then be placed in an extremely embarrassing and difficult position' (PSA, 2004c).

The working party considered what some of the key skills and requirements for a chair might be and listed the following:

- 'is a senior and eminent figure who is respected across the discipline;
- can provide effective leadership to the Association;
- can ably represent the Association nationally and internationally;
- is administratively and socially competent;
- can work effectively with the EC'.

There are, of course, some potential contradictions in these requirements. While the post requires someone who can exercise leadership, this has to be leadership of a particular kind. There are often tensions within the discipline, reflected in the EC, about the direction it should be taking. The role is not suitable for a large ego determined to push their personal agenda. The chair needs to have a strategic vision for the development of the PSA, but also needs to be a team player who is sensitive to different points of view and can use these to build a consensus that represents more than a 'lowest common denominator' position but allows both the PSA and the discipline to develop and take advantage of new opportunities.

The working party rejected the idea of a directly elected chair, commenting that 'it remains the case that Executive members have to work under the Chair. They have a clearer idea of what is involved and someone directly elected might not be suitable' (PSA, 2004c). They recommended 'regularising the status quo' with a search committee reporting to the EC with a nomination. It was this system that led to the appointment of Jon Tonge (2005), who was already a member of the EC. However, if the new chair is not a member of the EC, one consequence of the 2005 review is that they can be co-opted and appointed to the committee. This is what happened in the case of Vicky Randall (2008) who was not an EC member although she had been secretary of the PSA in the past.

Chairs of the association have their own particular style and set of priorities. Ian Forbes recalled:

> When I became chair I wanted to replicate some of the achievements and working practices of the APSA. The key things were that they were professional in their approach, supplied a diverse set of services, and worked hard to defend the profession. The big difference was their huge resources. My big thing was to professionalise the Association, and we did get the reputation for being very well run, and punching above our weight (Personal communication, 14 September 2009).

In his final report to the EC, Ian Forbes sounded a note of caution: 'The range of activities needs to be analysed carefully, in order to avoid creating expectations that are unreasonable, to guard against over-reaching ourselves and thereby getting a reputation for not delivering the goods, particularly in terms of policy-influence. We cannot do everything and maybe we should do more to allow other organisations to take the lead on some issues' (PSA, 1999c). One of these other organisations was the Association of Learned Societies in the Social Sciences (ALSISS) of which Ian Forbes was the last chair. In 1999 it was replaced by the Academy of the Social Sciences of which Forbes became the first chair.

When Rod Rhodes was asked to stand as chair in 1999, he recounted: 'I was told by the Executive Committee that it did not want someone to run the organisation but a chair who would work with and through members of the EC' (PSA, 1999d). He subsequently stated that 'he wished to be a "hands off" rather than a "hands on" chair as there were multiple talents around the table to carry out the PSA's activities' (PSA, 1999e). The task becomes something like that of a conductor: ensuring that all the talents and skills are harnessed to produce a harmonious whole which also progresses the work in hand.

When I became chair in 2002, it was evident that Rod Rhodes had established a strong momentum in the PSA and what was important was to maintain that and carry it forward. I therefore set myself four specific objectives which I pursued with mixed success. The first of these was 'Continuing to build on the support we offer postgraduates and assisting new entrants to the profession. The survey of the profession indicated that this area was of concern to PSA members'. While I think that the support to postgraduates did continue, I am not sure that we developed it significantly and it may be that I should have placed more emphasis on dialogue with the postgraduate network. The second objective was more international links for the Association. We did develop an effective working relationship with APSA, and started to raise the PSA's profile at its conference, but our relations with IPSA fell into disrepair through a series of accidents and were only restored when I stood down as chair and joined the IPSA executive. Since then work led by Terrell Carver has enabled the PSA successfully to develop bilateral relationships with associations around the world, in Asia and, most recently, in Latin America. The third objective was to encourage the study of politics in secondary schools and colleges, and although I gave a number of talks there myself, I was not successful in setting up a Web-accessible list of PSA members willing to undertake this work. The fourth objective was 'Helping departments meet the challenge of national standards' (PSA, 2002). We did establish a very effective working relationship with BISA in terms of nominations to the RAE panel and also with Tony Payne, the chair of the sub-panel, who had been a joint nominee of the two associations.

As noted earlier, one of the consequences of the Chester strategy review was the establishment of a system of sub-committees which formed part of the agenda for a two-day EC meeting. Reviewing the first three years of operation of this system, Ian Forbes noted: 'The subcommittees have been reasonably successful, although the system has come under pressure from the increasing demands on the time of the Executive members' (PSA, 1999c). Rod Rhodes began 'the process of reviving the sub-committees' (PSA, 1999d). However, he also made an important innovation in the form of a management committee of the chair, treasurer and secretary (later joined by the company secretary) to run the business of the PSA between its quarterly meetings which left too long a gap when decisions sometimes needed to be taken quickly. When I became chair, I used the Management group to review the sub-committee structure and they 'came up with a fairly radical set of proposals with the aim of aligning committees more closely with the Association's priorities to some aspects of our work, e.g., the creation of a Grants and Awards committee' (PSA, 2002). This process of regular review was continued by the new chair, Jon Tonge, who created a Research sub-committee.

The author as chair also established a comprehensive set of terms of reference for the work of the Management group. Its three main tasks were defined as:

(1) to progress and implement the policies of the Association between meetings of the Executive Committee and sub-committees;
(2) to ensure that decisions taken by the Executive Committee are put into effect promptly; and
(3) to prepare agenda items for the next meeting of the Executive Committee.

It was also empowered to undertake strategic reviews of the PSA's work; to oversee the operation of the national office; to make recommendations on the structure and membership of sub-committees; to handle requests for nominations to other bodies; and to ensure that the charitable objectives of the PSA were being properly pursued (PSA, 2003c). It was very much a strategy committee with a steering function in relation to the EC, but it had to take full account of the views of the EC and the membership of the Association as expressed through a series of membership surveys.

Conclusions

The increasing membership of the PSA is one indicator both of the strength of the Association in terms of undertaking the mix of activities that members think is appropriate and also of the growth of the discipline itself. There was a nearly 50 per cent increase in total members from 1,105 at the end of 2000 to 1,645 at the end of 2005. Membership continued to grow, but more steadily, to a total of 1,750 at the end of 2008. The strongest growth in percentage terms between 2000 and 2008 has been in the core category of full members in the UK and Europe whose numbers increased from 705 to 1,262 or by 79 per cent.

The contemporary PSA bears no resemblance to the elitist, club-like organisation of the 1950s. It is a modern, sophisticated organisation employing professional staff and providing a range of services to members. It has a thriving set of journals which underpin its financial model. Some of the deficiencies of the annual conference as a quality academic event have been tackled and its specialist groups are flourishing. There has been much more engagement with higher education policy and the development of more systematic relationships with practitioners. The annual awards ceremony has helped here, but there are other signs of progress. For example, the Association compiled a response to the Green Paper on Governance and Professor Jon Tonge, the chair of the Association, was appointed by the prime minister to chair the Youth Citizenship Commission. As befits the second largest professional body for political scientists in the world, reciprocal relationships have been developed with sister associations across the globe, with help given to delegates from countries such as Thailand to attend the annual conference. The PSA is a lead player in the new Confederation of European Political Studies Associations and enjoys a close relationship with APSA and IPSA. It is in good shape to face the challenge of what is likely to be a more difficult period for higher education in Britain.

Chapter 8

Women and Diversity in British Political Science

In 1961 members of the PSA were invited to a dinner with members of the Iron and Steel Board at the Reform Club. Margherita Rendel, subsequently a founder member of the PSA Women's group, was refused entry as at that time the Reform Club did not admit women. In a letter to the PSA secretary she explained:

> When I arrived for dinner, Mr Leslie stopped me on the steps and told me that I may not enter; apparently no women may be admitted. I think you may imagine my embarrassment at this public humiliation. I had to wait on the steps while it was decided that Mr Aylard [the press secretary of the Iron and Steel Board] should take me for dinner elsewhere. It was a pleasant dinner and Mr Leslie has since written to apologise to me, but, as you will appreciate, this does not compensate for being excluded from part of the programme (LSE, 1961a, PSA/3).

John Day, the secretary of the PSA, wrote back in apology, stating that he would scrutinise arrangements in future 'in order to avoid unpleasantness to any member . . . I must confess that it never occurred to me that you would be excluded from the Reform Club, although I have heard such clubs were masculine institutions' (LSE, 1961b, PSA/3).

Such examples of blatant sexism have largely disappeared (the Reform Club admits women as members), but political science in the UK 'is still a conspicuously male and white discipline – with women and ethnic minorities continuing to face that "glass ceiling" which, in so many professions, divides the junior from the senior ranks' (Harrison and Saez, 2009, p. 351). Thus, a number of outstanding challenges remain in relation to the role of women in British political science as well as other diversity issues relating to ethnic minorities and those with disabilities. It is perhaps a reflection of the prevalent conventionality of British political science that the PSA has no equivalent of APSA's Lesbian, Gay, Bisexual Political Science caucus which had over 200 members in 2009 or the organisation's Committee on the Status of Lesbians, Gays, Bisexuals and Transgendered in the Profession.

The benchmarking review of UK politics and international studies found that 'Research capacity in UK Politics and IS is most seriously diminished by the "missing" women and ethnic minorities'. It drew an unfavourable comparison with other disciplines in the social sciences:

> In terms of the number of women on staff, Politics and International Relations compares unfavourably to other social science disciplines in the UK . . . Sociology, Social Work, Social Policy/Administration and Anthropology have a larger proportion of women on staff than Politics and IS. Even Business/Management Studies and Accountancy have more. Among the core social science disciplines, only Economics has less – and then by two percentage points – than Politics and IS. While there are increasing numbers of women in the lower ranks, there are still way too few women in senior ranks (ESRC, 2007, p. 20).

In the early days of the discipline, the women's colleges at Oxford provided one source of employment for women political scientists, while there were a few at the LSE and Manchester. The percentage of women in the membership of the PSA declined from 7.3 per cent in 1953 to 5.2 per cent in 1959 and 5.6 per cent in 1963. As the number of politics academics grew slowly, the number of women did not increase as those employed in Oxford colleges remained steady and there was actually a slight decline at Manchester. Early women recruits, however, were often the product of very specific circumstances that assisted their career development and, even then, they did not necessarily remain in the study of politics (see Box 8.1).

Susan Saunders was the first woman to serve on the PSA committee from 1974 to 1975 and she was followed by Dilys Hill, who 'never found the PSA committee etc. anything other than straightforward or collegial'. There were few women in the wider profession and:

> I certainly know that some women within the profession felt they had been harassed, and many felt, myself included, that paths to promotion were slower. I also think that some women, again myself included, came across what might be called 'patronising' attitudes, solicitous and no doubt well-meaning, but irritating, and a feeling that you might not be taken as seriously as you should be (Personal communication, 11 May 2009).

The PSA Women's group was established at the 1977 annual conference. Among those involved in its formation were Margherita Rendel, Judith Evans, Joni Lovenduski, Annie Phizacklea, Vicky Randall and Jean Woodall. Among its objectives were 'to improve the opportunities and status of women in political science', 'to combat sexism in course content' and 'to generate discussion about the masculine assumptions of the discipline'. 'Sympathetic males' were welcome to attend (LSE, 1978i, PSA/17). Four meetings were held in London in 1977–78 to exchange information and provide a forum in which women could present papers. Jean Woodall, who eventually became Dean at Westminster Business School, recalls: 'Dragging ourselves up to London on a Saturday to discuss research, I recall we

Box 8.1:   Lucy Mair, 1901–86

Lucy Mair is of interest because she illustrates the favourable circumstances that allowed a woman to construct a career before the Second World War and because she switched from the study of international relations to another discipline. Mair was born into an upper-middle-class family and her mother, who was secretary of the LSE, made a second marriage to the school's then director, William Beveridge. Kuper (2005) portrays her as a rebel against her class and poses the question whether she was an insider because of her social class background or an outsider because she was a woman in the academic world of the 1930s and 1940s. Mair took a degree in classics at Cambridge and in 1927 she was appointed to a lectureship in international relations at the LSE: there is no record of any discussion of conflict of interest issues. Her task was to teach the training courses for colonial administrators and her particular research interest was the mandated territories in Africa. Her colleague Audrey Richards took the view that 'no one could understand Africa unless they understood anthropology' (Davis, 2009, p. 1). Her research then took an anthropological direction, although she worked in Chatham House during the war. She became a professor at the LSE in 1963. She continued to be interested in technical problems of colonial administration and published a book on *Primitive Government*. At the LSE she tried, without success, 'to turn applied anthropology into development studies' (Kuper, 2005, p. 55). Her move away from international relations was in part a consequence of serendipity and particular influences at the time, but it is worth noting that social anthropology continues to have a higher proportion of women academics than political science (ESRC, 2007, p. 20).

usually ended up in a small restaurant before everybody dashed back home to partners and families'.

She remembers: 'I recall a mixture of influences that propelled me into activism! I was a typical "second wave feminist", carried the usual insecurities about not being taken seriously by my immediate male colleagues, found my first PSA conference experience an unwelcoming experience, and I guess just wanted to get noticed and accepted!' Woodall did not specialise in gender politics, but found mainstream political science disappointing in its content: 'It was tiresome to read sweeping (and oh so frequently patronising) generalisations about women's political behaviour (both electoral and civic) in the scholarly texts and articles, and depressing to encounter the lack of curiosity around gender studies. So it was time for action!'

'Friendly male members of the PSA Executive' gained recognition for the group. What Woodall 'got out of it was a boost in confidence, as I slowly got drawn into organising our seminars and conferences and later became a member of the PSA Executive . . . I think the PSA Women's Group made a significant change to the wider PSA, and provided the basis on which a number of Women's Group members developed very distinguished careers – particularly Joni [Lovenduski], Vicky [Randall], Pippa [Norris], Elizabeth [McLeay] and Sue [Richards]' (Personal communication, 22 May 2009).

Joni Lovenduski was unsuccessful in securing election to the EC in 1977, but was elected in 1978, along with Vicky Randall as secretary, a post she held until 1981 when Jean Woodall succeeded her. She was an energetic individual with an American background who was well versed in the feminist views and literature that had developed there. Lovenduski took responsibility for the newsletter and the heads of department conference as well as working on the study of women in the profession, and her contribution was reflected in the fact that she came second in the EC poll in 1980 (the then chair came top) and again in 1981, although one woman candidate was defeated in 1980 by one vote. Lovenduski recalls that she and Vicky Randall were 'made very welcome' on the EC and Hugh Berrington, the then chair, 'wrote two years later to say that you have "proved yourself" ' (Interview with Joni Lovenduski, 12 May 2009).

Two motions relating to the status of women in the profession were passed at the PSA annual general meeting in 1978. The first, proposed by Jean Woodall and seconded by Vicky Randall, stated: 'This AGM declares its support for equal opportunities for women, and therefore calls for an inquiry into the status of women in the study and teaching of politics'. The second, proposed by Peter Willetts, an active supporter of the Women's group, and seconded by Sue Richards, called 'for the provision of crèche facilities at future conferences and the avoidance of conference locations where this facility is not available' (LSE, 1978j, PSA/17).

The issue of crèche facilities preoccupied the EC in subsequent years. In 1979 it was found that they were not required, nor was any provision made in 1980. In relation to that conference, it was reported that a woman participant in a panel who was not attached to any funding institution:

> would need to bring her young baby with her to the Conference and, in the absence of adequate child care facilities at the Conference would also be obliged to bring a nurse to look after the baby. It was agreed . . . the PSA should pay the nurse's board but that would in no way constitute a precedent. It was suggested that the PSA's Women's Group might pay the nurse's travel cost (LSE, 1980d, PSA/18).

In the event both baby and nurse were ill and the facility was not used.

Women in British Political Studies

The 1978 resolution was implemented through a series of studies carried out by Joni Lovenduski (Lovenduski, 1981). This involved a three-stage study between May 1978 and June 1980. First, there was a population study which sought to identify and locate political studies staff in the UK. Second, a postal survey was administered to all women and a control group of men employed in British universities, polytechnics and other higher education institutions. Third, a further postal survey was administered to the full-time higher education employees who had responded to the first postal survey. 'The questionnaire was designed to probe possible causes of the different research and publication performances and population prospects of men and women which had been striking findings of [the first postal survey]' (Lovenduski, 1981, p. 3). 'The objectives of the project were to test hypotheses that self-selection, domestic burdens and discrimination were factors accounting for the apparent low achievement of women in Political Science in the UK' (LSE, 1978k, PSA/17).

Women were found to comprise only 11 per cent of the political science profession in the UK. This overall figure needs to be qualified in so far as 'The Population Study located a higher proportion of women in polytechnic posts than in university posts in political studies (14 per cent and 9 per cent respectively)' (Lovenduski, 1981, p. 9). This contrasted with between 27 and 29 per cent of women in full-time university first degree courses that involved a major political studies component (31 per cent in polytechnics). The figures for universities rose to 38 per cent if one took into account those studying politics as a subsidiary component of their degree (Lovenduski, 1981, p. 3).

Less than a third of undergraduate students were women. Lovenduski commented:

> The peculiar nature of the study of politics is problematic here. The fact that it is a subject not normally taught in schools and often only chosen after the first year of a degree course undoubtedly distorts recruitment for both men and women and may explain why it is one of the two smallest social sciences when measured by student numbers (LSE, 1978j, PSA/17).

Having carried out the survey, Lovenduski observed:

> It is possible that Political Studies presents special problems for women, simply because of the nature of the subject with its strong orientation (particularly in the UK) toward 'elite' politics and its exclusive preoccupation with Public Power. Political Science looks very much like a male subject, concerned with the study of men rather than of persons. More than one critic has commented that references to 'Political Man' mean exactly that. It may be a perception of this on the part of both sexes which accounts for the fact that women are less well represented in Political Studies than they are in the other Social Sciences (LSE, 1981d, PSA/18).

Because of this under-recruitment of women into first degrees, the Women's group in its early years undertook a considerable amount of outreach work in schools, drawing attention to the role of women in politics and why women should study the subject. Women MPs were invited to talk at sixth form conferences (Interview with Joni Lovenduski, 12 May 2009).

The overall findings of the surveys were summarised by Lovenduski in a paper prepared for the PSA Executive:

> The low presence of women in employment as political scientists and a fall off in women's performance after first degree level are two of the most dramatic findings of the project. In addition, a pattern of disadvantage involving higher teaching loads, lower publication success, lower publication rates, lower earnings, lower levels of self-confidence, lower chances of promotion and a possible frustration arising from a contradiction between high valuations of and relatively poor performance for women already employed (compared to men) indicate that women are not fulfilling the potential suggested by their first degree performance (LSE, 1980j, PSA/18).

When women graduated from their first degree, they 'simply do not obtain proportionately as many firsts as men either in politics or in other subjects' (Lovenduski, 1981, p. 6). Women were then less likely to go on to postgraduate study, even though they obtained a first or upper second, in proportion to their presence on undergraduate politics courses. 'Overall women are at least 26 per cent of political studies "qualifiers" but comprise only 17 per cent of those obtaining higher degrees and 13 per cent of those obtaining doctorates in political science' (Lovenduski, 1981, p. 7). Thus, what the evidence suggested was 'that there exists a progressive fall-off in the proportion of women students of political studies as each identifiable stage in the hierarchy is passed' (Lovenduski, 1981, p. 9).

Lovenduski used a weighting system to provide a quantitative count of publications with, for example, sixteen points for a book and four for a journal article. Men's scores were well over twice those of women, although there were significant differences between universities and polytechnics. When scores were weighted for length of service, the difference between the sexes reduced, but remained substantial in universities, while in polytechnics they disappeared, in part because at least half of each sex had virtually no publications. There were no significant differences between publication scores for women and men who did or did not have children; nor did whether a respondent was single, cohabiting or married make any difference. Lovenduski concluded (1981, p. 20): 'The family or domestic circumstances of political studies academics do not appear to have an effect on the publication output of either sex. There is no evidence that those women who eschew marriage and children in order to pursue their careers are more successful in terms of publications despite attitudes to the contrary'.

Explanations of disadvantage

Lovenduski notes that 'Whilst the questionnaire turned up evidence of a small number of cases of discrimination against women there was no systematic evidence of direct discrimination against women' (LSE, 1980j, PSA/18). Also, '19.5 per cent of men and 37.93 per cent of women felt that their career had been adversely affected by discrimination on the basis of sex or marital status and 33.8 per cent of men and 32 per cent of women felt they had been discriminated against on other grounds, the most common of which were class or political beliefs' (LSE, 1980j, PSA/18). 'The possibility of indirect discrimination has proved more difficult to dismiss however and the data provide no reason to believe that Academic Institutions have escaped the absorption of sexist attitudes' (LSE, 1980j, PSA/18). In comparison to 'other careers, the Academic profession is particularly open to the possibility of capricious treatment of its members of either sex' (LSE, 1981d, PSA/18). Lovenduski referred here in particular to the absence of rules of procedure, codes of conduct and standardised criteria for the assessment of an individual's work. 'These features of the profession simultaneously facilitate the task of anyone who would like to actively discriminate purely on the grounds of sex and make it more difficult for those discriminated against both to perceive and prove such discrimination' (LSE, 1981d, PSA/18). Arguably, adherence to procedural norms has improved since the 1970s, although the existence of formal channels of complaint does not mean that they will necessarily be used by women for a variety of reasons or that when they are the process is free of personal costs.

What Lovenduski did find is that 'Women consistently carried higher teaching loads than men and their teaching apparently involved more hours of preparation. A possible explanation for this might be a greater "spread" in the subjects which women were required to teach – something which many women complained of' (LSE, 1980d, PSA/18). There was 'also evidence that women undertake their research under less favourable conditions than men. Sixty-five per cent of the women but only 50 per cent of the men have never held a research grant (excepting post-graduate awards)' (Lovenduski, 1981, pp. 24–5). Even more striking, '72 per cent of university women but only 30 per cent of university men have never had a sabbatical' (Lovenduski, 1981, p. 25).

While the study revealed that a complex mix of factors was holding back the progress of women in the discipline, what does emerge is the importance of the attitudes of both men and women. The argument was sometimes heard that women did not get jobs because they did not apply, but they seemed to have been adversely affected by deficient mentoring and the absence of the kind of informal encouragement that is so important in an academic career, particularly when setbacks are encountered, as they are invariably are. Lovenduski referred to the 'phenomenon of a failure to encourage capable women to seek academic careers with its implied attendant lack of access to the patronage which often characterises successful academic careers' (LSE, 1981d, PSA/18). 'Moreover, most departments employ one or possibly two women at the most and many of these women feel isolated and that they receive little support or understanding from their male colleagues' (Lovenduski, 1981, p. 33). That is why informal mutual support networks for women like that provided by the PSA Women's group were so important and helped to lay the foundation for successful careers. Elizabeth Meehan recalls:

Joni [Lovenduski] and the others started to organize a kind of specialist group conference on gender issues and politics. Indeed, I got my first 'break' by being asked by them to present a paper from my thesis on anti-discrimination politics in Britain and the US. This was intended to give space, not only for neglected topics, but also for young women to develop the skills and confidence to offer papers to the Annual Conference (Meehan, 2009).

Lovenduski concluded that 'The findings of the two surveys are in keeping with those of quite a large body of independent social psychology research which demonstrates women's greater tendency to undervalue themselves, women's lower levels of self-confidence and lower self-assertiveness in comparison to men'. Women were only half as likely as men to continue their academic training after first degree level and 'The reasons for a fall-off in women's performance after first degree level appear to be mainly located in the attitudes of both the men and the women employed in the political studies profession, and are particularly identifiable in women's diffidence about their own performance' (Lovenduski, 1981, p. 32).

Follow-up action

In 1981 Joni Lovenduski made four specific proposals to the EC outlining actions the PSA should take:

(1) 'Establish a prize designed to encourage more women to publish, either for the best article by a woman or the best women's studies article.
(2) Make special efforts to place women in positions of responsibility, for instance on editorial boards and working committees.
(3) Promote inclusion of material on sex-roles and politics, and non-sexist materials in politics courses.
(4) Include proposals for equal opportunity policies in reply to all requests for evidence and information from outside bodies, wherever relevant and possible' (LSE, 1981d, PSA/18).

The view taken by the EC was that the award of a prize should form part of a broader PSA prize strategy. In relation to the second recommendation, the EC approved a resolution that 'This Executive Committee urges political studies departments to give women positions of responsibility wherever appropriate'. This was rather vaguely worded as a position of responsibility could involve an onerous and academically unrewarding administrative task. Moreover, the PSA had little or no influence over the decisions taken by departments. It was also suggested that at the next heads of department conference 'a session could be devoted to the inclusion of material on women and the avoidance of sexism in politics courses' (LSE, 1981e, PSA/18).

One of the concerns that Lovenduski had expressed in her preliminary report was that the proportion of women higher degree graduates obtaining university political studies posts peaked in 1970–72. While the same trend was evident after 1972, they experienced a less marked decline after 1972. 'This suggests that women were able to exploit some of the opportunities offered by a period of expansion of

Political Studies, but were not able to maintain this once an employers' market reasserted itself' (LSE, 1981d, PSA/18). The cold climate that political science was experiencing for much of the 1980s was not a propitious one for the PSA to exercise leadership on the role of women in the profession. The 1987 survey of the profession found that, compared with their position in the discipline as a whole, a relatively high proportion of those who left were women (Berrington and Norris, 1988).

Geraint Parry was chair of the PSA in the early 1980s and recalls:

> A development which should be mentioned in this period was the growing involvement of women in the PSA. Feminism is certainly one of the most important intellectual and organisational movements during my professional life. At PSA elections a women's group had been putting up notices with questions for candidates on their views about such policies as positive discrimination through quota places on committees etc. (Parry, 2009).

One of the issues that had arisen out of the first postal survey 'concerned "blind" readership of articles submitted to journals. Research in the US indicated that blind readership did help women, but some British journals, such as *British Journal of Political Science*, preferred to inform reviewers of the identity of the author' (LSE, 1979h, PSA/18). The author was a member of the editorial team that took over responsibility for *Political Studies* with Jack Lively as editor in 1982 and one of the team's first actions was to seek a meeting with the Women's group at the annual conference to discuss procedures for refereeing articles. That meetings of this kind were sought illustrates how far the Women's group had become an integral part of the work of the PSA.

The Impact of Feminism on British Political Science

Feminist critiques raise fundamental questions about what we define as political, how we study these phenomena and the very boundaries of the discipline of political science itself. Feminism has certainly had an intellectual impact on political science, yet it has not been as transformative as many had hoped. Part of the explanation is the existence of a variety of feminist perspectives with different priorities and methodologies (Randall, 1991). There are also some aspects of political science and its professional organisation that remain very masculine. Randall notes (2002, p. 109): '[Feminism] has had, and still has, a great deal to say to political science, although it is not always apparent that mainstream political science is listening'. In her view, 'Political science, unlike sociology, say, or history, remains remarkably undented by the feminist perspective. Not only does political science remain a very "male-dominated" profession. But in addition to core subject matter, the world of "high politics" remains stubbornly masculine' (Randall, 2002, p. 129). This is not to say that there has been no impact. As Fiona Mackay points out (2004, p. 100), 'As a result, feminist political science has successfully reframed "private" issues such as domestic violence, reproductive rights and the sexual division of labour as public issues worthy of academic scrutiny'. More generally, 'it has broadened the scope of political studies to include unconventional politics such as grass-roots activism and social movements, micro politics and practices relating to the politics of difference and identity'.

Feminist political science has been 'much more modest and cautious' than feminism 'in its ambitions and prescriptions' (Mackay, 2004, p. 99). It has raised fundamental questions about what is public and what is private, but those traditional boundaries have been challenged in other ways in conventional political science through debates about the changing role of the state. Moreover, 'feminist political science never abandoned its interest in the political, conventionally defined' (Mackay, 2004, p. 100). As Randall points out (1991, pp. 530–1), 'Feminism's critique of the research methods, related methodology and underpinning conceptual assumptions of political science does not threaten (to borrow Engel's phrase), the "world historical defeat" of the discipline as we know it'. Political science in Britain in particular is a pluralist and eclectic target, and is more so in the United States (Harrison and Saez, 2009, p. 346). 'Political science is not sufficiently monolithic, either as a body of "knowledge" or in its identification with a rigorously "scientific" knowledge to come tumbling down after one well-aimed blow' (Randall, 1991, p. 531). The response of British political science to new approaches is to absorb them and, if they are sufficiently robust, to accord them sub-disciplinary status.

Where perhaps feminist perspectives might be seen to pose a particular challenge is in terms of the identity of the discipline itself. Randall asks (2002, p. 119):

> If, as the feminist critique implies, political science needs to take a much broader view of its subject matter, what does this mean for the relationship between political science and other disciplines? The boundary between political science and sociology appears particularly arbitrary: much of what sociology deals with – family relationships, sexual behaviour, welfare functions – looks pretty political to a feminist.

Randall then asks whether political science should expand to embrace these social questions, should one advocate the interdisciplinary approach associated with women's studies (generally not the preferred route) or 'is the problem more fundamentally the way traditional disciplines have been constructed around male understandings' (Randall, 2002, p. 119)? This is an important question to ask, but issues about disciplinary boundaries always carry with them an element of risk, particularly in a discipline like politics that has been afflicted by doubts about its own identity.

Randall distinguishes three stages in the application of feminism to political science. 'The first stage was mounting a critique of male political science for its virtual exclusion of women as political actors' (Randall, 2002, p. 113). It was this stage in the 1970s which required women to organise within the PSA to change the dominant assumptions of a world in which 'political scientists were almost all men and the spheres of public politics they studied were likewise overwhelmingly male' (Randall, 2002, p. 113). The second stage 'entailed a much more systematic investigation into the extent of women's under-representation and its institutional and non-institutional causes' (Randall, 2002, p. 114). This involved gathering data much as one might do in any branch of political science, although the data would be interrogated in new ways. The third stage raises more fundamental questions about the discipline: 'about limitations of the characteristic methodologies employed in political science, about the way that politics is conceptualised; and about the "gendered" character of political institutions and processes' (Randall, 2002, p. 114).

For all the theoretical, conceptual and empirical work that has been undertaken, 'We are at a relatively early stage of carrying out systematic research in the UK on gender and political institutions' (Mackay, 2004, p. 112). 'The field is not as well developed as in the US and Scandinavia' (Mackay, 2004, p. 113), although that partly reflects slow progress in the political sphere. Since 1997 more women have been involved in political institutions but solutions to under-representation like 'women only' shortlists for parliamentary candidatures remain contested.

What has happened is that a sub-discipline has been established, which is not a trivial outcome in a discipline where 'More than elsewhere perhaps, the primary attachments of scholars of Politics and IS in the UK are to sub-disciplines rather than some larger, overarching discipline' (ESRC, 2007, p. 11). As Mackay puts it (2004, p. 113), 'there is a coherent sub-field developing which consists of a contextualised examination of women in conventional politics'. The PSA Women and Politics specialist group 'is the second most active in the PSA with a membership of approximately 60 and its Annual Conference routinely attracts more than 40 women, including overseas visitors' (Childs and Krook, 2006, p. 18). Among the other groups it works closely with is one of the largest specialist groups, EPOP. The substantive political representation of women has been an important field of activity which has produced high-quality work, although, of course, being a woman political scientist does not mean that one works on topics that are deemed in some way to be particularly relevant to women; one could equally well be an expert on international security. Sarah Childs commented: 'My perception is that there's still very much a shared sense that gender and political research is somewhat marginalised in the discipline and there are concerns amongst women regarding the promotion of senior women within the profession'. However, she also noted: 'Individuals have received support from particular male academics over the years; and institutional support from, for example, PSA specialist groups' (Personal communication, 21 September 2009).

Women in the Contemporary PSA

In 1993 Elizabeth Meehan became the first woman to chair the PSA. Michael Goldsmith recalled: 'It took some effort to persuade colleagues to have a female chair after me – but they did finally accept Liz Meehan. It's taken over 15 years to get a woman in the same job!' (Goldsmith, 2009) Elizabeth Meehan herself saw this as part of a process of modernisation within the PSA, 'coming to realise that women were half the human race' (Meehan, 2009). Over the period since 1993, four presidents of APSA have been women, one of them (Dianne Pinderhughes) an African-American.

When one looks at the description provided by Sarah Childs of her work as convenor of the Women and Politics group in the middle of the first decade of the twenty-first century, some of the challenges, such as raising the profile of work by women and ensuring that they did not find the conference intimidating, seem remarkably similar to those faced by the pioneers of the 1970s:

> Mainstreaming gender and politics research by co-hosting panels at PSA, e.g., with EPOP and legislative studies specialist groups; mainstreaming at EPOP annual conference by co-hosting panels there; adding drinks or tea and cakes receptions at PSA annual conference for members and to pick up members/women who might have felt the Conference rather intimidating (Personal communication, 10 April 2009).

Around three-quarters of politics and international studies staff are male and they are overwhelmingly white. The ESRC benchmarking survey commented: 'We know perfectly well why that happens, at least as regards women. Women take a series of temporary positions initially, which require more teaching than research . . . Women who choose to have children will likely do so at a time in their lives that corresponds to the early stage of their careers' (ESRC, 2007, p. 21). Universities have relaxed their geographical residence requirements, which were often not that strictly enforced anyway, and improved communications means that it is possible for partners to work at two different universities, particularly if they can find a convenient mid-point location. Modern technology means that preparation and research work can often be done from home, although some universities are responding to student demands by requiring a greater physical presence by staff. Nevertheless, the strains arising from physical separation of a couple can be considerable and life becomes more complicated if there are children (Grant and Sherrington, 2006, pp. 24–5).

In 2004 David Marsh supervised a project that carried out focus group research with final-year undergraduate students to investigate the perceived obstacles of proceeding to postgraduate research and how those might differentially affect men and women. This research revealed some persistent problems in terms of the likelihood of women proceeding beyond undergraduate study. Four main factors influenced both men and women in deciding whether to continue to postgraduate work: financial considerations; the desire to make a difference (working for organisations such as NGOs was seen to offer greater potential to bring about change than academic life); information/awareness; and self-confidence. Four factors 'were very clearly gendered, only being identified by women: stereotypes; role models; family responsibilities; and time constraints'.

A stereotype of the academic as male clearly emerged from the research. Most of the academics they came into contact with were male and they tended to teach the core courses in Politics or International Studies. Female academics tended to be concentrated in specific spheres of the discipline. 'There was a sense in which women were on the margin of the discipline, as token feminists, or in softer areas, such as international development'. Women were disadvantaged because 'They generally knew less about academia, largely because staff (in most cases of course male staff) appear less likely to approach them to undertake graduate work. At the same time, they are less self-confident' (Akhtar *et al.*, 2004).

The ESRC benchmarking panel recommended 'vigorous proactive strategies to remedy the under-representation of women, particularly in senior ranks, and ethnic minorities across all ranks' (ESRC, 2007, p. 6). Joni Lovenduski made the point in interview that the political class was now more feminised than political science: the voluntary sector, think tanks and the civil service were all more feminised. 'It has been very slow work to feminise political science, taking years and years. Apart from political theory, the feminine dimension was still given insufficient attention; for example, transport policies took no account of the fact that women are the main users of public transport and have particular needs' (Interview, 12 May 2009). None of this is to undervalue the achievements of the Women and Politics group which in particular supports people coming into the subject very well.

Towards the end of 2008 the PSA established a Diversity working party chaired by Vicky Randall. It is intended that this will form the basis for an Equality and Diversity sub-committee in the longer run. The working party is concentrating on the issue of ethnic minority representation in the discipline and it has been agreed to gather information about ethnicity when registering or re-registering members, and to signal interest in improving minority representation when inviting nominations to the EC or editorial teams. In the absence of data, it is difficult to say anything concrete about numbers and experiences of ethnic minority members. It may be that British Asians are more present (but not proportionate to their numbers in the population) than Afro-Caribbeans.

One way in which political science in the UK has become more diverse is through its internationalisation. English is the global working language of the discipline and in many respects the labour market in the UK is more open than in some continental European countries as it is less dependent on hierarchy and patronage. A well-qualified candidate from elsewhere in the EU will be assessed on their merits. Among politics and international studies 'staff over 55, some 86 per cent are UK nationals: among those under 35 that proportion shrinks to 63 per cent. This is nothing short of a sea-change in the UK profession' (ESRC, 2007, p. 14). The trend is predominantly one of Europeanisation. 'About half of the non-UK nationals in that youngest cohort are from other EU countries, and a quarter from North America. A quarter of them are from elsewhere in the world, however'. The benchmarking study concludes:

> UK Politics and International Studies is now, quite possibly, the most cosmopolitan in the world. For those working within it, it must be like what it was to be in the US in 1938, when all the big brains started arriving in droves as refugee scholars from Europe. It is an exciting time, indeed, to be in the UK working in Politics and International Studies (ESRC, 2007, p. 35).

Although welcome, this development does not resolve the other diversity challenges the discipline faces.

Chapter 9

Conclusions: Confronting the Challenges

Throughout this book a process of modernisation and professionalisation of political science in the UK has been analysed. From a preoccupation with historical accident, constitutional quirks and the exceptionalism and innate superiority of the British model, and a sluggish and reluctant response to external pressures, particularly from the USA, British political science has become more comparative, more cosmopolitan, more methodologically sophisticated and more adept at developing and applying theory. The PSA has mirrored those developments, at times stimulated and accelerated them and provided an organisational framework within which political scientists can share their intellectual interests and develop links with practitioners and higher education funding bodies. As Dunleavy (1994, p. vi) has argued, 'We need to carry on insisting that the mainsprings of professional advance lie with the discipline itself, that only autonomous developments can genuinely raise standards and promote new intellectual development. The Political Studies Association fulfils a key role here'.

Strengths and Weaknesses

The ESRC benchmarking study found 'a discipline in robust good health'. There was 'considerable evidence of research quality across almost all the principal sub-disciplines'. While some weaknesses were noted, 'the much larger story is one of considerable strengths: in political theory; in electoral studies; in the "English school" of international relations; in European Union studies; in "critical" security studies; in political economy, domestic and especially international; and in certain areas of public policy and administration and of comparative and area studies' (ESRC, 2007, p. 5). This picture was confirmed by the 2008 RAE where the sub-panel for politics and international studies 'formed a view of the discipline as energetic, ambitious and producing research of very high quality' within a 'vigorous and innovative profession' (RAE, 2008, p. 6).

A recurring theme of this book has been the efforts of political science to establish an effective working relationship with reticent practitioners. This is an area in which the PSA has made particular progress in recent years, and some of the results are evident in the benchmarking study, which 'found considerable evidence of engagement with end-users in the policy community, narrowly construed' (ESRC, 2007, p. 5). 'UK Politics and IS scholars have a truly distinguished record of providing research-based advice to public policymakers' (ESRC, 2007, p. 25). There is a substantial record of engagement with government departments and parliamentary committees (in all four parliaments of the UK) and political scientists are in demand from the media and not just at election times. 'The policy community is getting quite extraordinarily good value out of UK Politics and International Studies. We would be hard-pressed to name any other country in which a larger proportion of the Politics and IS profession was directly engaged with high-level policymakers in this way' (ESRC, 2007, p. 25). This is, of course, a story of individual, research team, departmental and university effort, but the PSA has played a substantial facilitating role.

The subject's popularity with students is growing. In 2007 there were 23,000 politics undergraduates and 9,625 postgraduates, many of them from outside the UK. The number of students taking up undergraduate places in politics and international studies increased in the first decade of the twenty-first century from 2,741 in 2000 to 4,366 in 2005. Perhaps because of the '9/11 effect', 'this has tended to favour courses in international relations, rather than traditional political studies/ science' (Harrison and Saez, 2009, p. 349). This has been reflected in a growth in research-active staff: the 2008 RAE saw the number of researchers in politics and international studies submitted increase from 1,076 in 2001 to 1,269 in 2008 (RAE, 2008, p. 5) out of an estimated total of 1,400 full-time equivalent staff, making the discipline the same size as sociology and only slightly smaller than economics (ESRC, 2007, pp. 7–8).

There are some signs of weakness, however. If one examines the expectation that 10 per cent of UK politics and international studies articles are among the 10 per cent most cited worldwide, 'it seems that at the ten per cent threshold UK politics and IS performs just about as should be expected'. The record of very high impact articles is less good: in other words, the discipline is not producing as many paradigm-shifting 'big ideas' as one might expect: 'It seems much more comfortable concentrating on high quality work that is more modest in scope' (ESRC, 2007, p. 14). 'Only 4.1 per cent of UK Politics and IS articles are among the world's five per cent most highly cited. Only 0.7 per cent are among the world's one per cent most highly cited' (ESRC, 2007, p. 15). While the discipline was performing on a par with some cognate disciplines such as sociology, it fell short 'of the much-higher-than-expected citation rates of others' such as history, philosophy and economics/business (ESRC, 2007, p. 11).

The benchmarking study speculates that some of this might have to do with the self-deprecating, eclectic, tolerant, pluralist character of the UK discipline. As noted in Chapter 5, the relative absence of risky research recalls the debates of the 1970s with the SSRC when Jim Sharpe urged them to chance their arm on more risky research. It is perhaps easier for private foundations to do this and the UK has fewer and less-well-funded ones than the USA. Research councils are understandably influenced by their accountability for public funds and peer review practices perhaps tend to reward the conventional which builds on existing literature rather than more unorthodox work. It is perhaps in the interdisciplinary work funded by the research councils in combination that there is more opportunity for 'blue skies' work.

The Hix global rankings of political science departments have proved controversial and the author himself would admit that any pioneering ranking of this kind is going to have shortcomings (Bull and Espindola, 2005; Erne, 2007; Haverland, 2005; Hix, 2004; 2005). While UK departments make up 48, or 24 per cent, of the top 200 political science departments and thus are ranked second after the USA (Dunleavy and Kelly, 2004, p. 290), no UK departments are ranked in the top ten global departments (and only one European department, the entirely postgraduate European University Institute in Florence). According to the Hix rankings for 1998–2002, the only three UK departments in the top twenty are the LSE (ranked fifteenth), Essex (ranked sixteenth equal) and Oxford (ranked nineteenth equal).

In the 2001 RAE, 24 units received a 3a grade and another three received even lower. 'That suggests more dispersion of research quality in Politics and International Studies than in cognate social science disciplines. Such a tail of departments scoring below 4 is less in evidence in Economics, Anthropology or Sociology' (ESRC, 2007, p. 10). In the controversial 2008 RAE, the discipline was ranked 62 out of 67 submissions. 'For example a middle ranking in Politics and International Studies is 2.15; in sociology, 2.40; in business and management studies, 2.35; in social work, 2.50' (Russell and Croft, 2009, p. 6). As Andrew Russell and Stuart Croft point out, 'the GPA or National Profile is a very poor indicator, and it is one that could move significantly if any of the high volume departments had achieved only a marginally different result. It was never designed to provide a comparative tool across disciplines; the purpose has to be to standardise procedures' (Russell and Croft, 2009, p. 6). Nevertheless, there was a certain amount of discontent expressed about the alleged failure of the sub-panel to 'defend' the discipline. Perhaps the real target should have been the HEFCE's oversight of the 'main' panels spanning a number of disciplines which seemed to become preoccupied with procedures rather than reining in those disciplines that were inclined to be overgenerous in their assessments rather than thorough and scrupulously fair like the politics sub-panel.

A Discipline of Sub-disciplines?

Brian Barry (1999, p. 447) drew an important distinction between specialisation and fragmentation in a discipline. He saw specialisation as:

> the elaboration and extension of a common body of ideas to different aspects of the subject. The specialities radiate out from the hub like the spokes in a wheel . . . In

contrast fragmentation might be defined as what happens when the centrifugal tendencies inherent in specialization are not reined in by the gravitational pull of the central core.

Barry concluded that 'For better or worse, the study of politics in Britain surely approximates to the model of fragmentation rather than that of specialization'.

The ESRC benchmarking panel implicitly agreed with this analysis by arguing that the strength of political science in Britain resided with the sub-disciplines and it was with them that the funding agencies and others should engage. The strength of these sub-disciplines reflects in part the effort that the PSA has made since the 1970s to sustain and develop its specialist groups, although in doing so it may have caused the unintentional consequence of undermining its own authority and legitimacy. In the view of the benchmarking panel, 'UK scholars in Politics and IS identify primarily with their sub-discipline, rather than the discipline as a whole. Nurturing the discipline in the UK requires building on the sub-disciplines'. This has implications for the standing and role of discipline-wide organisations. The benchmarking panel saw a tension between the role of disciplinary associations as membership organisations seeking to serve the interests of all their members, whereas funding agencies 'more generally are supposed to be concentrating resources on the best'. Funders should therefore convene select workshops of the dozen or so leaders in a sub-discipline. They should 'work more with innovative leaders of sub-disciplines in developing research agendas', while consulting with professional associations on developments of more general sorts' (ESRC, 2007, p. 25). In other words, cutting edge research is done by the sub-disciplines, while disciplinary associations are best suited to deal with more routine or procedural matters.

Dunleavy, Kelly and Moran (2000, pp. 7–8) take a somewhat more optimistic view of the health of the discipline as a whole, arguing that 'Vigorous "generalist" journals and conferences provide an acute public barometer of the health of different areas and perspectives, and maintain a sharp competitive edge that might get lost in a more segmented and specialized structure'. For all the importance of links with people in the same sub-field elsewhere in Europe, 'Linkages between different parts of the British discipline remain more important than the USA because specialization has been less hyper-developed' (Dunleavy *et al.*, 2000, p. 7). There is still a shared interest in narratives about democracy, justice, power and conflict.

There are three reasons for being relatively optimistic about the condition of political science as a whole. First, while eclecticism is still present, its nature has changed. In so far as it was a product of the way in which 'The relatively small size of the majority of departments encouraged colleagues to collaborate across different subject boundaries' (Dunleavy *et al.*, 2000, p. 7), departments have become larger as is shown by the increase in the mean size of departments submitting to the 2008 RAE. The discipline has become less inclined towards a tolerant and uncritical acceptance of anything that appears to be political so that one ends up with 'description that . . . is too out-of-date for journalism but not long enough ago for history' (Barry, 2007, p. 38). Analysis now has to meet higher standards of theoretical and methodological rigour. Eclecticism 'remains built in to the intellectual substructure of the discipline, but now in a more intellectually productive way' (Dunleavy *et al.*, 2000, p. 7). It is reflected in the call by Nicola Phillips (2004, p. 15) for a 'controlled eclecticism'. This is set in juxtaposition to 'a "kitchen sink" kind of eclecticism that rides roughshod over the limits of theoretical or conceptual commensurability'. Openness to other disciplines is preserved, but care is taken in selecting the terrains to utilise. Burnham, Gilland Lutz, Grant and Layton-Henry (2008, pp. 29–30) develop this concept in terms of three checks to be applied as controls on eclecticism: parsimony, commensurability and coherence.

Second, the strength of normative political theory is an asset that the American discipline does not possess, particularly as it has developed a harder and more philosophical character under the influence of Barry and Rawls (Kelly, 2000) and has developed a focus on topics such as justice that can inform policy debates. Paul Kelly argues (2000, p. 13) that political theorists 'manage to inform, challenge and influence each other in ever more subtle and sophisticated ways', but in fact this influence extends to the discipline as a whole. It may help to explain the extent to which 'the power of critique remains a strong force for good in the British discipline' (Dunleavy *et al.*, 2000, p. 7). Political theory obliges us to think about our assumptions, the language we use and the analytical rigour of our arguments.

Third, there are advantages in being a subject matter rather than a discipline with distinctive methods, even if there is still a case for more definition of boundaries. 'The advantage is that it cannot simply abandon the questions that people would like answers to. Economics – to make the obvious contrast – simply writes off topics if they cannot fit into its theoretical frameworks' (Barry, 2007, p. 38). Barry points out that 'The downside of defining politics as a subject matter is obvious: can it be ever more than the composite of a lot of bits of information?' (Barry, 2007, p. 38) The answer is that politics maintains a fine balancing act: between being a discipline that is open to new perspectives generated both within the discipline and elsewhere, yet has some agreed criteria by which to assess their value; by tolerating a variety of approaches, yet sharing some common ground about how one should proceed; and by insisting on core themes and topics, while encouraging specialisation.

Challenges

One of the greatest challenges that the discipline faces is financial. The allocation of funds following the 2008 RAE was influenced by a government decision to protect research funding for science, technology, engineering and medicine, the so-called STEM subjects. Politics departments that had done well in the RAE nevertheless found their research funding from the HEFCE (and the equivalent bodies in the devolved regions) cut back. In addition, higher education is likely to face a round of public expenditure cuts that could rival those of the 1980s. There is a certain irony in funding for research and teaching politics and international studies being cut when there is widespread concern about the health of the democratic polity and the need for more effective international cooperation to deal with challenges such as financial crises and climate change. One ground for relative optimism is that many universities are less dependent on public funding than they were in the 1980s, but HEFCE core funding is still very important.

The subject remains popular with students: the declining reputation of the political class does not seem to have affected interest in the subject; rather the contrary, with students interested in newer forms of political expression such as non-governmental organisations. One way to sustain funding is to increase student numbers, taking in more students on first degree courses and taught masters' programmes, including overseas students. The overseas student market is, however, increasingly competitive. As students pay higher fees for their education, they understandably scrutinise more carefully what they receive in return, demanding more personal contact. Moreover, these additional students may have to be taught without an increase in the unit of resource, making it more difficult to undertake research, thus affecting performance in the Research Excellence Framework (REF) that is to replace the RAE. Barry argues (2007, p. 38) that 'There are too many undergraduates, too few academics. When I joined up in 1960, the student/staff ratio was seven and a half to one: now it exceeds twenty to one'. He concludes: 'In Britain, at least, unless pay and working conditions improve drastically, political science will go down the drain along with every other subject' (Barry, 2007, p. 39). This is probably too gloomy a view. The ESRC (2007, p. 5) benchmarking review drew attention to 'some stunning recent hires. The quality of these outstanding young scholars, as much as anything else we observed, convinces us that Politics and International Studies has a very bright future indeed in the UK'. As far as teaching is concerned, the innovative use of new technology can both reduce the burden and increase student satisfaction.

Changes in the internal organisation of universities can also challenge the study of politics. Following the 2008 RAE, the University of Liverpool mooted closure of the Department of Political Theory and Institutions, but this proposal was not pursued after a strong campaign by the discipline in which the PSA was actively involved. A more common trend has to be to merge politics departments into broader schools, submerging the identity of politics. This is usually done for management rather than academic reasons. It is claimed that economies of scale can be achieved, although these usually seem to be small, and probably the main incentive is that it reduces the number of middle-level line managers in a university, making control by the central management easier. The benchmarking panel warns that 'there is the danger that those schools may weaken disciplines, without promoting effective interdisciplinary research. On balance, the Panel bemoans these managerial innovations that undermine disciplinary integrity' (ESRC, 2007, p. 25). In 2009 it was the HEFCE's intention to reduce the number of sub-panels from 67 in the RAE to 30 in the REF and it is therefore encouraging, and a recognition of the strength of the discipline, that a distinctive politics sub-panel is to survive.

In terms of research in the discipline, it is strongly networked into Europe through the ECPR and more personal networks. 'That European connection is one of the most distinctive features of UK Politics and IS and it is an important source of its comparative advantage *vis-à-vis* its North American counterpart' (ESRC, 2007, p. 8). At the same time, existing links with American political science have been developed further, again encouraged by the PSA through initiatives that have assisted British scholars to attend APSA conferences and vice versa. The PSA has not neglected links elsewhere in the world and has been active in developing relationships with its counterparts in Asia and, more recently, in Brazil. This process of internationalisation is a strength of the discipline and reflects the changing nature of its subject matter, global politics.

However, two notes of caution are necessary. A capacity to study the UK needs to be retained, if only because it is much in demand from a range of practitioners including the media and is therefore relevant to success in terms of 'impact', which is likely to be a significant aspect of the REF. In the case of Australasia, 'something is being lost as political science becomes increasingly specialised and oriented to international communities of scholars rather than towards informing debate at home' (Sawer, 2008, p. 9). Of course, the foundation of *The British Journal of Politics & International Relations* represented a significant act of encouragement by the PSA for work on the UK. Nevertheless, the author has heard the view argued that the study of single-country politics is an obstacle to the development of comparative politics, but comparison surely requires a thorough understanding of particular national polities.

The balance between the study of politics and international relations also needs to be kept in mind. An understanding of domestic politics and how this affects the international actions of that persistent form of political organisation, the nation state, is still very much required. Distinct politics and international studies have merged in most universities (the LSE is an exception) but there remain two distinct associations. That is unlikely to change and the emphasis has been on ensuring that they have an effective working relationship.

What of the future of the PSA itself? It has undergone a complete transformation from the club-like association of the 1950s to a highly professional organisation that provides a wide range of services to its members. Those services are, however, highly dependent on the income from its journals and in the long run changes in the format of academic publishing may place that at risk. The Trustees' Report for 2008 notes:

> One issue that has been of concern to the charity is the question of on-line open-access 'free-to-read' publications. Over several years there has been continuing discussion about the development of such publications. Sales of the Association's journals might be adversely affected were the latest research to appear in free publications. As yet, this does not appear to be happening but the matter is being kept under review (PSA, 2008, p. 14).

It should also be noted that many universities are insisting that 'pre-print' versions of publications should be made available on their websites, while research councils require ready access to publications arising from work they have funded. In the long run, universities may increasingly resist the high sums they pay for journal subscriptions.

The PSA also has to make decisions about how it can most effectively service its members and maintain links with decision makers and funding bodies. The range of the Association's work would increasingly seem to require someone who can work as a chief executive, possibly based in London given the metropolitan character of Britain. Helena Djurkovic was appointed chief executive in 2010.

Throughout its history the PSA has been fortunate to draw on the voluntary efforts of academics who consider that having an effective professional association is important to the well-being and success of the discipline. The PSA was effectively reborn in 1975. The 1980s were a difficult time for universities and the discipline and there may be another difficult period ahead. If that proves to be the case, the discipline will have even more need of an association that is resilient, well resourced, shows foresight and has a capacity to innovate. The subject association does not create the discipline, but it is difficult to envisage a discipline without it.

References

Adcock, R. and Bevir, M. (2007) 'The Remaking of Political Theory', in R. Adcock, M. Bevir and S. C. Stimson (eds), *Modern Political Science: Anglo-American Exchanges since 1980*. Princeton NJ: Princeton University Press, pp. 209–33.

Adcock, R., Bevir, M. and Stimson, S. C. (2007) 'A History of Political Science. How? What? Why?', in R. Adcock, M. Bevir and S. C. Stimson (eds), *Modern Political Science: Anglo-American Exchanges since 1980*. Princeton NJ: Princeton University Press, pp. 1–17.

Akhtar, P., Fawcett, P., Legrand, T., Marsh, D. and Taylor, T. (2004) 'The Relative Absence of Women in the Political Science Profession'. Working Paper, Department of Political Science and International Studies, University of Birmingham.

Alderman, G. (2009) 'Simplistic View of Insider Betrayal', *Times Higher Education*, 30 July, 46.

Almond, G. (2004) 'Who Lost the Chicago School of Political Science?', *Perspectives on Politics*, 2 (1), 95–8.

Arthur, P. (2009) 'Professor Sir Bernard Crick 1928–2008', *Political Studies Association News*, 20 (1), 8.

Ashworth, L. M. (2009) 'Interdisciplinarity and International Relations', *European Political Science*, 8 (1), 16–25.

Bamford, E. C. (1963) Letter to Colin Seymour-Ure, 30 April, Seymour-Ure Collection.

Barber, B. (1984) *Strong Democracy*. Berkeley CA: California University Press.

Barry, B. (1965) *Political Argument*. London: Routledge and Kegan Paul.

Barry, B. (1975) Letter to J. E. S. Hayward, 21 February, accompanied by list of nominations and campaign statement.

Barry, B. (1999) 'The Study of Politics as a Vocation', in J. Hayward, B. Barry and A. Brown (eds), *The British Study of Politics in the Twentieth Century*. Oxford: Oxford University Press, pp. 425–67.

Barry, B. (2007) 'Leaders of the Profession: An Interview with Brian Barry', *European Political Science*, 6 (1), 34–40.

Beith, A. (2008) *A View from the North*. Newcastle on Tyne: Northumbria University Press.

Beloff, M. (1975) 'The Politics of Oxford "Politics" ', *Political Studies*, 23 (2–3), 6–17.

Berrington, H. and Norris, P. (1988) 'Political Studies in the Eighties'. Political Studies Association, typescript.

Bevir, M. and Rhodes, R. A. W. (2007) 'Traditions of Political Science in Contemporary Britain', in R. Adcock, M. Bevir and S. C. Stimson (eds), *Modern Political Science: Anglo-American Exchanges since 1980*. Princeton NJ: Princeton University Press, pp. 234–58.

Birch, A. H. (2009) 'Thoughts on the History of the PSA', unpublished notes.

Birch, A. H. and Spann, R. N. (1974) 'Mackenzie at Manchester', in W. J. M. Mackenzie, B. Chapman and A. Potter (eds), *WJMM, Political Questions: Essays in Honour of W. J. M. Mackenzie*. Manchester: Manchester University Press, pp. 1–23.

Boncourt, T. (2007) 'The Evolution of Political Science in France and Britain: A Comparative Study of Two Political Science Journals', *European Political Science*, 6 (3), 276–94.

Boncourt, T. (2008) 'Is European Political Science Different from European Political Sciences? A Comparative Study of the *European Journal of Political Research, Political Studies* and the *Revue Française de Science Politique*, 1973–2002', *European Political Science*, 7 (3), 366–81.

Boncourt, T. (2009) 'Political Science, a Postwar Product (1947–1949)', *Participation*, 33 (1), 3–7.

British Association (1943) 'Scientific Research on Human Institutions', *Advancement of Science*, 8.

Brown, C. (2006) 'IR Theory in Britain – the New Black?', *Review of International Studies*, 32 (4), 677–87.

Buckler, S. (2002) 'Normative Theory', in D. Marsh and G. Stoker (eds), *Theory and Methods in Political Science*, second edition. Basingstoke: Palgrave-Macmillan, pp. 172–94.

Budge, I. (2006) 'Jean Blondel and the Development of European Political Science', *European Political Science*, 5 (3), 315–27.

Bull, M. and Espindola, R. (2005) 'European Universities in a Global Ranking of Political Science Departments: A Comment on Hix', *European Political Science*, 4 (1), 27–9.

Burnham, P., Gilland Lutz, K., Grant, W. and Layton-Henry, Z. (2008) *Research Methods in Politics*, second edition. Basingstoke: Palgrave-Macmillan.

Butler, D. and Stokes, D. (1969) *Political Change in Britain: Forces Shaping Electoral Choice*. New York: St Martin's Press.

Chapman, R. A. (1992) 'The Demise of the Royal Institute of Public Administration (UK)', *Australian Journal of Public Administration*, 51 (4), 519–20.

Chapman, R. A. (2007) 'The Origins of the Joint University Council and the Background to *Public Policy and Administration*: An Interpretation', *Public Policy and Administration*, 22 (1), 7–26.

Chester, D. N. (1975) 'Political Studies in Britain: Recollections and Comments', *Political Studies*, 23 (2–3), 151–64.

Chester, D. N. (1986) *Economics, Politics and Social Studies in Oxford, 1900–85*. London: Macmillan.

Childs, S. and Krook, M. L. (2006) 'Gender and Politics: The State of the Art', *Politics*, 26 (1), 18–28.

Cmd. 6868 (1946) *Report of the Committee on the Provision for Social and Economic Research*. London: The Stationery Office.

Collini, S., Winch, D. and Burrow, S. (1983) *That Noble Science of Politics*. Cambridge: Cambridge University Press.

Committee on Graduates Council of Junior Members (1962) *Oxford Graduates Survey 1962*, Oxford.

Crick, B. (1959) *The American Science of Politics*. London: Routledge.

Crick, B. (1968) *The Reform of Parliament*, second edition. London: Weidenfeld and Nicholson.

Crick, B. (2009) 'William Alexander Robson (1895–1980)', *Oxford Dictionary of National Biography*. Available from: http://www.oxforddnb.com/articles/31/31622-article.html [Accessed 23 June 2009].

Crossman, R. H. S. (1951) 'Review of "Political Education" ', *New Statesman and Nation*, 42, 60–1.

Dalyell, T. (2009) 'John Pitcairn Mackintosh', *Oxford Dictionary of National Biography*. Available from: http://www.oxforddnb.com/articles/31/31393-arrticle.html [Accessed 28 August 2009].

Davis, J. (2009) 'Lucy Philip Mair', *Oxford Dictionary of National Biography*. Available from: http://www.oxforddnb.com/articles/63/63455-article.html [Accessed 14 September 2009].

Den Otter, S. M. (2007) 'The Origins of a Historical Political Science in Late Victorian and Edwardian Britain', in R. Adcock, M. Bevir and S. C. Stimson (eds), *Modern Political Science: Anglo-American Exchanges since 1980*. Princeton NJ: Princeton University Press, pp. 37–65.

Dowding, K. (2009) 'Obituary: Brian Barry (1936–2009), *Political Studies*, 57 (2), 459–63.

Dreijmanis, J. (1983) 'Political Science in the United States: The Discipline and the Profession', *Government and Opposition*, 18 (2), 194–217.

Dunleavy, P. (1994) 'Foreword', in P. Dunleavy and J. Stanyer (eds), *Contemporary Political Studies, Volume 1*. Belfast: Political Studies Association, pp. vi–vii.

Dunleavy, P., Kelly, P. J. and Moran, M. (2000) 'Characterizing the Development of British Political Science', in P. Dunleavy, P. J. Kelly and M. Moran (eds), *British Political Science: Fifty Years of Political Studies*. Oxford: Blackwell, pp. 3–9.

Dunleavy, P. and Kelly, P. J. (2004) 'Editorial: Political Science in a Globalizing Era', *Political Studies Review*, 2 (3), 289–92.

Editors (1999) 'Editorial: Studying British Politics', *British Journal of Politics & International Relations*, 1 (1), 1–11.

Englefield, D. (2009) *The Study of Parliament Group: The First Twenty-One Years*. Available from: http://www.spg.org.uk/details.htm [accessed 20 July 2009].

Erne, R. (2007) 'On the Use and Abuse of Bibliometric Performance Indicators: A Critique of Hix's "Global Ranking of Political Science Departments" ', *European Political Science*, 6 (3), 306–14.

ESRC (2007) *International Benchmarking Review of UK Politics and International Studies*. Swindon: Economic and Social Research Council.

Fairlie, H. (1968) *The Life of Politics*. London: Methuen.

Fourcade, M. (2009) *Economists and Societies: Discipline and Profession in the United States, Britain and France, 1890s to 1990s*. Princeton NJ: Princeton University Press.

Freedman, L. (2006) 'Confessions of a Premature Constructivist', *Review of International Studies*, 32 (4), 689–702.

Gaber, A., Gaber, I. and Fox, S. (n.d.) *SSRC/ESRC: The First Forty Years*. Swindon: ESRC.

Goldsmith, M. (2009) 'Personal Recollections' provided to the author.

Goodin, R. E. (2009) 'The British Study of Politics', in M. Flinders, A. Gamble, C. Hay and M. Kenny (eds), *The Oxford Handbook of British Politics*. Oxford: Oxford University Press, pp. 42–55.

Grant, W. and Sherrington, P. (2006) *Managing your Academic Career*. Basingstoke: Palgrave-Macmillan.

Greaves, J. (2008) 'Is Political Science a Discipline?' Unpublished paper, University of Warwick.

Gunnell, J. G. (2005) 'Political Science on the Cusp: Recovering a Discipline's Past', *American Political Science Review*, 99 (4), 597–609.

Hansard (1982) HC Deb., 18 October, vol. 29, cc. 38–9W.

Harrison, L. and Saez, L. (2009) 'Political Studies in the UK: A Twenty-First Century Health Check', *European Political Science*, 8 (3), 345–55.

Harrison, W. (1953) 'An Editorial Note', *Political Studies*, 1 (1), 1–5.

Harrison, W. (1975) 'The Early Years of *Political Studies*', *Political Studies*, 23 (2–3), 183–92.

Haverland, M. (2005) 'A Comment on Simon Hix: "European Universities in a Global Ranking of Political Science Departments" ', *European Political Science*, 4 (1), 25–6.

Hayward, J. (1975) Letter to Brian Barry, 21 February.

Hayward, J. (1991a) 'Political Science in Britain', *European Journal of Political Research*, 20 (3–4), 301–22.

Hayward, J. (1991b) 'Cultural and Contextual Constraints upon the Development of Political Science in Great Britain', in D. Easton, J. G. Gunnell and L. Graziano (eds), *The Development of Political Science: A Comparative Survey*. Abingdon: Routledge, pp. 93–107.

Hayward, J. (1999) 'British Approaches to Politics: The Dawn of a Self-Deprecating Discipline', in J. Hayward, B. Barry and A. Brown (eds), *The British Study of Politics in the Twentieth Century*. Oxford: Oxford University Press, pp. 1–35.

Hayward, J. (2001) 'Sammy Finer', in *Political Studies Association of the United Kingdom, 50th Anniversary*. Newcastle: Political Studies Association, p. 13.

Hayward, J. and Norton, P. (1986) *The Political Science of British Politics*. Brighton: Harvester Wheatsheaf.

Hirst, P. (2001) 'Harold J. Laski', in *Political Studies Association of the United Kingdom: 50th Anniversary*. Newcastle: Political Studies Association, p. 12.

Hix, S. (2004) 'A Global Ranking of Political Science Departments', *Political Studies Review*, 2 (3), 293–313.

Hix, S. (2005) 'European Universities in a Global Ranking of Political Science Departments: A Reply to Bull and Espindola', *European Political Science*, 4 (1), 30–2.

Jeffery, C. (2009) 'Obituary: Sir Bernard Crick (1929–2008)', *Political Studies*, 57 (2), 464–8.

Jones, D. (1969) *Borough Politics*. London: Macmillan.

Kavanagh, D. (2003) 'British Political Science in the Inter-war Years: The Emergence of the Founding Fathers', *British Journal of Politics & International Relations*, 5 (4), 594–613.

Kavanagh, D. (2007) 'The Emergence of an Embryonic Discipline: British Politics without Political Scientists', in R. Adcock, M. Bevir and S. C. Stimson (eds), *Modern Political Science: Anglo-American Exchanges since 1980*. Princeton NJ: Princeton University Press, pp. 97–117.

Kelly, P. J. (2000) 'Political Theory: Introduction', in P. Dunleavy, P. J. Kelly and M. Moran (eds), *British Political Science: Fifty Years of Political Studies*. Oxford: Blackwell, pp. 11–13.

Kennedy-Pipe, C. and Rengger, N. (2006) 'BISA at Thirty: Reflections on Three Decades of British International Relations Scholarship', *Review of International Studies*, 32 (4), 665–76.

Kenny, M. (2004) 'The Case for Disciplinary History: Political Studies in the 1950s and 1960s', *British Journal of Politics & International Relations*, 6 (4), 565–83.

Kenny, M. (2007) 'Birth of a Discipline: Interpreting British Political Science in the 1950s and 1960s', in R. Adcock, M. Bevir and S. C. Stimson (eds), *Modern Political Science:*

Anglo-American Exchanges since 1980. Princeton NJ: Princeton University Press, pp. 158–79.

Kuper, A. (2005) 'Alternative Histories of British Social Anthropology', *Social Anthropology*, 13 (1), 47–64.

Lee, J. M. (2009) 'Mackenzie, William James Millar (1909–1996), Political Scientist', *Oxford Dictionary of National Biography*. Available from: http://www.oxforddnb.com/articles/63/63210-article.html [Accessed 22 June 2009].

Lovenduski, J. (1981) *Women in British Political Science*. Glasgow: Centre for the Study of Public Policy, Studies in Public Policy No.78.

LSE (1949) PSA/15, 'Memorandum on the Proposed Formation of a British Political Studies Association'.

LSE (1950a) PSA/15, Letter from Harold J. Laski to 'Willy' (W. A. Robson), 22 March.

LSE (1950b) PSA/15, Minutes of the conference held at the London School of Economics and Political Science, 23 and 24 March 1950.

LSE (1955a) Oakeshott, Correspondence, 11/3.

LSE (1955b) PSA/15, Minutes of the Annual General Meeting, 25 March.

LSE (1958) PSA/15, Minutes of the Executive Committee, 2 January.

LSE (1959a) PSA/15, Minutes of the Executive Committee, 8 July.

LSE (1959b) PSA/15, Minutes of the Executive Committee, 3 January.

LSE (1960a) PSA/15, Minutes of the Executive Committee, 8 January.

LSE (1960b) PSA/15, Minutes of the Executive Committee, 30 March.

LSE (1960c) PSA/15, Minutes of the Executive Committee, 27 September.

LSE (1960d) PSA/15, Minutes of the Tenth Annual General Meeting, 31 March.

LSE (1961a) PSA/3, Letter from Margherita Rendel to John Day, 13 October.

LSE (1961b) PSA/3, Letter from John Day to Margherita Rendel, 16 October.

LSE (1961c) PSA/15, Minutes of the Executive Committee, 21 January.

LSE (1961d) PSA/15, Minutes of the Executive Committee, 27 March.

LSE (1963) PSA/15, Minutes of the Executive Committee, 4 January.

LSE (1964) PSA/15, Minutes of the Fourteenth Annual General Meeting, 24 March.

LSE (1965a) PSA/15, Minutes of the Fifteenth Annual General Meeting, 30 March.

LSE (1965b) PSA/15, Minutes of the Executive Committee, 20 December.

LSE (1966a) PSA/15, Minutes of the Sixteenth Annual General Meeting, 29 March.

LSE (1966b) PSA/15, Minutes of the Executive Committee, 4 February.

LSE (1966c) PSA/15, Minutes of the Executive Committee, 19 December.

LSE (1967a) PSA/15, Minutes of the Executive Committee, 3 April, including Editorial Report on *Political Studies*.

LSE (1967b) PSA/15, Minutes of the Executive Committee, 14 April.

LSE (1967c) PSA/15, Minutes of the Seventeenth Annual General Meeting.

LSE (1968a) PSA/15, J. Blondel, 'Extension of Activities of the PSA', November.

LSE (1968b) PSA/15, Minutes of the Executive Committee, 2 April.

LSE (1968c) PSA/15, Minutes of the Annual General Meeting, 3 April.

LSE (1968d) PSA/15, Minutes of the Executive Committee, 18 October.

LSE (1968e) PSA/15, 'Report of the First Postgraduate Conference on "The Study of Politics" held 16–18 December 1968 at the Carr-Saunders Hall, London'.

LSE (1968f) PSA/15, Letter from Bernard Crick, 6 January.

LSE (1968g) PSA/15, Minutes of the Executive Committee, 4 April.

LSE (1969a) PSA/15, Minutes of the Executive Committee, 24 January.

LSE (1969b) PSA/15, Minutes of the Executive Committee, 7 July.

LSE (1969c) PSA/15, Minutes of the Executive Committee, 10 October.

LSE (1969d) PSA/15, Minutes of the Executive Committee, 7 March.

LSE (1969e) PSA/15, Minutes of the Nineteenth Annual General Meeting, 1 April.

LSE (1969f) PSA/15, Letter from Sammy Finer to Geoffrey Alderman, 19 September.

LSE (1970a) PSA/15, Minutes of the Executive Committee, 13 April.

LSE (1970b) PSA/15, Minutes of the Executive Committee, 9 January.

LSE (1970c) PSA/15, Minutes of the Twentieth Annual General Meeting, 15 April.

LSE (1970d) PSA/15, Letter from Professor Finer to Professor Moodie, 6 January.

LSE (1970e) PSA/15, Minutes of the Executive Committee, 21 May.

LSE (1971a) PSA/15, Letter from Brian Barry to Professor G. Moodie, 18 January.

LSE (1971b) PSA/15, Letter from Graeme Moodie to Professor Barry, 10 March.

LSE (1971c) PSA/15, Letter from the Department of Education and Science, 2 June.

LSE (1972) PSA/15, 'Report on the Graduate Students' Conference sponsored by the PSA at the Carr-Saunders Hall, 11–13 December 1972'.

LSE (1973a) PSA/15, Letter from B. Crick to A. H. Birch, 1 March.

LSE (1973b) PSA/15, Letter from A. H. Birch to B. Crick, 2 March.

LSE (1973c) PSA/15, Letter from B. Crick to A. H. Birch, 19 March.

LSE (1973d) PSA/20, Letter from A. H. Birch to Peter Woodward.

LSE (1974a) PSA/15, 'Political Studies Association: Election Procedures', undated.

LSE (1974b) PSA/15, Minutes of the Executive Committee, 26 September.

LSE (1974c) PSA/15, Letter from Bernard Crick to Peter Woodward, 26 February.

LSE (1975a) PSA/16, Letter from Jim Sharpe to Rod Rhodes.

LSE (1975b) PSA/16, Minutes of the Executive Committee, 21 April.

LSE (1975c) PSA/16, Memorandum from Dennis Kavanagh to Search Committee, 6 May.

LSE (1975d) PSA/16, Minutes of the Executive Committee, 31 October.

LSE (1975e) PSA/15, Memorandum from Ian Budge to Academic and Research Staff, PhD Students, Department of Government, University of Essex.

LSE (1975f) PSA/15, Memorandum from Bob Dowse on selective benefits, undated.

LSE (1975g) PSA/16, Minutes of the Executive Committee, 31 October.

LSE (1975h) PSA/16, Letter from Mick Ryan to Ian Budge, 14 November.

LSE (1975i) PSA/16, Circular letter from Bob Dowse to eight bloc convenors (copied to R. Rhodes).

LSE (1975j) PSA/16, Letter from D. Hill to R. Rhodes, 7 April.

LSE (1975k) PSA/16, Letter from I. Budge to D. Hill, 17 April.

LSE (1975l) PSA/16, Letter from A. H. Birch to D. Hill, 11 April.

LSE (1976a) PSA/16, 'Draft Statement to be distributed at the Nottingham Conference, 1976'.

LSE (1976b) PSA/16, Minutes of the Executive Committee, 23 January.

LSE (1976c) PSA/16, Ian Henderson, 'The Role of the Political Studies Association in the Polytechnics'.

LSE (1976d) PSA/16, D. Donald, 'Teaching and Research in the Polytechnics: Some Comments on a Discussion Paper'.

LSE (1976e) PSA/16, D. Donald, 'Political Studies in the Public Sector of Higher Education: An Analysis of a Survey'.

LSE (1976f) PSA/16, 'Conference of Heads of Departments. Report by L. J. Sharpe to Executive Committee', 6 July.

LSE (1976g) PSA/16, Letter from W. Grant, Acting Honorary Secretary to John Mackintosh MP.

LSE (1976h) PSA/16, Bernard Crick, 'Memorandum on possible mutual help between the Politics Association and the Political Studies Association', May.

LSE (1977a) PSA/16, 'Political Studies Association. Election to the PSA Executive. Liverpool, 1977'.

LSE (1977b) PSA/16, Minutes of the Executive Committee, 19 December.

LSE (1977c) PSA/16, Minutes of the Annual General Meeting, 5 April 1977.

LSE (1977d) PSA/16, D. Donald, 'The PSA and the CNAA'.

LSE (1977e) PSA/16, Minutes of the PSA Executive Committee, 21/22 October.

LSE (1977f) PSA/16, Ian Budge, 'Political Science as Discipline, Profession and Career'.

LSE (1977g) PSA/16, Letter from Hugh Berrington to the Secretary, Area Studies Panel, SSRC, 29 July.

LSE (1977h) PSA/16, Letter from Saul Rose to Hugh Berrington, 14 September.

LSE (1977i) PSA/16, Letter from Wendy A. Thompson to Hugh Berrington, 27 October.

LSE (1977j) PSA/16, 'PSA Executive Committee, Birmingham, 21–2 October 1977', Paper on internships by Ivor Crewe.

LSE (1977k) PSA/16, 'Links with Influentials', Memorandum by L. J. [Sharpe], October.

LSE (1978a) PSA/17, 'Politics and International Relations', presentation by Jack Spence to the Conference of Political Science Department Heads, Birmingham.

LSE (1978b) PSA/17, '1979 PSA Conference', Memorandum from Ivor Crewe, 30 March.

LSE (1978c) PSA/17, Minutes of the special policy review meeting of the Executive Committee, Wast Hills, 17–18 November.

LSE (1978d) PSA/17, 'The Problem of Undergraduate Recruitment', presentation by A. Barker to the Conference of Political Science Departmental Heads, Birmingham.

LSE (1978e) PSA/17, 'Meeting between Chairman and L. J. Sharpe and the Political Science Committee of the SSRC, 6 May 1978 at Ware'.

LSE (1978f) PSA/17, Minutes of the Executive Committee, 2 June.

LSE (1978g) PSA/17, Memorandum to meeting of the EC from Tony Birch, 11 September.

LSE (1978h) PSA/17, Minutes of the Executive Committee, 22 September.

LSE (1978i) PSA/17, 'Political Studies Association. Women's Group'.

LSE (1978j) PSA/17, Minutes of the Annual General Meeting, 21 March.

LSE (1978k) PSA/17, Joni Lovenduski, 'Proposed PSA Enquiry into the Status and Recruitment of Women in the Study and Teaching of Political Science'.

LSE (1979a) PSA/18, 'Manifesto for Elections to Executive Committee'.

LSE (1979b) PSA/17, Minutes of the Executive Committee, 2 February.

LSE (1979c) PSA/18, Minutes of the Executive Committee, 19 July.

LSE (1979d) PSA/17, 'PSA Study Groups 1979'.

LSE (1979e) PSA/18, 'Discussion between Chairman of Political Studies Association and members of Political Science Committee of the Social Science Research Council at Greenwich on May 12th, 1979'.

LSE (1979f) PSA/18, Minutes of the Executive Committee, 24 May.

LSE (1979g) PSA18, Minutes of the Annual General Meeting, University of Sheffield, 10 April.

LSE (1979h) PSA/18, Minutes of the Executive Committee, 7 December.

LSE (1979i) PSA/18, Letter from Patrick Dunleavy to L. J. Sharpe and Ken Newton, 6 December.

LSE (1980a) PSA/18, Memorandum from Ivor Crewe to PSA Executive, 'PSA Parliamentary Assistantship Scheme', 11 February.

LSE (1980b) PSA/18, 'Political Studies Executive Elections. Manifesto of Pat Dunleavy, David Marsh, Hugh Ward'.

LSE (1980c) PSA/18, Letter from Peter Nailor to Joni Lovenduski, 2 January.

LSE (1980d) PSA/18, Minutes of the Executive Committee, 22 February.

LSE (1980e) PSA/18, Minutes of the Executive Committee, 22 September.

LSE (1980f) PSA/18, Letter from Martin Holmes, finance director of Martin Robertson and Company, to Jim Sharpe, 21 August.

LSE (1980g) PSA/18, 'Report on SSRC/PSA Graduate Students' Conference held at the LSE 11–13 December 1980'.

LSE (1980h) PSA/18, Letter from Adrian Shaw, Secretary, Political Science and International Relations Committee, SSRC, to George Philip, 30 June.

LSE (1980i) PSA/18, Minutes of the Executive Committee, 31 March.

LSE (1980j) PSA/18, Joni Lovenduski, 'Report to PSA Executive on the Survey of the Position of Women in Political Science. Policy Review Meeting: 22 September'.

LSE (1981a) PSA/18, Meetings of the Executive Committee, 2 July.

LSE (1981b) PSA/18, Report of the Executive Committee to the Annual General Meeting, 7 April.

LSE (1981c) PSA/18, 'Government and Political Science. Report of a Conference held under the auspices of the PSA and the RIPA in December, 1980. For Executive Meeting on 27 February 1981'.

LSE (1981d) PSA/18, Joni Lovenduski, 'Summary of Preliminary Report on Women as Academic Staff and as Students in Political Studies'.

LSE (1981e) PSA/18, Minutes of the Executive Committee, 27 February.

Macintyre, S. and Clark, A. (2003) The History Wars. Carlton: Melbourne University Press.

Mackay, F. (2004) 'Gender and Political Representation: The State of the "Discipline"', British Journal of Politics & International Relations, 6 (1), 99–120.

Mackenzie, W. J. M. (1975a) 'Introduction', in W. J. M. Mackenzie (ed.), Explorations in Government, Collected Papers: 1951–68. London: Macmillan, pp. ix–xxxvi.

Mackenzie, W. J. M. (1975b) 'Sighting Shots', in W. J. M. Mackenzie (ed.), Explorations in Government, Collected Papers: 1951–68. London: Macmillan, pp. 1–3.

Mackenzie, W. J. M. (1975c) 'Public Administration in the Universities', in W. J. M. Mackenzie (ed.), Explorations in Government, Collected Papers: 1951–68. London: Macmillan, pp. 4–16.

March, J. G. and Olsen, J. P. (1984) 'The New Institutionalism: Organizational Factors in Political Life', American Political Science Review, 78 (3), 734–49.

Meehan, E. (2009) 'Musings on PSA', notes provided to the author.

Miall, L. (1994) 'Obituary: Sir Stanley Tomlinson', The Independent, 5 October. Available from: http://www.independent.co.uk/news/people/obituary-sir-stanley-tomlinson-14440983.html [Accessed 21 July 2009].

Minogue, K. (2009) 'Oakeshott, Michael Joseph (1901–1990), Philosopher', Oxford Dictionary of National Biography. Available from: http://www.oxforddnb.com/articles/39/39816-article.html [Accessed 24 June 2009].

Monroe, K. R. (2004) 'The Chicago School: Forgotten but Not Gone', Perspectives on Politics, 2 (1), 95–98.

Moran, M. (2003) The British Regulatory State. Oxford: Oxford University Press.

Moran, M. (2006) 'Interdisciplinarity and Political Science', Politics, 26 (2), 73–83.

NA (1944a) PRO, T 161/1301, Letter from Clement Attlee to the Rt Hon. Sir John Anderson, 20 September.

NA (1944b) PRO, T 161/1301, Letter from Sir John Anderson to the Rt Hon. C. R. Attlee MP, 12 October.

NA (1944c) PRO, T 161/1301, 'Deputy Prime Minister. Note for interview with Sir John Clapham. E. F. M. D.', 27 November.

NA (1945) PRO, T 161/1301, Letter from Sir John Clapham, 7 July.

NA (1946a), PRO, T 161/1301, Letter from J. A. [Sir Alan] Barlow to Sir Henry Clay, 22 July.

NA (1946b) PRO, T 161/1301, Letter from Sir Henry Clay to Sir Alan Barlow, 24 July.

NA (1946c) PRO, T 161/1301, Memorandum from Sir Alan Barlow to Sir Edward Bridges, passed to Mr Trew for comment, 8 August.

NA (1947) PRO, RG 25/1, Minutes of meeting of Standing Interdepartmental Committee on Social and Economic Research held 9 May.

NA (1948) PRO, RG 25/1, Minutes of meeting of Standing Interdepartmental Committee on Social and Economic Research held 16 January.

NA (1949) PRO, RG 25/1, Minutes of meeting of Standing Interdepartmental Committee on Social and Economic Research held 9 December.

NA (1961) PRO, ED 87/375, 'Anderson Committee Report to Grants on Students in Training'.

NA (1963a) PRO, C (63) 173, 'Cabinet: The Robbins Report. Memorandum by the Chief Secretary to the Treasury and Paymaster-General'.

NA (1963b) PRO, ED 188/12, '1. Mr Clarke, 2. Mr Burrett'.

NA (1967) FCO 13/497, Letter from D. N. Chester to the Rt Hon. George Brown, Secretary of State for Foreign Affairs, 12 December.

NA (1969a) PRO, CAB 152/151, Letter from J. F. Embling, Department of Education and Science, 3 December.

NA (1969b) PRO, CAB 152/151, Letter from Sir David Serpell, Ministry of Transport, 13 December.

NA (1971a) PRO, FCO 13/441, Letter from Professor Graeme Moodie to Sir Denis Greenhill, 14 September.

NA (1971b) PRO, FCO 13/441, 'Approaches on Behalf of the Political Studies Association of the United Kingdom for Assistance'.

NA (1971c) PRO, FCO 13/441, Memorandum from R. A. Fyjis-Walker, Information Administration Department, 25 February.

NA (1971d) PRO, FCO 13/441, Memorandum from Mrs C. M. Hart to Mr Crook, 26 February.

NA (1971e) PRO, FCO 13/441, 'Note of a Meeting Held in Sir S. Tomlinson's Office', 20 October.

NA (1971f) PRO, FCO 13/441, 'International Political Science Association', Memorandum from C. Spearman, Cultural Relations Department to Sir S. Tomlinson and Mr Daunt.

NA (1971g) PRO, FCO 13/441, 'International Political Science Association', Memorandum from R. A. Fyjis-Walker, Information Administration Department to Mr Shawyer, 21 September.

NA (1971h) PRO, FCO 13/441, 'Note of a Meeting Held in Sir S. Tomlinson's Office', 20 October.

NA (1972a) PRO, UGC 8/268, 'Allocation of Studentships and Bursaries for 1972/3: Appendix A, Political Science'.

NA (1972b) PRO, FCO 13/497, Letter from Sir S. Tomlinson, Foreign and Commonwealth Office, to Mrs E. H. Boothroyd, Treasury, 6 March.

NA (1972c), PRO, FCO 13/497, Letter from Mrs E. H. Boothroyd, Treasury, to Sir S. Tomlinson, Foreign and Commonwealth Office, 14 April.

NA (1972d) FCO 13/497, 'International Political Science Association', Memorandum from D. H. C. Phillips, Cultural Relations Department, to Mr Morgan and Mr Reddaway, 4 September.

NA (1972e) PRO, FCO 13/497, Letter from Mrs E. H. Boothroyd, Treasury, to G. F. Reddaway, Foreign and Commonwealth Office, 21 August.

NA (1973) PRO, BA 21/73, 'Professor Ridley's Letter on the Teaching of Public Administration'.

NA (1974a) PRO, BA 21/73, 'Teaching Public Administration', Memorandum from I. P. Bancroft to Mr Grebenik.

NA (1974b) PRO, BA 21/73, 'Mr Bancroft's Forthcoming Meeting with Mr Dunsire'.

NA (1974c) PRO, BA 21/73, 'Meeting with Mr Dunsire'.

NA (1974d), PRO, BA 21/73, 'Note for the Record'.

NA (1974e), PRO, BA 21/73, J. C. Whiting, 'Royal Institute of Public Administration'.

NA (1974f), PRO, BA 21/73, C. Priestley, 'Appointments: In Confidence. Royal Institute of Public Administration'.

NA (1982a), PRO, UG 8/276, Letter from Professor Peter Campbell to G. E. Higgins, UGC, 'UGC Social Studies Sub-committee: The Impact of the Cuts', 1 November.

NA (1982b) PRO, UG 8/276, 'Universities Restructuring Bids, Appendix D, Politics'.

NA (1982c) PRO, UG 8/276, Letter from Professor Peter Campbell to T. Grant, UGC, 18 November.

NA (1982d) PRO, UG 8/276, 'Social Studies Sub-committee, Report on Subject Review'.

NA (1982e) PRO, UG 8/276, 'Comments on the Rothschild Report'.

NA (1982f) PRO, 82/212/1, Memorandum to Sir Geoffrey Otton (name of sender obscured).

NA (1982g) PRO, 82/212/1, Memorandum from Sir Robert Armstrong, 12 March.

National Institute (1945) *Register of Research in the Social Sciences: In Progress and in Plan*. London: National Institute for Economic and Social Research. Marked 'for private circulation'.

Newman, M. (2009) 'Laski, Harold Joseph (1893–1950), Political Theorist and University Teacher', *Oxford Dictionary of National Biography*. Available from: http://www.oxforddnb.com/articles/34/33412-article.html [accessed 22 June 2009].

Newton, K. (1976) *Second City Politics*. Oxford: Clarendon Press.

Norris, P. (1988) 'Survey of Political Studies, 1988'. Edinburgh University, typescript.

Norris, P. (1989) 'Survey of Political Studies, 1989'. Edinburgh University, typescript.

Norris, P. (1990) 'Survey of Political Studies, 1990'. Edinburgh University, typescript.

Olson, M. (1965) *The Logic of Collective Action*. Cambridge MA: Harvard University Press.

Parekh, Lord (2001) 'Michael Oakeshott (1901–1990)', in *Political Studies Association of the United Kingdom, 50th Anniversary*. Newcastle: Political Studies Association, p. 14.

Parry, G. (2009) 'PSA Chairmanship', notes provided to the author.

Peters, B. G. (1999) *Institutional Theory in Political Science*. London: Pinter.

Phillips, N. J. (2004) *The Southern Cone Model: The Political Economy of Regional Capitalist Development in Latin America*. London: Routledge.

PSA (1964) 'The Political Studies Association's Evidence to the Committee on Social Studies', *Political Studies*, 12 (2), 265–6.

PSA (1995a) Minutes of the Executive Committee, 1 July.

PSA (1995b) 'PSA Strategy Meeting, Chester, Rough Notes from Plenary Sessions', 22 September.

PSA (1995c) 'Report of the Working Group on Administration as established by the PSA Strategy Meeting'.

PSA (1996a) Minutes of the Executive Committee, 20 January.

PSA (1996b) Minutes of the Executive Committee, 28 September.

PSA (1998a) 'Political Studies Report', 30 September.

PSA (1998b) Minutes of the Executive Committee, 7 April.

PSA (1999a) Minutes of the Executive Committee, 16 January.

PSA (1999b) 'Report of the Local Organiser for the 49th Annual Conference'.

PSA (1999c) Ian Forbes, 'Chair's Report', March.

PSA (1999d) Rod Rhodes, 'Chair's Report', October.

PSA (1999e) Minutes of the Executive Committee, 26 June.

PSA (2000) Rod Rhodes, 'Chair's Annual Report, 2000'.

PSA (2002) Chair's Report to PSA Executive, 2 November.

PSA (2003a) 'Preliminary Editors Report 2003'.

PSA (2003b) 'Education and Research Sub-committee Report', November.

PSA (2003c) 'Terms of Reference for the Management Group of the PSA'.

PSA (2004a) 'Proposals for *Political Studies* 2nd term'.

PSA (2004b) 'Attitudes towards the Political Studies Association (UK): Findings from the PSA Survey of Profession 2002 and 2003'.

PSA (2004c) 'Evolving Chairs: Strategy for the PSA Executive'.

PSA (2005) 'Report from the PSA Chair to the EC, 30 October'.

PSA (2006a) 'Conference and Events Sub-committee Report, PSA Executive meeting, 21 January'.

PSA (2006b) Richard Topf, 'PSA Conferences', 7 December.

PSA (2007) Minutes of the Executive Committee, 3 February.

PSA (2008) *Trustees' Report and Financial Statements for the Year ended 31 December 2008*. Newcastle: Political Studies Association.

Pulzer, P. (2009) 'Finer, Samuel Edward (1915–1993), Political Scientist', *Oxford Dictionary of National Biography*. Available from: http://www,oxforddnb.com/articles/51/51914-article.html [Accessed 24 June 2009].

RAE (2008) 'Subject Overview: J39 Politics and International Studies'. Available from: http://www.rae.ac.uk/pubs/2009/ov/ [Accessed 15 September 2009].

Randall, V. (1991) 'Feminism and Political Analysis', *Political Studies*, 29 (3), 513–32.

Randall, V. (2002) 'Feminism', in D. Marsh and G. Stoker (eds), *Theory and Methods in Political Science*, second edition. Basingstoke: Palgrave-Macmillan, pp. 109–30.

Redcliffe-Maud, J. (1981) *Memoirs of an Optimist*. London: Hamish Hamilton.

Rhodes, R. A. W., 't Hart, P. and Noordegraaf, M. (eds) (2007) *Observing Government Elites: Up Close and Personal*. Basingstoke: Palgrave Macmillan.

Ricci, D. M. (1984) *The Tragedy of Political Science*. New Haven CT: Yale University Press.

Richardson, J. and Jordan, G. (1979) *Governing Under Pressure*. Oxford: Martin Robertson.

Rose, R. (1999) 'William James Millar Mackenzie, 1909–1996', *Proceedings of the British Academy*, 101, 465–85.

Ross, D. (2007) 'Anglo-American Political Science, 1880–1920', in R. Adcock, M. Bevir and S. C. Stimson (eds), *Modern Political Science: Anglo-American Exchanges since 1980*. Princeton NJ: Princeton University Press, pp. 18–36.

Russell, A. and Croft, S. (2009) 'The End of the RAE, and Onwards to the REF', *PSA News*, March, 1 and 6.

Sawer, M. (2008) 'The State of the Discipline: Australasian Political Science'. Unpublished paper, Australian National University, Canberra.

Seymour-Ure, C. (1963) 'Post-graduate students', *Aspect*, 7, 31–7.

Sharpe L. J. (1990) *The Anglo-American Lexicon of the Social Sciences*. Oxford: Trulex.

Shattock, M. (1991) *Making a University: A Celebration of Warwick's First 25 Years*. Coventry: Warwick University.

Smith, T. (1986) 'Political Science and Modern British Society', *Government and Opposition*, 24 (4), 420–36.

Somit, A. and Tanenhaus, J. (1967) *The Development of American Political Science: From Burgess to Behavioralism*. Boston MA: Allyn and Bacon.

Stanyer, J. (1994) 'Introduction', in P. Dunleavy and J. Stanyer (eds), *Contemporary Political Studies, Volume 1*. Belfast: Political Studies Association, p. viii.

Stapleton, J. (1994) *Englishness and the Study of Politics*. Cambridge: Cambridge University Press.

Stapleton, J. (2009) 'Barker, Sir Ernest (1874–1960), Political Theorist', *Oxford Dictionary of National Biography*. Oxford: Oxford University Press. Available from: http://www.oxforddnb.com/articles/30/30588-article.html [Accessed 23 June 2009].

Stears, M. (2009) 'Cole, George Douglas Howard (1899–1959), University Teacher and Political Theorist', *Oxford Dictionary of National Biography*. Oxford: Oxford University Press. Available from: http://www.oxforddnb.com/articles/32/32486-article.html [Accessed 23 June 2009].

Stoker, G. and John, P. (2009) 'Design Experiments: Engaging Policy Makers in the Search for Evidence about What Works', *Political Studies*, 57 (2), 356–73.

Strange, S. (2002) 'I Never Meant to Be an Academic', in R. Tooze and C. May (eds), *Authority and Markets: Susan Strange's Writings on International Political Economy*. Basingstoke: Palgrave-Macmillan, pp. 19–25.

The Times (2009) 'Sir Derek Mitchell: Treasury Mandarin', 21 August. Available from: http://www.timesonline.co.uk/tol/comment/obituaries/article6804335.ece [Accessed 28 August 2009].

Tooze, R. and May, C. (2002) 'Personal Values: Introduction and Commentary', in R. Tooze and C. May (eds), *Authority and Markets: Susan Strange's Writings on International Political Economy*. Basingstoke: Palgrave-Macmillan, p. 17.

Trent, J. E. (2009) 'Developments in Political Science: Report on the IPSA Montreal Conference, May 2008'. Paper prepared for the Santiago, Chile Congress of the International Political Science Association, July.

Warleigh-Lack, A. and Cini, M. (2009) 'Interdisciplinarity and the Study of Politics', *European Political Science*, 8 (1), 4–15.

Weale, A. (2009) 'Obituary for Brian Barry: 1936–2009', *PSA News*, 20 (2), 22.

Whiteley, P. (2009) 'Political Insight', *PSA News*, 20 (3), 17.

Wright, T. (2001) 'G. D. H. Cole (1899–1959), in *Political Studies Association of the United Kingdom, 50th Anniversary*. Newcastle: Political Studies Association, pp. 13–14.

Index

JOIN THE

POLITICAL STUDIES ASSOCIATION

The Political Studies Association (PSA) is the UK's leading body for scholars and students of politics, the largest of its kind in Europe, and aims to link teachers, students, academics, policy makers and journalists together in the study of politics.

For just £74 per year, membership of the Political Studies Association provides:

- *Political Studies* – 4 times a year
- *Political Studies Review* – 3 times a year
- *POLITICS* – 3 times a year
- *The British Journal of Politics and International Relations* – 4 times a year
- *Political Insight* – 3 times a year
- **Newsletter** – 4 times a year
- **Annual Directory** – listing all political scientists in the UK and Ireland
- **Members' discounts on conference and workshop fees**
- **Access to grants to attend overseas conferences**
- **Exclusive online members-only resources at www.psa.ac.uk**
- **Access to a network of 40 specialist research groups**
- **Opportunities to compete for annual Political Studies Association prizes**
- **Discount on books and journals from Wiley and Polity Press**

Only £64 if paying by direct debit

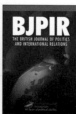

For more details please email **psa@ncl.ac.uk** or **call +44 (0)191 222 8021**

Political Studies
Association
60 years of political studies
1950–2010

www.psa.ac.uk